William Hudson

Leet Jurisdiction in the City of Norwich during the XIIIth and XIVth Centuries

With a Short Notice of its Later History and Decline, from Rolls in the Possession of the Corporation

William Hudson

Leet Jurisdiction in the City of Norwich during the XIIIth and XIVth Centuries
With a Short Notice of its Later History and Decline, from Rolls in the Possession of the Corporation

ISBN/EAN: 9783337086541

Printed in Europe, USA, Canada, Australia, Japan

Cover: Foto ©ninafisch / pixelio.de

More available books at **www.hansebooks.com**

THE
PUBLICATIONS
OF THE
Selden Society

περὶ παντὸς τὴν ἐλευθερίαν

VOLUME V.

FOR THE YEAR 1891

Selden Society

FOUNDED 1887

TO ENCOURAGE THE STUDY AND ADVANCE THE KNOWLEDGE
OF THE HISTORY OF ENGLISH LAW.

Patron:
HER MAJESTY THE QUEEN.

President:
THE LORD CHIEF JUSTICE OF ENGLAND.

Vice-President:
THE RIGHT HON. SIR EDWARD FRY.

Honorary Secretary for America:
EZRA R. THAYER, Cambridge, Mass.

Honorary Secretary and Treasurer:
P. EDWARD DOVE, 28 Old Buildings, Lincoln's Inn.

Leet Jurisdiction

IN THE CITY OF NORWICH

Selden Society

LEET JURISDICTION IN THE CITY OF NORWICH

DURING THE XIIITH AND XIVTH CENTURIES

WITH A SHORT NOTICE OF ITS

LATER HISTORY AND DECLINE

FROM ROLLS IN THE POSSESSION OF THE CORPORATION

EDITED

FOR THE SELDEN SOCIETY

BY

WILLIAM HUDSON

VICAR OF ST PETER PERMOUNTERGATE, NORWICH
HON. SEC. OF THE NORFOLK AND NORWICH ARCHÆOLOGICAL SOCIETY

LONDON
BERNARD QUARITCH, 15 PICCADILLY
1892

All rights reserved

CONTENTS.

	PAGE
MAP OF THE CITY OF NORWICH . . . . . *To face p.* vii	
INTRODUCTION ix	
FACSIMILE OF A PORTION OF A TITHING ROLL OF THE LEET OF MANCROFT . . . . *To face p.* xlvii	
LOCAL MANUSCRIPTS AND BOOKS lxxxiv	
NOTES lxxxv	

A. PRESENTMENTS AND AMERCEMENTS AT THE LEETS HELD BEFORE THE BAILIFFS OF THE CITY OF NORWICH.

 I. LEET ROLL OF THE SIXTEENTH YEAR OF THE REIGN OF KING EDWARD I. (A.D. 1288) 1

 II. LEET ROLL OF THE SEVENTEENTH YEAR OF THE REIGN OF KING EDWARD I. (A.D. 1289) 20

 III. LEET ROLL OF THE EIGHTEENTH YEAR OF THE REIGN OF KING EDWARD I. (A.D. 1290) 33

 IV. LEET ROLL OF THE NINETEENTH YEAR OF THE REIGN OF KING EDWARD I. (A.D. 1291) 37

 V. LEET ROLL OF THE TWENTY-FIRST YEAR OF THE REIGN OF KING EDWARD I. (A.D. 1293) 42

 VI. LEET ROLL OF THE TWENTY-FOURTH YEAR OF THE REIGN OF KING EDWARD I. (A.D. 1296) 46

 VII. LEET ROLL OF THE TWENTY-EIGHTH YEAR OF THE REIGN OF KING EDWARD I. (A.D. 1300) 50

 VIII. LEET ROLL OF UNCERTAIN DATE (? *c.* A.D. 1307) . . 54

 IX. LEET ROLL OF THE SIXTH YEAR OF THE REIGN OF KING EDWARD II. (A.D. 1313) 55

VOL. V.   a

CONTENTS.

		PAGE
X.	LEET ROLL OF THE FORTY-NINTH YEAR OF THE REIGN OF KING EDWARD III. (A.D. 1375)	62
XI.	LEET ROLL OF THE FOURTEENTH YEAR OF THE REIGN OF KING RICHARD II. (A.D. 1391)	69
XII.	ACCOUNT RENDERED OF AMERCEMENTS AT THE LEETS IN THE THIRTY-SEVENTH YEAR OF THE REIGN OF KING EDWARD III. (A.D. 1364)	77
XIII.	TITHING ROLL OF THE LEET OF MANCROFT IN THE CITY OF NORWICH (c. A.D. 1311)	79
XIV.	INQUISITIONS BEFORE THE BAILIFFS OF THE CITY OF NORWICH (A.D. 1350)	80

B. PRESENTMENTS AND AMERCEMENTS AT THE TOURNS AND LEETS HELD BEFORE THE SHERIFFS OF THE CITY OF NORWICH.

XV.	LEETS AND TOURNS IN THE FIFTH YEAR OF THE REIGN OF KING EDWARD VI. (A.D. 1551)	85
XVI.	TOURNS IN THE FIRST AND SECOND YEARS OF THE REIGN OF PHILIP AND MARY (A.D. 1554 AND 1555) .	90
XVII.	TOURNS AND LEETS (A.D. 1681 AND 1682) . . .	93
XVIII.	TOURNS AND LEETS (A.D. 1608)	97
XIX.	AMERCEMENTS FOR NON-ATTENDANCE AT THE LEETS (A.D. 1698)	100
XX.	PRESENTMENTS OF THE QUEST OF WARDS (A.D. 1629) .	101
XXI.	THE SAME (A.D. 1802)	101

GLOSSARY	103
INDEX OF MATTERS	105
INDEX OF PERSONS	111
INDEX OF PLACES	123

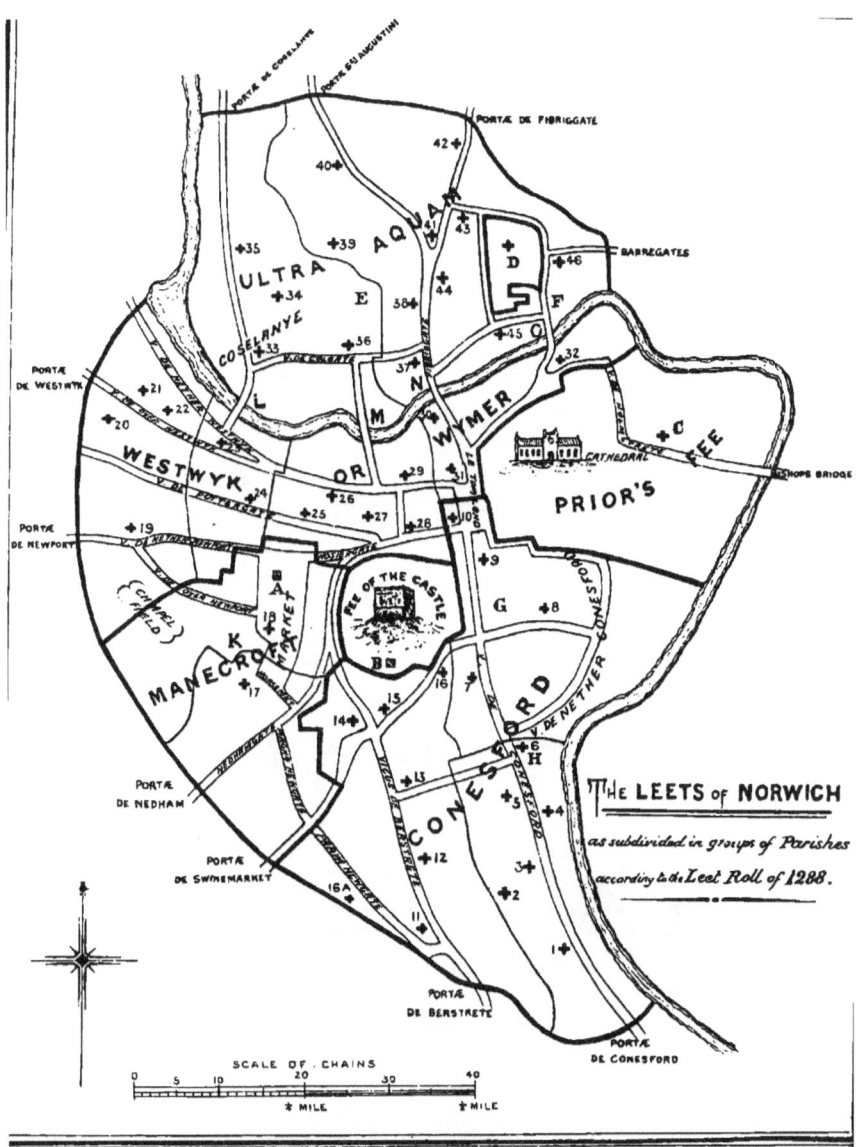

THE FOUR LEETS OF NORWICH IN 1288.

I.—LEET OF CONESFORD.

Subleet (as named in later Rolls) — *Parish.*

S. CONESFORD
 1. St. Peter de Southgate.
 2. St. Edward.
 3. St. Etheldreda.
 4. St. Clement de Conesford.
 5. St. Julian.
 6. St. Michael de Conesford.

N. CONESFORD
 7. St. Peter de Parmentergate.
 8. St. Vedast.
 9. St. Cuthbert.
 10. St. Mary the Little.

BERSTRETE
 11. St. Sepulchre.
 12. St. Bartholomew.
 13. St. Michael de Berstrete.
 14. All Saints de Berstrete.
 15. St. John de Berstrete.
 16. St. Martin in Ballia.
 [16A. St. Winwaloy. Roll VIII.]

II.—LEET OF MANECROFT.

ST. STEPHEN — 17. St. Stephen.
ST. PETER DE MANECROFT — 18. St. Peter de Manecroft.

III.—LEET OF WYMER OR WESTWYK.

ST. GILES
 19. St. Giles.
 20. St. Benedict.
 21. St. Swithin.
 22. St. Margaret de Westwyk.

Subleet — *Parish.*

ST. GREGORY
 23. St. Lawrence.
 24. St. Gregory.

ST. ANDREW
 25. St. John de Maddermarket.
 26. St. Cross.
 27. St. Andrew.
 28. St. Michael de Motstowe.
 29. St. Peter de Hungate.

ST. GEORGE
 30. SS. Simon and Jude.
 31. St. George before the Gates of the Holy Trinity.
 32. St. Martin before the Gates of the Bishop.

IV. LEET OVER THE WATER.

ST. MICHAEL
 33. St. Michael de Coselanye.
 34. St. Mary de Coselanye.
 35. St. Martin de Coselanye.
 36. St. George de Colegate.

ST. CLEMENT
 37. St. Clement de Fibriggate.
 38. St. Mary Combust.
 39. St. Olave.
 40. St. Augustine.
 41. St. Botulph.
 42. St. Margaret.
 43. All Saints de Fibriggate.
 44. St. Saviour.
 45. St. Edmund.
 46. St. James.

A. The Tolhouse, Theolonium, Curia Theolonii.
B. The Shire House, Curia Comitatus.
C. Hospital of St. Giles.
D. Normanspitel.
E. First site of the Black Friars.
F. Site of the White Friars.
G. Site of the Grey Friars.
H. Site of the Austin Friars.
K. Chapel of St. Mary in the Fields.
L. Bridge of Coselanye.
M. Bridge of Newbrigge.
N. Bridge of Fibrigge.
O. Bridge of St. Martin.

V. in the map is used for Vicus (Street).

INTRODUCTION

    I. Leet Jurisdiction in Norwich. The Leet Rolls.
    II. The Leet Divisions and Subdivisions.
    III. Place and Time of holding the Leets.
    IV. The Constitution of the Court.
    V. The Offences presented.
    VI. The Amercements.
    VII. The Frankpledge System. The Capital Pledges.
    VIII. The Mancroft Tithing Roll.
    IX. The original Number of the City Tithings and Formation of the Subleets.
    X. Capital Pledges and Tithingmen: their social position, residence etc.
    XI. Frankpledge in Norwich and London.
    XII. The Decadence and later History of the Leets.

    NOTES :—
        A. Citizenship in Norwich in the thirteenth Century.
        B. Craft Gilds in Norwich.
        C. The City Court of Norwich in the thirteenth and fourteenth Centuries.
        D. The Dean of the City of Norwich.
        E. Surnames in the thirteenth Century.
        F. The Leet of the New Fee of the Castle.
        G. Some Words explained.

I. Leet Jurisdiction in Norwich. The Leet Rolls.

1. Among the documents preserved in the Record Room of the Guildhall in the City of Norwich are thirteen Rolls connected with the Leet Courts in the City during the thirteenth and fourteenth centuries while the Frankpledge System on which they were based was still in full operation. After this time the power of these Courts to a great extent passed away from the popular bodies who had hitherto composed them. It was partly superseded by the general authority of the Municipal Assembly which was organised in the early part of the fifteenth century. This Assembly consisted of twenty-four

Aldermen, and sixty Common Councillors under the presidency of a Mayor and two Sheriffs and was supreme in all municipal affairs, including those which had come under the cognisance of the Leets. More particularly the twenty-four Aldermen, the successors of a body of twenty-four representative citizens which had come into existence during the fourteenth century, were in the course of the fifteenth century endued with permanent magisterial authority corresponding to that exercised by the Justices of the Peace in the country districts. Moreover the City Sheriffs from the time of their first appointment in 1403 held their Tourns as the County Sheriffs did. At a later time inquiries were also made by sworn inquests in each of the four Great Wards (quite independently of the Leet inquests) for the purpose of making presentments to the Justices at Quarter Sessions. Nevertheless the Leet juries continued to be appointed and made their presentments to the City Sheriffs down to at least 1700, though finally nothing was left for them to deal with but nuisances and unpaved streets and defective weights and measures. The name survive in the City even down to the Municipal Reform Act of 1835, but the institution which then bore it could claim only the very slightest resemblance to its original predecessor.

In fifteenth century Norwich assimilated itself to London, and the common type of Borough organisation

2. The oligarchical development effected at the beginning of the fifteenth century was the result of a great tide of similar influence which had been gradually spreading over the country. Judging by the language used in contemporary charters and municipal documents, as well as by the names adopted under the new organisation ('Wards' instead of 'Leets,' 'Aldermen' instead of '24 Citizens,' 'Guildhall' instead of 'Tolhouse'), the form it assumed in Norwich was copied from the organisation of London. It was the common form which may be found, with a few variations, in almost all the chartered boroughs from the fifteenth century to 1835, except that Norwich was one of those boroughs which were 'counties of themselves.'

Leet system specially seen in operation in

3. The special interest attaching to Norwich is that in it the older Leet jurisdiction survived so long, and may be

seen at work under circumstances which can hardly be paralleled elsewhere. The field of its operations here was, not a country manor where it dealt with the incidents of agricultural life, but one of the largest and most prosperous cities of the kingdom. Moreover, in this case, time has dealt favourably with our sources of information. The most abundant and the most fruitful are also the earliest, and in addition some other contemporary documents have been preserved which throw further light upon them. We are able, therefore, to see how the system adapted itself to the requirements of a large town population. *Norwich as applied to a large town*

4. Of the thirteen Rolls referred to, eleven are strictly proceedings of the courts. They are of two kinds. Some are Rolls of Presentments and others are Rolls of Amercements. The former have no amercements entered in the thirteenth century; in two later Presentment Rolls of the fourteenth century the amercements are given. The Amercement Rolls are (at least in some cases) records of the whole proceedings from the first presentment to the final balancing of their accounts by the appointed collectors of the amercements. *The Rolls here edited*

Although the words 'Presentationes' and 'Amerciamenta' are sometimes both used in the same Roll, yet the two kinds of Rolls invariably differ in form. The Presentment Rolls have their membranes fastened at the top. In the Amercement Rolls they are fastened lengthwise so as to form one long Roll.

The special features of each Roll will be found noted where it is given in the course of the volume. It will be sufficient here to observe that the earliest is of 16 Edward I. (1288) and that the seventh is of 28 Edward I. (1300), the whole seven falling within the limited period of thirteen years. Then there is a fragment of *c.* 1307 and a very full Roll of 1313. After this there is a long interval followed by two interesting Rolls of 1375 and 1391.

The remaining two of the thirteen Rolls are of a different character. One is an Account Roll of 1364, apparently an account rendered by the collectors at the Leets. The

other is one of very special value, a Tithing Roll, or list of all persons enrolled in tithings in the Leet of Mancroft. Its date (which is not given) is *circ.* 1311. It stands entirely by itself and is fully described in Section VIII. of this Introduction.

These are all the early Leet Rolls which have survived. But with a view to completing the subject by giving some account of the later history of the Leets and of the institutions which co-existed with them from the fifteenth century onwards, some extracts have been added from later Rolls, chiefly Rolls of the Tourns and Leets held before the City Sheriffs who took the place of the Bailiffs.

II. The Leet Divisions.

The Leet divisions and subdivisions

1. The earliest Leet Roll (followed, with more or less fulness of detail, by all the rest) presents us with a view of the City as divided into four large divisions called 'Leets.' They are named, 1. The Leet of Conesford; 2. The Leet of Manecroft; 3. The Leet of Wymer or Westwyk; 4. The Leet 'Ultra Aquam,' or Over-the-Water. These four Leets, however, are not separately utilised for the purpose of making presentments, but are unequally subdivided, at first into eleven and afterwards into ten smaller divisions, for which separate presentments are made.

In the thirteenth century Rolls these subdivisions are not distinguished by any special names. But in the Account Roll of 1364 and in the two later Leet Rolls of 1375 and 1391 they are not only distinguished by names but are themselves called Leets, no notice being taken of the four larger divisions to which that title was usually restricted.

formed the basis of the organisation of the City till 1835

2. As these divisions, both large and small, formed the basis of all the municipal organisation of the City of Norwich from an unknown time of origin down to 1835, it is most important to ascertain, if possible, how far the Leet organisation made use of previously existing divisions, and how far the divisions arose out of the requirements of the Leet organisation. To form a judgment on this question (in

the absence of any distinct evidence as to the origin of the divisions as official districts) is impossible without some little knowledge of the topography and early history of the City.

3. At the close of the thirteenth century the City of Norwich formed what may be roughly described as a pear-shaped pyramidical figure with the apex at the south, slightly inclined to the south-east. The river Wensum crossing the upper part from west to east divided it into two unequal portions, of which the southern was much the larger and more important. A small piece on the north-west was bounded by the river which also partly formed the boundary on the north-east and wholly on the eastern side of the City. The remainder of the boundary on the south, west and north was defined by a bank and ditch which had been made in pursuance of a royal licence in 1253. The wall was begun on this bank in 1294. *Early topography of the City*

4. The City, which was thus enlarged and rounded off in 1253, much to the detriment of many people's rights (so the injured parties alleged) had been growing up in the course of some seven centuries. The first settlers had been Angles, who penetrated up a great estuary the broad entrance of which had not yet been blocked up by the sand-bank where Great Yarmouth was afterwards built. They formed a settlement at one of its northern heads on the bank of the Wensum just where the estuary ceased and the river was entered. Possibly from its situation in regard to this estuary the settlement obtained its name of 'Northwic.' One of the early chiefs or kings must have thrown up the great artificial mound on which was afterwards placed the Keep of the Norman Castle. This mound forms the northern end of a high ridge of ground which, parting from the river at the extremity of what I have called the apex of the inverted pyramid, runs parallel with the river for some distance, leaving at the foot of its steep eastern escarpment a strip of meadow ground, narrow towards the south but afterwards broadening out towards the north into a large expanse of marshy land, which was *Growth of the four Divisions: 1. Conesford*

called the 'Cowholm,' the site in later times of the Cathedral. On this river-side meadow south of the Cowholm was the earliest Angle settlement. Somewhere here the early Angle kings had a ford over the river and the district therefore became known as 'Conesford,' originally 'Cyningesford,' the king's ford. The settlers gradually pushed up the hillside to the top of the ridge, on which was an ancient road called 'Berstrete,' *i.e.* Berg or Hill Street.

2. Westwyk

5. Meanwhile either the Angles or at all events at a later time the Danes ascended the river, passed the abrupt bend which it takes to the west at the north of the Cowholm, and settled on either bank. The southern settlement was called 'Westwyk,' evidently in reference to the earlier settlement of Conesford, which lay to the east on the other side of the Castle Hill. The settlement on the northern bank had no such distinctive name. The earliest name of a portion of it was 'Coselanye,' the latter syllable of which must have been derived from an island in the river. But although the name has lasted to this day it never was used for the whole district.¹

3 Ultra Aquam

All these three settlements had grown together into a flourishing 'burgus' by the time of King Edward the Confessor, when the Domesday Survey records 1238 burgesses as resident 'in burgo,' besides 32 belonging to Harold as Earl of East Anglia in the neighbourhood of the Castle, and 50 belonging to Stigand, Bishop of Thetford, in a small district to the north-west of the Cowholm.

4. Manecroft

6. About the time of the Norman Conquest, by the joint action of the king and the earl, a 'novus Burgus' was added for the benefit of the 'Frenchmen.' It lay to the west of the Castle and was at first called 'Newport,' *i.e.* 'novus burgus,' but afterwards took the name of 'Manecroft' from a great croft near the church of St. Peter which was founded simultaneously with the new burgh. This district became the site of the great market, and by the

---

¹ The name 'Ultra Aquam' must have been given in Norman times when Mancroft had become the centre of the borough.

thirteenth century had grown to be the centre of the life of the whole community.

It is plain from this statement that the four great divisions which the Roll of 1288 describes as four 'Leets' were divisions of great antiquity. The question, however, remains, When were they formed into administrative districts? and, When did they become 'Leets' or sections of criminal jurisdiction? For the solution of this question we have no documentary evidence to guide us, and can only catch at any clue that offers itself. *When first organised as the four 'Leets'*

7. The first is afforded by the fact that in 1223 the government of the City was placed in the hands of four Bailiffs. In the earliest existing evidence bearing on the subject we find that one of these Bailiffs was chosen for each Leet. Although this information begins at a late date (Assembly Roll, 1365), yet there is every reason to suppose that such had been the practice from the first. We may therefore take for granted that the number of four Bailiffs was fixed upon to correspond with these four divisions. It would seem to follow that at the time of the first appointment of four Bailiffs the four divisions were already recognised as so many integral units of municipal organisation. Assuming, however (as I hope to show), that the authority to hold courts for criminal presentments coincided with the appointment of Bailiffs (p. xviii.), we must either presume that these four divisions were not called 'Leets' till 1223, or that the word had before that time another meaning. Professor Maitland, in Vol. II. of this series (p. lxxiii) has pointed out that to hold a Leet meant originally no more than to hold the 'view of frankpledge.' In this sense these divisions may have been called 'Leets' in the twelfth century. Blomefield in his 'History of Norwich' at the close of King Henry II.'s reign gives what seems to be such a use of the word. He says that in 1184 the citizens claiming exemption from serving at Leets belonging to the Fee of the King's Castle or in some other places 'were commanded to serve for the future in that leet or view wherein they dwelt.' This, however, might only mean that they *Either co-incidently with the appointment of four Bailiffs in 1223,* *or at close of twelfth century*

were to attend the court of the lord in whose jurisdiction they lived, the burgh itself being part of the king's demesne.

8. It is quite possible that from the time when Henry I. ordered the enforcement of frankpledge these four districts may have been treated as separate units. A town with 1238 burgesses, if each one had a separate household, could hardly have been dealt with all at once. If, however, the word 'leet' was used only in the case of a privileged lord or a chartered borough to distinguish a franchised court from the Sheriff's Tourn, we must seek for some time when the privilege of holding the view of frankpledge may *perhaps in 1194 (5 R. I.)* be supposed to have been granted to the citizens. This can only have been in 5 R. I. (1194). In that year they obtained by royal charter leave to elect their own Provost, and by his hands to pay their 'firma burgi' into the king's exchequer. Perhaps the privilege of holding their own view of frankpledge was included in that grant.

I conclude, therefore, that the four leets, though of much greater antiquity, were not called 'Leets' till at least 1194, and if so called then it was because they were the divisions according to which the citizens then first began to hold their own view of frankpledge.

The subdivisions formed for Leet purposes

9. When we pass from the four great divisions to consider the smaller subdivisions as they are seen to have existed in 1288 the problem presented to us is of a different character. They were not old divisions that had grown up with the growth of the town like the four large ones. On the contrary, the evidence seems distinctly to warrant the belief that they arose out of the combined requirements of the frankpledge system and the duty of making criminal presentments.

The divisions and subdivisions as shown in Roll I. (1288) A. Conesford

An analysis of the first Roll will show the character of the evidence.

Its first heading is 'Leet of Conesford on Monday next after Ash Wednesday in the 16th year of the reign of King Edward.'

Subdiv. 1

On that day twelve Capital Pledges make presentment on their oath of various offences.

They are followed (the days are not here specified) by twelve other Jurors who do the same. Subdiv. 2

It is not stated in this Roll for what districts these two sets of presentments are made. The defect, however, is remedied by the fragment called 'Roll III.' (p. 33). From that it appears that the first set of Capital Pledges answered for the southern end of Conesford Street, the district including six parishes. The other set answered for the northern end of the street, including four parishes.

After this twelve Jurors make presentments for a district called 'Berstrete.' Subdiv. 3

The Roll next proceeds to presentments headed 'Manecroft,' and first 'Parish of St. Stephen,' for which twelve presenters appear. B. Manecroft
Subdiv. 1

Then comes the 'Parish of St. Peter de Manecroft,' the most important parish in the City, including the market. For it thirty persons make presentments. Subdiv. 2

Next follow the 'Parishes of St. Giles, St. Margaret, St. Swithun and St. Benedict.' These were in the Leet of Wymer[1] or Westwyk. In this Roll the heading of the Leet is inadvertently omitted. For these parishes twelve presenters appear. C. Wymer
Subdiv. 1

Next for the two 'Parishes of St. Lawrence and St. Gregory' twelve persons answer; Subdiv. 2

And then thirteen for the 'Parishes of St. John de Madermarket, St. Cross, St. Andrew, St. Michael de Motstowe and St. Peter' [Hungate]; Subdiv. 3

And then twelve for 'SS. Simon and Jude, St. George before the gates of Holy Trinity, and St. Martin before the gates of the Bishop.' Subdiv. 4

Then the Roll crosses over to the 'Leta ultra Aquam,' and records first the presentments made for the 'Parishes of St. Michael de Coselanye, St. George, St. Mary and St. Martin' by eighteen persons; D. Ultra
Aquam
Subdiv. 1

---

[1] Wymer was originally the name of part of this district, near the parish of St. Andrew. It had by this time nearly supplanted the older name of Westwyk, which belonged originally to the western part of the district, St. Margaret and the adjoining parishes.

xviii ORIGIN OF THE SUBDIVISIONS.

Subdiv. 2. And then those made by fifteen others for the remaining ten parishes in that Leet.

The existence of the organisation thus revealed is fully confirmed by the other Rolls of Presentments, and by incidental notices occurring in the Rolls of Amercements.

10. The following observations suggest themselves :—

(1) The presentments are made by the Capital Pledges of the tithings. This will be more fully shown further on.

(2) The subdivisions are composed of groups of parishes and are of unequal size, sometimes containing one parish, sometimes many.

(3) The number of presenters is never less than twelve, and in three districts considerably more.

A subdivision contained at least twelve tithings.

These considerations obviously point to the theory that the subdivisions of the Leets were so organised originally that each should contain at least twelve tithings, and therefore be able to make presentments through twelve Capital Pledges, the minimum number which the commonly accepted custom of the country, confirmed by royal ordinance [1] only a few years before the date of this Roll, held to be essential for the presentment of criminal offences. Hence a populous parish could stand alone, and less populous parishes had to be associated with one or more of their neighbours.

This organisation coincided with appointment of Bailiffs who were officers of a Hundred to which Leet jurisdiction appertained.

11. Can we say when this organisation first originated? I cannot doubt that the answer is, At the time of the appointment of four Bailiffs in 1223. This, I think, was what led to the substitution of Bailiffs for a Provost, viz. because the citizens were then authorised to hold their own courts for presentment of offences and take the profits themselves. The Assize of Clarendon had ordered the Sheriff to receive such presentments annually in the Hundred Court. Norwich was a Hundred of itself, and presumably the Sheriff would summon the responsible presenters to attend his court in the Castle enclosure for the purpose.

---

[1] 13 Ed. I. c. 3. After the order given to the Sheriffs is added, 'And as it hath been said of Sheriffs so shall it be observed of every Bailiff of Franchise.'

But when this privilege was granted to the citizens, and the business was carried to their own private court, the proper president would be the Bailiff of the Hundred, representing the lord as the sheriff represented the king, the lord in the case of Norwich being the king himself. In accordance with this view we find in 1288 each of the four Leets organised as a Hundred with its Bailiff, Constable, and criminal court, though, on the one hand, the unity of the City was preserved by the Bailiffs sitting together, and, on the other, the court of each Leet was subdivided for convenience of administration. The title of 'Leet' was not given to the subdivisions till a later period.

12. The subdivisions shown in the Roll of 1288 appear to have remained unaltered till after the date of the Roll of 1313. But in the Account Roll of 1364 and in the two Leet Rolls of 1375 and 1391 a noticeable change is found. The number of subdivisions for which separate presentments are made is reduced from eleven to ten. This arises from the fact that the two districts which were previously formed out of the parishes in Conesford Street are at these dates represented by only one set of Jurors. A reason for this may be found in the circumstance that during the close of the thirteenth and the early part of the fourteenth centuries, first the Grey Friars and then the Austin Friars had enclosed two large spaces in this locality, thus considerably reducing the number of persons in tithings. It is instructive to observe that before this was done permanently it appears to have been done on at least one occasion for passing convenience. In the Rolls for 1288 and 1290 a set of Jurors appears for each of these subleets. The Roll for 1289, the intervening year, is one of Amercements, and only mentions the Capital Pledges when they are amerced. A set of thirteen was amerced in that year in the (Great) Leet of Conesford, and from the first names would be at once taken for the Jury of South Conesford. A closer examination, however, reveals the curious fact that the first eight names correspond with eight of the jury of South Conesford for the previous year, while the last five similarly

Reduction in the number of subdivisions in the fourteenth century

correspond with five of the jury of North Conesford. Evidently they had formed but one jury on that occasion, for they are amerced as one body for the concealment of a specified offence.

They are thenceforward treated as separate Leets

It has already been mentioned that up to 1313 the subdivisions are not called by any special names and are not described as 'Leets.' In the later Rolls of 1375 and 1391 they have distinctive names applied to them and are spoken of as the Leets, no notice being taken of the four large divisions to which the title had formerly been restricted. We may gather that by this time the character of a Leet as a portion of a Hundred had become forgotten. The names of the ten subdivisions are evidently selected for mere convenience, and are mostly those of the principal parish in each district. They are :—1. Conesford; 2. Berstrete; 3. St. Stephen; 4. Mancroft; 5. St. Giles; 6. St. Gregory; 7. St. Andrew; 8. St. George; 9. St. Michael [in Coslany]; 10. St. Clement.

The four Leets became the four Great Wards

13. Although the subsequent history of these divisions and subdivisions belongs rather to the municipal history of the City than to the Leets, yet the two subjects are so closely connected together that no account of the earlier 'Leet' divisions would be complete without a notice of their subsequent adaptation to municipal purposes.

In 1403-1417,

When the constitution of the City was remodelled between 1403 and 1417 the four great Leets retained their position as the principal divisions. They were called the four Great Wards, with the old names of Conesford, Mancroft,[1] Wymer, and Over-the-Water. The electors of each Great Ward chose six Aldermen and an unequal number of the sixty Common Councillors.

and the subdivisions the twelve Small Wards before close of the fifteenth century

The subdivisions were also retained, and at first in the form last mentioned. They were, however, treated as mere subdivisions. St. Giles's Parish was reckoned as a third subdivision of Mancroft Ward.[2] In Over-the-Water 'St.

---

[1] About this time the 'e' began to be omitted from this word. Account Roll, p. 70: Landgable List temp. R. II. in City Domesday, fol. xlvi.
[2] This had been done earlier.

Michael' was called 'Coslany,' and 'St. Clement' was called 'Fibrigge.' The retention of the number ten at first is curious, and shows that the 'Aldermen' had not yet acquired their full magisterial maturity. This development was not long after effected, for in an undated document [1] (probably soon after 1450), the City is described as 'quadripartita' into four Wards (with the four old names) and each Ward is divided into 'three Aldermanries.' These districts are the old subdivisions with only such modifications as were necessary to make three in each Ward. Unfortunately the latter part of this interesting document is lost. Before the end of the fifteenth century, however, we find them called 'the twelve Wards,' and bearing the names which continued till 1835. The Great Ward of Conesford was subdivided into the three Small Wards of South Conesford, North Conesford, and Berstreet; the Great Ward of Mancroft into the three Small Wards of St. Stephen, Mancroft, and St. Giles; the Great Ward of Wymer into the three Small Wards of West Wymer, Middle Wymer, and East Wymer, and the Great Ward Over-the-Water into the three Small Wards of Coslany, Colegate, and Fybridge. Two Aldermen were elected for (not by) each Small Ward. They were elected for life. Each was a magistrate for his own Small Ward, and when he had passed the chair of mayoralty he was a magistrate for the whole City.

14. This account of the final organisation of the City into four great divisions, each subdivided into three small divisions, raises a question which can hardly be passed over. The account I have given of the probable origin of the four great divisions, and still more of the twelve subdivisions is irreconcileable with a statement which at first sight might seem to furnish a satisfactory explanation of the somewhat peculiar double organisation which existed so many centuries in Norwich. I allude to a statement made by Sir Francis Palgrave in 'The Rise and Progress of the English Commonwealth,' i. 97 :—' In East Anglia

Was the original set of subdivisions one of twelve (4×3)?

[1] Old Free Book, fol. clx. There is another instance in Assembly Book 11 H. VII. fol. xx.

there existed a duodenary division, the Hundred being distributed into twelve Leets or Tribes: that is to say, into four head Leets, each containing three subordinate Leets.' He gives no instance of this arrangement. About 1184 the Hundred of Thingoe in Suffolk was divided into twelve Leets, of which the Abbot of St. Edmund held nine (Gage's 'History of Suffolk,' p. xii). Palgrave was well acquainted with East Anglia, and refers to the Norwich Records. When his book was published, Norwich was still divided into four Great and twelve Small Wards. He probably knew that these divisions had once been called Leets, and perhaps he founded his statement chiefly on the case of Norwich, especially as Yarmouth and Ipswich were also divided into Leets. This is the more probable as the statement is modified in the Table of Contents (p. xii), by being referred to the '*Borough* Hundreds of East Anglia.' If this statement is to be accepted it would be necessary to suppose that the double set of divisions in the Leet Rolls was a relic of a more uniform system of earlier days which was once more restored during the fifteenth century. With regard, however, to the four Leets of Norwich, the late settlement of Mancroft makes it almost impossible that there should have been such an arrangement before the Conquest. With regard to twelve divisions symmetrically arranged, the Norwich records show no such arrangement till well into the fifteenth century. In 1288 there are eleven, and they are arranged in two sets of three, one of four, and one of two. Afterwards, one of the first sets is reduced to two, and the whole number to ten. Nevertheless it may be true that originally the number of subdivisions had been twelve. Twelve was a number most closely associated with the Hundred. Some further observations on this point may be reserved till we come to consider the working of the tithing system (see below, Section X. 3).

III. Place and Times of Holding the Courts.

1. The Rolls make no reference to the place where the presentments were made. Only in the general heading to the Roll of 1375 it is described as the Roll of the Verdicts of the Leets *before* the Bailiffs ('coram Ballivis'). This must mean in the Bailiffs' Court. This would of course be the natural place, unless each Leet had a separate court of its own, of which there is no evidence whatever. The Bailiffs' Court in the thirteenth century was held in a building which occupied the site of the later Guildhall, and was called the 'Tolboth,' or the 'Tolhus.' It is frequently alluded to in the contemporary Conveyance Rolls under the name of 'Theolonium,' or 'Domus' or 'Curia Theolonii,' and is so distinguished from the Sheriffs' Court, which stood within the exempt precinct of the Castle, and was called 'Curia Comitatus.' When spoken of simply as a Court the former is called 'Curia Norwici' or 'Curia Civitatis.' The Tolhouse is said to have been a small thatched building, and must have been altogether inadequate to the requirements of the City at the close of the thirteenth century. It was, however, the chief official building of the City and was certainly used for public judicial business. Pleas in pursuance of the king's Writs of Right are said to be held 'in Theolonio Norwici.'[1] A prisoner is said to be tried 'coram Ballivis et tota communitate totius civitatis in Tolboth.'[2] Here the Bailiffs must have sat almost daily to hear pleas or try issues or record recognitions of bonds and deeds of conveyance, and also, as it seems, to hear 'appeals' from injured complainants. In the Leet Roll of 1288 (p. 5), the Capital Pledges of Berstrete present that Beatrice daughter of Robert Beumund 'levavit hutesium et secuta fuit usque ad Teolonium.' This must surely imply that she expected to find a sympathetic court sitting there, and not merely an official to take down the charge. The entry may be compared with another in

Proceedings took place in the Bailiffs' Court, or 'Tolhouse'

---

[1] Conveyance Rolls. [2] Crown Plea Roll, 34 H. III.

xxiv   TIME OF HOLDING THE COURTS.

a surviving Roll[1] which states that in the 48 Henry III. Katerine, wife of Stephen Justice, having had her house burglariously entered ' statim levavit hutesium et clamorem de vico in vicum de parochia ad parochiam de domo ad domum quousque venit in presentia Ballivorum et Coronatorum.' Here, then, no doubt the Bailiffs sat to receive the presentments of the Capital Pledges; and the business occupied them for portions of at least four or five weeks.

Sessions held during Lent   2. The time when the Courts were held may be roughly described as the season of Lent. Only one Roll, that for 1891 (p. 69), gives the days of the different sessions throughout. The practice, however, had evidently not changed. In all the other Rolls there are only three notices of the day of sitting. In Roll I. the Leet of Conesford is stated to be held on the 'Monday next after Ash Wednesday' (*post carniprivium*). In Roll III. the presentments for (South) Conesford (p. 88) are made on the Monday next after the Feast of St. Valentine. This, being 20 Feb. 1290, would again be the first Monday in Lent. On that occasion the presentments for (North) Conesford are recorded as being taken on the following day.

But most of the early Rolls have a set of entries from which we may judge of the duration of the business. It was the custom to appoint two collectors to gather in the fines, and at the end of each of the four Great Leets is entered an account of the moneys they have received and the dates when they have paid them over. Thus in Roll II. (1289: p. 27) the payments were made for Conesford on Saturday after the Feast of St. Gregory the Pope (19 March), Saturday after the Feast of the Annunciation of the Blessed Mary (26 March), Thursday after the same feast (81 March), Saturday on the vigil of Palm Sunday (2 April), Thursday next following (7 April), and on Saturday before the Close of Easter (16 April). Those for Mancroft were made on the same days, omitting Thursday, 31 March. Those for Wymer were made on three Saturdays,

---

[1] Catalogued as a Coroner's Roll.

19 and 26 March, and 2 April, and on Thursday 7 April. Those for Over-the-Water, on the four Saturdays and the second of the two Thursdays. The first of these Saturdays (19 March) was the third Saturday in Lent. Certain fines on forestallers and others, not presented in particular Leets, were paid in on Saturday before the Feast of SS. Philip and James (30 April). In Roll IV. (1291 : p. 38) the payments were all made on Saturdays: Over-the-Water from Saturday 3 March to Saturday 24 March; Wymer, the same; Manecroft, from Saturday 10 March to Saturday 7 April; and Conesford from Saturday 17 March to Saturday 7 April. In this year 3 March was the Saturday before Lent, which fell very late. In 1293 they extended from Saturday 7 March (fourth Saturday in Lent), to Saturday 28 March (Easter Eve). In 1300 they are unusually late—from Saturday 2 April (Vigil of Palm Sunday) to Saturday 23 April.

3. It is a little difficult to understand from the payments how the sessions had been taking place. If each subleet had a separate day to itself, it might have been expected that they would occupy four weeks. But in 1289, all the four Leets have fines paid in on 19 March (third Saturday in Lent). If, therefore, the sittings had commenced, as in 1288 and 1290, on the first Monday in Lent, either they must all have been finished in three weeks, or perhaps a Great Leet was not taken all at once, but the subleets were mixed together, and so some out of each Leet may have been taken in the course of the three weeks, though all perhaps were not finished. *Subleets taken on separate days, but not always in order*

That this may have been the case is rendered probable by the precise notices given in Roll XI. for 1391. As already explained, there are only ten sets of presentments made then, and the districts are treated as separate Leets. They follow the almost invariable order from Conesford to Over-the-Water in their sequence on the Roll, but the dates of session are curiously intermixed. The weeks are specified as the weeks in Lent, and the days of sitting are as follows, arranged chronologically:— *Dates of sessions in 1391*

2nd week in Lent . .	Monday	. St. Stephen
	Tuesday	. Conesford
	Thursday	. Berstrete
	Friday	. St. Gregory
3rd week in Lent. .	Thursday	. St. Peter de Manecroft
4th week in Lent. .	Monday	. St. Andrew
	Thursday	. St. Michael (Coslany)˙
	Friday	. St. Giles
5th week in Lent. .	Monday	. St. Clement
	Tuesday	. St. George (Tombland)

In this year Easter fell on 27 March and the Monday in the 2nd week in Lent was 28 Feb.

The holding of the Leets in Lent is a proof of their antiquity; for if the privilege had been granted subsequently to Magna Charta they would have had to be held after Easter.[1]

IV. **The Constitution of the Court.**

1. The two matters of most importance to be considered under this head are, Who made the presentments and to whom were they made?

The Bailiffs presided over the Court, sitting together throughout Taking the latter first, there can be no reasonable doubt that the presiding officials in the Court were the four Bailiffs and that they sat together throughout the whole of the sessions. The only place where this is distinctly stated, in the heading to the Roll of 1375, has been already quoted. The first heading on Roll VII. for 1300 (p. 50) probably implies the same thing: 'Presentaciones Lete de Conesford Anno xxviii° temporibus Johannis Clerici, Rogeri de Tudenham et sociorum eorum.' But throughout all the Rolls the Bailiffs are mentioned as the supreme authority whose rights were being vindicated. The constantly recurring phrase 'per quod Ballivi amittunt theolonium' may be taken as evidence of this. Still more direct evidence of their authority in the Court is another phrase which is frequently used of some offender who has been presented: 'condonatur per Ballivos.' In Roll I. (p. 4) William Calf, a Capital Pledge of Berstrete, is in mercy 'pro magno con-

---

[1] Scriven, *Law of Copyholds*, p. 354. The Confirmation of Magna Charta was in 9 H. III. (1225).

temptu *facto Ballivis* quia noluit prestare sacramentum. Postea juravit.' His name immediately afterwards occurs among the jurors and is marked 'jur.'

The question, however, arises, In whose name was the authority exercised—in the name of the king, or in the name of the citizens? The court was the court of a privileged franchise and the holders of the franchise were the citizens. If, therefore, the citizens as a body occupied the position of the lord of a manor, the Bailiffs in presiding at the Leets might have corresponded to the lord's steward. But the case of a borough which was itself a Hundred was not that of a Manor cut off from the jurisdiction of the Hundred but of a Hundred where this particular jurisdiction was transferred from the Sheriff to some other nominees of the king. Remembering also that Norwich formed part of the king's demesne, and that he had a double lordship over it, it seems likely that the king rather looked upon himself as foregoing the profits than as altogether parting with the jurisdiction. In other words, I think that the Bailiffs sat in the court as the representatives of their lord the king, and that no nice distinction was drawn between his seignorial and royal rights. An entry near the beginning of the first Roll confirms this view. The Capital Pledges of Conesford say (p. 2), 'De tesauro invento sciunt set presentare contempnunt;' which seems to mean that they were willing to make presentment of offences to the Bailiffs so far as they acted for the benefit of the city but declined to give information to them as inquisitors acting on behalf of the king. Whether the Bailiffs had any assessors is a matter to be considered elsewhere (Section VII. 5).
_{as the king's officers in the Hundred, not as chief citizens}

2. As to the persons by whom the presentments were made, the Rolls give very clear evidence that they were made by the Capital Pledges of the tithings.
_{Presentments made by the Capital Pledges of the tithings}

The first Roll begins 'Cap̄ pleg'[then follow twelve names] presentant per sacramentum suum' etc. In the first of the Wymer subleets is the entry, 'Omnes capitales plegii in mīā pro concelamento' etc. (p. 12). In the other districts the jurors are not so described, but in 'Manecroft, Parish of

xxviii THE CAPITAL PLEDGES.

St. Stephen' is the note (p. 7) 'Laurence de Takelston cap: pleg: for extreme contempt. In mercy. Afterwards he took the oath.' His name accordingly occurs amongst the rest.

The second Roll, which is one of Amercements, only contains the names of the jurors incidentally when they are amerced. When mentioned they are plainly called Capital Pledges. Thus of Conesford (p. 22) : 'De Radulpho de Suthgate capitali plegio pro concelamento etc. xij d.' Then follow the names of twelve other persons fined 'pro eodem.' A similar entry (p. 25) is made with regard to the jurors of Berstrete. Still more explicit is the entry in reference to the jurors of the first of the subleets Over-the-Water (p. 31), 'De Rogero de Honeworth [and 15 others] capitalibus plegiis [written in full] de fine pro concelamento, dī marc'.' Similar entries are found in the Roll of Amercements IX. The fragment for Berstrete (Roll VIII.) and Rolls X. and XI., which are in the form of presentments, begin in all the subleets, 'Capitales plegii presentant' etc.

The Capital Pledges sworn, but not all who were present   3. Before making their presentments the Capital Pledges were sworn. The first and third Rolls are here of special value, for they specify the number of those who were sworn by adding 'jur:' after the name. Not all whose names are entered are so marked, although the words 'presentant per sacramentum suum' are made to apply to all alike. The following is a statement of the number of Capital Pledges entered in each district in Roll I.

	Number of names entered	Number marked 'sworn'
Leet of Conesford		
1. [South Conesford]	12	[12 [1] : 'jur' is omitted]
2. [North Conesford]	12	12 (one other in default)
3. Berstrete	13	12 (one discharged)
Leet of Manecroft		
1. [St. Stephen]	12	11 (the twelfth described as 'clericus')
2. [St. Peter]	30	22 [2] (one marked with a + ; seven not marked)

[1] In Roll III. twelve are sworn. Of the seven unsworn six come at the end. The seventh is in the middle of those that are sworn, and as no explanation of the omission is given it is probably a mistake.

[2] I think this should be 23.

[Leet of *Wymer*]	Number of names entered	Number marked 'sworn'
1. [St. Giles]	12	12
2. [St. Gregory]	12	12
3. [St. Andrew]	15	12 (one struck out; one marked with a + as absent; one unmarked)
4. [St. George]	12	12
Leet Over-the-Water.		
1. [St. Michael]	18	17 (one not marked; he and another are substitutes for two who are absent)
2. [St. Clement]	15	15
	163	149

4. The relation of the Capital Pledges to their tithings belongs rather to the general working of the tithing system. It may, however, be observed here that before appearing in court the Capital Pledges of each subleet must have come to some agreement as to the presentments to be made. The presentments are, with very rare exceptions, given as the common verdicts of the whole body. One of these exceptions is in the Roll of 1288. Under the subleet of S. Conesford it is stated (p. 2) : ' Omnes in mīa pro concelamento. Presentat etiam Ricardus Erych quod Alanus de Catton invenit ix bidentes submersos ' etc. Richard Erych was one of the Capital Pledges. More curious is an entry in the Wymer Leet in 1293 (p. 44) : ' De Martino de Tudenham pro falsa presentatione eo quod presentavit quod quedam mulier que vocabatur Lecia occidit Olivam de Hemelington . que quidem presentatio non fuit advocata de decennariis suis nec de capitali plegio.' Then follows ' De Ricō de Ho pro eodem. De Rado Russell pro eodem.' The first of these entries, that in 1288, is so vague that it is not safe to found any argument upon it. There is nothing to show why in this particular case one Capital Pledge alone should have made the presentment. The other entry, in 1293, is a very suggestive one. First, it is the only place in the Rolls where the word ' decennarius ' occurs. Its conjunction with ' capitalis plegius ' plainly shows that in Norwich it meant a ' member of a tithing,' not ' the tithingman,' as in some other places. Next it must be asked, Whose decennaries and Capital Pledge are intended, those of Martin de Tudenham, or those

The Capital Pledges in a subleet acted as one body.

of the woman called Lecia. If those of Martin de Tudenham, then we should apparently have the case of a presentment being made by a private person (not a Capital Pledge) and unsupported by his fellow-tithingmen and his own Capital Pledge. This is quite inconsistent with the practice disclosed in these Rolls. The 'decennarii sui' must, in my opinion, be those of Lecia and an explanation of what happened may, I think, be found. Martin de Tudenham occurs among the Capital Pledges of St. Laurence and St. Gregory in the Roll of 1288. It may be presumed, therefore, that he and the other two persons fined with him made their false presentment in that capacity. The omission of any surname for the woman Lecia makes it impossible to identify her. But the surname 'de Hemelington' occurs only in this Leet Roll and in the Conveyance Roll for the previous year. In both cases it is the same person who is mentioned—Nicholas de Hemelington. In the year before this presentment he and his wife Cecillia had a messuage conveyed to them in St. Michael de Coslany. There they no doubt resided, for in this Leet Roll the 'wife of Nicholas de Hemelington' is among those fined for breaking the assize of beer in the Leet Over-the-Water. We may be justified, therefore, in concluding that the Oliva who was killed belonged to this family. If so the entry may be thus explained. The three Capital Pledges of the second subleet of Wymer made presentment of an offence committed possibly in their district and charged it upon a woman living in another Leet. The tithingmen of the particular district inculpated, supported by their Capital Pledge, refused to believe in Lecia's guilt, and therefore the three presenters were amerced for false presentment. This explanation assumes that Lecia lived in the same district as Oliva. It is at all events probable that she lived in some other district than the one for which the presentment was made.

and in concert with their tithingmen The entry is interesting as disclosing some part of the process of preparing the presentments for the court. The Capital Pledge was not only nominally but actually the mouthpiece of the members of his tithing. All his present-

INTRODUCTION, IV. 5.   xxxi

ments had received their assent before he and his fellows delivered them in the court. In the present case the 'decennarii' with their Capital Pledge acted the part of compurgators. Their refusal to support it cleared Lecia from a serious charge. The question as to how Oliva had come by her death must have previously been discussed before the Coroner. Perhaps the evidence then given may have guided the 'decennarii' in refusing to admit Lecia's guilt.

It was not unusual for Capital Pledges to present offences belonging properly to another Leet or at least having no apparent connection with their own.

5. It is clear that as a general rule all Capital Pledges were bound to attend the court. How far this obligation was in practice strictly insisted on will appear to some extent in the Mancroft Tithing Roll. All required to be present, in theory,

One subject, however, belongs to their action as sworn presenters. They were sworn not only to make true presentments but to hide or keep back no offence. For neglecting this latter duty they were frequently amerced: 'Omnes capitales plegii [*or* juratores,] in mīa pro concelamento' is an entry of frequent occurrence. It is mostly (though not always) followed by some specified offence which they have neglected to present. On one occasion (p. 12), in 1288, the Capital Pledges of the subleet of St. Giles were declared 'in mercy' 'quia Johes Swynesheved levavit hutesium super Melisentiam Attethates et non presentaverunt.' Then it is added: '·Postea presentant quod Johes Swynesheved levavit hutesium super Melisentiam Attegates et Johem le Graunt et Ricardum servientem Melisentie Attegates.' Can they possibly have been ignorant of what must at the time have been notorious throughout the neighbourhood? The mention of their subsequently making a due presentment is unusual and suggests the inquiry whether such a sequel is to be understood in other similar cases. One would suppose that the only object of forcing the jurors to make presentment of an offence would be to obtain the amercement of the offender through the affeerers, which presumably could only follow on formal presentment and required to know and present every offence

by the jury. Yet these entries of amercements of the jurors for 'concealment' are not followed by any amercement of the person who is said to have committed the offence 'concealed.'

It appears from these instances that as on the one hand it was necessary for at least twelve presenters to agree in the presentment of an offence which most of them cannot have been personally acquainted with, so on the other hand they were held collectively responsible for a knowledge of all the offences committed in their district. This implies much previous inquiry amongst their own body and also amongst their tithingmen. Every adult male must have been under the obligation of disclosing every offence known to him. The process of preparation for the annual Leet can hardly have been agreeable to any of the parties concerned.

<small>Affeerers,</small>

6. *Affeerers and Collectors.*—The names of Affeerers are only twice entered. On Roll VII. (p. 50), at the head of the first membrane, is 'Affer' Matheus Thusceyns, Rogerus de Batesford.' The Roll begins as usual with the Leet of Conesford. To that Leet Roger de Batesford belonged. Matthew Tusceyns, however, certainly belonged to the Leet of Mancroft. It appears unlikely, therefore, that he should be appointed for Conesford alone, and it might be thought that these two were appointed to serve for all the four Leets, as no other names are given for the other Leets.

<small>probably taken from amongst the Capital Pledges</small>

The other instance is much clearer and points to a different practice. It is in the fragmentary Roll for the two subleets of Conesford, marked Roll III. At the foot of the first membrane dealing with (South) Conesford is this entry (p. 38): 'Afferatores, Ric̄us Botman, Witts King, Silvester Siger, Radulphus de Suthgate.' All these four had been sworn in as jurors for this subleet on this occasion. It seems certain, therefore, that they were intended to act for their own subleet alone. Whether they were appointed by the Bailiffs from among the sworn Capital Pledges or by the jurors themselves does not appear.

7. The Collectors are more frequently mentioned, and were evidently permanent servants or serjeants. Roll II. is precise on this point as on several others. At the commencement of the Leet of Conesford are the words 'Pre' Michi, Rado.' At the end certain moneys are accounted for as 'Recepta per manus Michis.' Similarly the names of two persons are given at the head of the other Leets, and amounts are accounted for at the end by one or both of them. The contraction 'Pre'' is sometimes followed by the contraction for 'est.' No doubt the meaning is 'preceptum est.' Though these headings do not occur in other Rolls, the payments do, and the names of the persons by whom they were made. From a comparison of the various occurrences of the names it appears that the same names recur in different years and sometimes for one Leet, sometimes for another. One of the persons so named (p. 47) is in one case described as 'Ricūs serviens.' Another, 'Witts de Keteringham,' may be assumed to be the same as a person of that name presented with his wife in the following year for breaking the assize of ale and excused 'quia serviens.' They were probably the permanent serjeants of the Bailiffs. *Collectors, serjeants of the Bailiffs*

8. *Constable and Sub-Constable.*—It may be here mentioned that a Leet had its own constable. This official is only once mentioned, viz. in Roll I. (p. 1) where Hugo de Bromholm is described in one of the entries as 'Constable of the Leet of Conesford.' It is a case of assault, of which presentment is made by the jurors of (South) Conesford. He was at the time one of the acting Capital Pledges for that subleet. Presumably he had been appointed at the view of frankpledge. He must have held office for the whole Leet and not for the subleet only. Constables were officers of a Hundred, created by the Statute of Winchester (13 Ed. I.) and the occurrence of the office here is an incidental proof that each Leet was an integral section of a Hundred. *Constable of a Leet*

In the same Roll in the first subleet Over-the-Water is the entry (p. 18) : 'De Simone de Melton pro maximo contemptu facto Ballivis quia noluit prestare sacramentum *Sub-constable, perhaps of a subleet*

suum cum electus fuit subconstabularius per omnes juratores.' This is entered as a presentment by the jurors, so that the offence had occurred previously, and probably that election also had taken place at the view of frankpledge, the sub-constable holding office for the subleet.

V. Offences presented and amerced.

1. The offences presented and amerced at the Leets embraced a very wide area of criminal and correctional jurisdiction, including matters personal, social, commercial and municipal.

Murder, violent death   One class of offences may be at once set aside. Murder, manslaughter or death by misfortune did not come under the cognisance of the court, having been sufficiently dealt with by the Coroner. Yet it would appear that, if foul play were suspected of having taken place, though no evidence of it in the shape of a dead body had been found, it was the duty of the Capital Pledges to report it. Such was the view taken by the jury of South Conesford in 1289 (Roll III.: p. 35) when they reported the murder of a child. The court ordered the arrest of the incriminated person. The case of Oliva de Hemelington mentioned above (p. xxix) must have been one where the murder (if one had been committed) had not been brought home to anyone.

Nuisances, weights, unwholesome food   2. Among cognisable offences may be taken, first, those which almost always continued to be dealt with by Leet presentments and amercements in all places. Such were especially nuisances and the use of defective weights and measures, besides market offences, as selling unwholesome meat and fish. Of these nothing further needs to be said. About one, however, an important observation must be made. It is held that a Leet jury could only present a *public* nuisance and not a private one, in which an action would lie for a remedy.[1] This was not the early practice in Norwich, private nuisances as well as public being presented.[2]

---
[1] Scriven on *Law of Copyholds*, p. 353.
[2] Roll I. (St. Stephen), p. 8 etc.

The distinction between a tort and a common nuisance had not yet been realised.

3. Next there was a large catalogue of offences which in the thirteenth and fourteenth centuries were presented at the Leets, but were afterwards taken out of their hands. They may be described as offences both against the common law of the land and also against the customs of the city. The most serious of these offences was theft. This *Larceny* was always presented, and occasionally dealt with by amercement. But as a rule it was treated as a felony, and the thief was ordered to be arrested and to be reserved for trial before the Coroners and Bailiffs in the City Court if he were taken with the mainour and the charge were supported by a suit; otherwise he was to be kept for the next visit of Justices assigned for gaol-delivery. (Customs, ch. 4.) Receivers of stolen goods were merely amerced.

4. Next to larceny may be named assaults. In the *Assaults* thirteenth century Rolls these are almost invariably described as 'blood-drawing' and are dealt with by amercement. An exception to this rule occurs at the Leet of 1313 (p. 57), when all such offenders, except in the Leet of Conesford, are ordered to be arrested instead of being amerced. In the two later Rolls of the fourteenth century this offence is described in much fuller detail.

5. The raising of the hue is a very frequent subject of *Hue and cry* presentment. In some of the Rolls it is specified that an amercement is imposed for *wrongfully* raising the hue. In most cases it is not so specified, but, as an amercement follows, it is doubtless so to be understood. Where the hue is said to have been justly raised and yet an amercement follows, it will be found that an offence is also mentioned, to which the amercement must be taken as referring. It is probable that it was the duty of the Capital Pledges to make presentment of all raising of the hue, whether rightful or wrongful. The first Roll, being in the form of presentments, would include both. The second and others, which are in the form of amercements, contain only the cases of wrongful raising.

Being out of tithing

6. Another offence which belonged to the general law of the land and was especially within the province of Leet jurisdiction was that of not being in a tithing. The court was responsible for enforcing the obligation on all who had been resident one year in the city, being of the age of twelve years, and not coming under the category of any of the classes who claimed exemption. In close connection with this offence the two later fourteenth century Rolls classify that of 'not coming to the Leet.' This offence is hardly ever mentioned in the earlier Rolls. Perhaps it is included under the head of 'defaults,' but they are not numerous. In the two later Rolls a considerable number of persons are fined under this head.

Non-attendance at the Leet

Purprestures etc.

Purprestures, removing bounds, altering watercourses and similar offences against the common law need no remark.

Forestalling etc.

7. One other class of offences belongs rather to common than to municipal law, for they were breaches of rules of universal obligation,[1] those of forestalling, or in any other way interfering with the freedom of the public market; and the breaking of the assize of ale and bread. It is a curious feature in these Rolls, that while the breaches of the assize of ale furnish an inordinate proportion of the whole number of amercements, the assize of bread is only incidentally mentioned, and no account is taken of defective or fraudulent loaves or the other offences for which the London bakers of this period were so vigorously dealt with. It would almost seem as though some other authority took such offences under its cognisance. The 33rd Chapter of Customs provides for four inspectors of bread, two bakers and two citizens of good repute.

8. There remain offences which may be called strictly municipal, or breaches of the Custom of the City.

Unlawful trading, and Gilds of separate crafts

The most obvious of these was that of merchandising without having been admitted to the freedom of the city. With this may be mentioned the offence of defrauding the Communitas of its rightful dues by the establishment of

[1] Ordinance of 51 H. III.

private gilds for individual trades or crafts. The light thus thrown upon the commercial constitution of the City in the thirteenth century is one of the most valuable contributions which these Rolls make to our knowledge. It is clear that while the *admission* to citizenship was in the hands of the community in general (Customs, ch. 36), the Leet was the authority which took cognisance of its rightful *exercise*. There is no trace of a gild merchant undertaking either of these offices. It is clear also that admission to citizenship meant full freedom to exercise any sort of trade, and that the formation of separate craft gilds was resented as an interference with the general interests of the whole body of citizens. In spite, however, of prohibition and amercement the craft gilds flourished, and finally impressed their stamp on the City constitution, so that to become a citizen it was necessary to be enrolled in one of the trade companies. This development was not fully matured till the middle of the fifteenth century; but it had begun to work in the fourteenth. A slight indication of the change is revealed in the Leet Rolls. The expression of the early Rolls 'emit et vendit tanquam concivis' becomes in the Roll of 1391 (p. 72) 'utitur arte sua.'[1]

Other breaches of the Customs of the City consisted of fraudulent manufacture, such as that of the tanners in the preparation of leather; and fraudulent dealings in trade, of which the instances are very numerous. *Fraudulent work*

9. One more is worthy of notice, the impleading a citizen in the Court Christian in matters which did 'not touch marriage or wills.' It seldom happened that a jury failed to present some offender of this sort. The Rolls of 1375 and 1391 show that there were persons who made a profit out of 'procuring' cases for the ecclesiastical courts (p. 71). It would not be difficult in numerous instances so to interpret the circumstances of a claim as to bring it under ecclesiastical cognisance, especially when the claimant had failed to get what he thought were his rights in a secular court. *Impleading in the Court Christian*

[1] On this whole subject see Notes A and B after the Introduction.

VI. Amercements.

Amercements

1. Roll II. is very valuable for its precise entries, not only of the amercements, but of the amounts paid in whole or in part, or excused, or for which gages were taken, or which were left in arrears. The state of affairs thus disclosed is decidedly curious. (The other Rolls entirely correspond with this one, omitting the precise details.)

Amount of separate amercements

The amercements in the earlier Rolls vary from 6 d. to 4 s. They rarely go beyond that. Occasionally 'half a mark' is imposed, and very rarely 10 s. or even 20 s. No definite relation between an offence and the amount of the amercement can be detected. It cannot be doubted that, according to the known practice in other matters, such as admissions to the freedom of the City, the affeerers estimated the amount of the fine according to the presumed capacity of the offender to pay. Every now and then some unusually heavy amercement seems to mark a special aggravation of the offence.

Analysis of amercements in Leet of Conesford in 1289

2. The financial results are very curious and worthy of attentive consideration. Take the Leet of Conesford. First come the general offences, as assaults, purprestures, breaches of City customs and privileges etc. The amount of amercements assessed for these offences is £8 4 s. The amount actually recorded as paid is £1 2 s. 4 d. Besides the amercements excused or pledged (the terms employed are ' *condonatur* ' and ' *vadiatur* ') amercements to the amount of

Breakers of assize of ale

£4 7 s. are marked with 'd' (*debet*). After this the breaches of the assize of ale are dealt with and mixed up with them (in small proportion) the creating a nuisance by putting refuse heaps (*fimaria*) in the highway. Here matters assume a more businesslike aspect, though the method is peculiar. Almost every well-to-do housewife in the City must have been in the constant habit of brewing and selling beer, and breaking the assize. Their annual amercement assumed very much the character of an excise duty. The usual form of entry is, ' De Johe de Morle et uxore eius pro assissa cervisie non observata.' Then follow the names of

numerous husbands and wives 'pro eodem.' From time to time 'et pro fimario' is thrown in as a kindred offence. The numbers are remarkable. In this Roll they are, in Conesford 57, Mancroft 84, Wymer 81, Ultra Aquam 64: total 286. A similar number is found in other Rolls. The amount of assessed amercements under this head in Conesford is £8 6 s. Of this £1 17 s. is recorded as paid, but only 13 s. are marked as 'owing.' The rest is almost entirely excused. The practice was this. An amercement is assessed at 4 s. This is accompanied by the entry 'solvit ij s. residuum condonatur' (or frequently with an amercement of 2 s. 'solvit vj d.'), and at the commencement of the entry 'quietus est.' Every single amercement is thus in some way accounted for. The authorities were quite satisfied to get, at the most, from one quarter to one half of the amount as assessed. Putting all the offences together, the total amount of amercements assessed for that Leet was £16 10 s.; the money actually paid £2 19 s. 4 d., and the amount marked as still owing £5. The collector, Michaelis, accounts for £3 11 s. 3 d. His accounts, which are intended for records of payment to some official, are rendered on four successive Saturdays and two intervening Thursdays. On the first day 16 s. is accounted for, and on the second 37 s. 11 d. The others are smaller sums. This looks as if at the end of a certain term the defaulters passed out of his hands to be dealt with, probably, by the Bailiffs. How much of the arrears they ever succeeded in obtaining is extremely doubtful.

3. The Leet of Manecroft in the same Roll rather strengthens the features thus disclosed. In that Leet the amount of assessed amercements for general offences is £6 16 s., and of this only the paltry sum of 6 s. 9 d. is accounted for as paid. The amount for breaches of the assize of ale is £12 11 s., of which £3 9 s. 6 d. is accounted for; and for 'fimaria' 19 s., of which only 3 s. 3 d. is received. In all, the assessed amercements are £20 6 s.; the amount received £3 19 s. 6 d. Brid and Makabe, the collectors, account for £4 3 s. 3 d. at various intervals as before.

Of the Leet of Manecroft

Of Wymer

4. The Wymer accounts are :—Assessed for general offences, £4 6 s. 8 d.; for breaking the assize, £10 6 s. 0 d. : £14 12 s. 8 d. The collectors account for £3 1 s. 10 d.

Of Ultra Aquam

In Ultra Aquam :—For general offences, £2 7 s. 8d.; for breaking the assize, £11 18 s. 0 d.; accounted for by collectors, £4 2 s. 6 d.

Miscellaneous

Certain trade offences committed by whole trades were dealt with for the whole City and not in Leets. The assessed amount for these is £7 4 s. 6 d., of which £2 1 s. 4 d. is accounted for.

Of the City

The totals for the whole City are :—Assessed amercements, £72 18 s. 10 d.; accounted for by collectors, £17 0 s. 2 d. Even allowing for the debts which may have been got in, the result can hardly be called satisfactory. The Account Roll for 1364 (p. 77) gives some insight into the collection of amercements.

Inadequate result

'Pardoning' of amercements

5. '*Condonatur.*'—Mention has several times been made of the fact that amercements after being assessed were either wholly or in part excused or pardoned. In many cases this is simply expressed by the note 'condonatur,' without any reason being assigned. Sometimes the reason 'quia pauper' is added, or some special reason as 'quia amens,' 'quia serviens,' or 'quia janitor' (at one of the City gates). Sometimes 'per Ballivos' is added : whether this expresses anything more than the simple 'condonatur' is not clear. No one else but the Bailiffs can be supposed to have had the requisite authority.

Besides these reasonable causes of pardon there are two of great interest, for they touch upon cardinal principles in the working of the frankpledge system in the City.

Intervention of leading citizens

The first is this. In twenty different cases in this Roll of 1289 it is noted against an amercement 'condonatur ad instantiam Henrici clerici,' or of some other person. These entries are not found so frequently in the other Rolls but they are not unknown. There are several in Roll V. and Roll VII. In this last the practice is to put only the name of the person intervening without the preliminary 'ad instantiam,' except in two instances, where the full

expression is used. The intention is evidently the same. These interventions occur most frequently, as might be supposed, in breaches of the assize of ale, but also in the amercements for general offences. Altogether the number of persons who thus intervened is twenty-five. A brief analysis will show who and what they were. Two may be dismissed as not leading to any conclusion, 'Fratres Minores' and 'Prior Predicatorum.' They may be supposed to have made interest with the Bailiffs on behalf of a friend or dependent. Two others also seem to involve no principle. They are Michaelis and Ranulphus Belle, two of the collectors whom I have presumed to have been serjeants of the Bailiffs. Of the twenty-one who remain, it is plain at first sight to anyone acquainted with the citizens of that period that nearly all of them were among the very foremost. No less than eleven of them were Bailiffs : some several times over. Three others were men who at various times held positions of official influence.· Gervase le Graunt was advocate for the city in a Plea held at Westminster between the citizens and the Prior in 1292.[1] Thomas Wisse acted as Clerk of the Bailiffs in 1287 when the Common Clerk was at Westminster 'super compotum suum.'[2] Thomas de Framingham is described in 1290 as Attorney for the Commonalty 'pro libertatibus calumpniandis.'[3] Of the other seven, Nigel de Foxclee was a 'merchant, citizen of Norwich.' Another was 'Master John Man, clerk.' 'Master' was, I think, an academic and not an ecclesiastical title, and John Man, though a clerk, was married. Of four more I can find no trace. There remains one who stands alone, 'Is' de Tudenham.' This cannot be any other than Isabella de Tudenham, wife of Roger de Tudenham, one of the then Bailiffs.

6. It is of course a fair argument that all these were instances of persons using their private interest with the Bailiffs for their own friends. But, considering how many of them belonged to the highest official class, the question *Were these present as part of a class above frank-pledge?*

[1] Book of Pleas, fol. xxiv.   [2] Conveyance Roll, 10 June.
[3] Conveyance Roll, 9 March.

certainly suggests itself, Have we here a trace of a class who were above the obligation of frankpledge and were present in the court as informal Assessors to the Bailiffs, or, in other words, forming the court of which the Bailiffs were the sole executive ? It may be observed that although four of those who thus intervened in 1289 were the Bailiffs presiding at the time, the personal intervention of a single one is clearly distinguished from the official and combined action of the four, which is expressed as 'condonatur per Ballivos.' (Only very rarely is the word 'per' used of a single person.) The importance of the question is seen by reference to a statement made by Bracton who says (f. 124 b) that a man need not be in frankpledge if he has 'quod sufficiat pro francoplegio sicut dignitatem vel ordinem vel liberum tenementum, vel in civitate rem immobilem.' One would have thought this last clause would have exempted nearly all the citizens of Norwich.[1] Yet it is plain from the instances given below in William Bele's tithing in St. Stephen (Section X. 8), and also from many of the names entered in the Tithing Roll, that no such broad exemption could have existed in Norwich. Still we know that there was a class who went by the vague description of 'probi homines' or 'discretiores' or other terms of similar import. These interveners are for the most part the persons who would be reckoned in such a class, and to find them intervening in the Leet court certainly suggests that they may have been there for some other purpose than merely to assist a friend. The question might be almost decided by the expression 'de diversis cruce signatis' used in Roll XII. (p. 77), if only we could be sure of its meaning in that place. The mark of a cross ordinarily means absence without excuse, and the 45th Chapter of Customs so uses it in a very important connection. Public business, it says, was hindered by the bad attendance of citizens at public meetings. Therefore substantial citizens from each Leet (*i.e.* each of the four Great Leets) were to be served with notices to attend on particular days. A serjeant was to come pre-

[1] A large number of the citizens were apparently freeholders.

pared with a panel and if any thus specially summoned failed to attend he was to have a cross set against his name with a view to his subsequent amercement. If we knew that this was the meaning of the expression in the Account Roll it would go far to prove that substantial citizens were required at the Leets to form a court. Unfortunately, as noticed in that Roll, the meaning there is too uncertain to form the basis of such a conclusion.

7. The other special cause assigned for the pardoning of amercements is also of much interest. In eleven instances of amercements in Roll II. (pp. 26, 27) is added the note 'condonatur quia causa non est vera.' This actual expression occurs only in this Roll, but in Roll V. (pp. 43, 45) are the similar notes 'quia non braciat'—'quia tenuit assissam.' The law, at least of a later time, held that a presentment at a Court Leet (not touching freehold) made by a jury of twelve persons could not be traversed. In the cases here referred to the presentments were received and the amercement assessed, and after that an appeal must have been made to the Bailiffs, who, perhaps with the help of a special jury, decided that the charge was not true. Kitchin states [1] that a presentment could not be traversed if the day were passed on which it was made; but 'on the same day a man might have an action of false presentment against the jurors and have recovery.' These instances, however, seem to indicate that a rather more summary course of procedure was the practice in these Norwich courts in the thirteenth century.

Amercements overruled on appeal

VII. The Working of the Frankpledge System. The Capital Pledges.

1. Having now gathered up the various fragments of information which may be obtained from these Rolls with respect to the Leet organisation of the City, the courts and their proceedings, and the character of the offences presented, we may next inquire what light they throw on

[1] *Le Courte Leete*, 42 b.

the organisation and working of the frankpledge system. What can be learned as to the number and composition of the tithings and as to the office of Capital Pledge? It will, I think, save repetition and add clearness to our view of the existing evidence if we start with the Capital Pledges, for they run through the whole of our evidences, whereas our special knowledge of the composition of the tithings is almost exclusively to be derived from the Mancroft Tithing Roll.

Lists of Capital Pledges

To begin with, then, we have a satisfactory foundation to work upon in the detailed lists of Capital Pledges for all the subdivisions of the City in the Roll of 1288. To compare with these we have lists of Capital Pledges amerced in 1289 in Conesford and Berstrete and in the second subleet Over-the-Water. Then there are two lists for the two subleets of South and North Conesford in 1290, and a list for the second subleet Over-the-Water in 1291. The evidence of these various lists is still further confirmed by another list which may be put together without any difficulty. In 14 Edward I. (1286), just two years before the date of the Roll of 1288, there had been held a very searching inquiry in the City by the Itinerant Justices. No previous Eyre had been held since 53 Henry III. (1269), after which, in 1272, had occurred the disastrous riot between the citizens and the monks of the cathedral which amongst other results had led to the flight of many of the citizens. The Judges in 1286 made diligent inquiry concerning the chattels of the fugitives and in each case is recorded either the name of the person in whose tithing the fugitive was, or else why he was not in a tithing at all. Several copies of the proceedings exist, in the Crown Plea Roll [1] in the Public Record Office, in the Book of Pleas [2] in the Guildhall at Norwich, in an isolated Roll [3] wrongly catalogued among the Leet Rolls, and in a Roll classed with some early Coroners' Rolls. They are all evidently taken from the

[1] M 4 2, memb. 88.
 3

[2] Book of Pleas, fol. xxix.
[3] Catalogued as Court Leet Roll 2.

same source, but occasionally supplement one another. From these sources may be derived a list of fifty persons from whom tithings were named throughout the city in 1286. At least twenty-five out of the fifty are found among the Capital Pledges of 1288.

A distinct source of information after a lapse of several years is to be found in a list of the Capital Pledges of the Mancroft subleet who were amerced in 1313. For the present it is sufficient to observe that this list almost exactly tallies with the names of some of the Capital Pledges in the Mancroft Tithing Roll.

2. A very cursory comparison of these lists, especially the earlier ones, will inevitably lead to the conclusion that a Capital Pledge once appointed remained in office for at least several years. The fact just mentioned, that of fifty Capital Pledges in 1286 no less than twenty-five are found still serving in 1288 is of itself sufficient to prove this. Or again, the same conclusion may be drawn from the otherwise inexplicable custom of calling a tithing from the name of a person and not of a locality, which would seem to be the natural use. The personal responsibility is what the law took notice of. It might be objected that the use of a personal name to describe a tithing does not of necessity imply that the person was still its head, or even that he was still alive, just as in these early documents we constantly find a lane called by the name of a leading resident who has long been dead. But when we find at least twenty-five out of fifty persons from whom tithings are named actually serving as Capital Pledges two years and more afterwards, it is strong evidence in favour of the conclusion that the tithings were called from them because they were the recognised officers who, until some other took their place represented in the eyes of the law the collective responsibility of the tithing.

A Capital pledge continued in office for several years

3. To make it clear that the office of Capital Pledge was held with some degree of permanence, the evidence of one subleet will be sufficient. Here are the lists of the Capital Pledges who answered for the second subdivision

of the Leet Over-the-Water in the three years, 1288, 1289, and 1291.

Three years' lists of same subject compared	16 Ed. I.	17 Ed. I.	19 Ed. I.
	Roger' de Huneworthe	Roger' de Honeworth	Rad' de Hevingham
	Rob¹ᵘ fil' Gervasii	Rob¹ᵘ fil' Gervasii	Roger' de Huneworthe
	Rob¹ᵘ de Donewyc'	Rob¹ᵘ de Donewyc'	Walter' fil' Henrici
	Joħes Knicht loksmicht	Hen. fil' capellani	Joħes Knyth le loc-smyth
	Joħes de Brandon	Thōs. Spik	
	Hen. le Stotrere	Reginald' de Catton	Joħes le mareschal
	Hen. fil' capellani	Ad. ffege	Joħes Waryn
	Hen. de Monjoye	Riĉus de Stalham	Rob¹ᵘ. fil' Rici
	Reginald' de Catton	Reyner' de Schuldham	Hen. fil' capellani
	Adam ffegge	Joħes le Skinnere	Pħs de Pulham
	Riĉus de Stalham	Rad. de Hevingham	Reginald' de Catton
	Reyner' de Schuldham	Rob. le Miteynmaker	Riĉus de Stalham
	Warin' le Skynnere	Hen. le Stotere	Reginald' de Schuldham
	Roger' Abbott	Joħes le loksmith	Thom' de Sc̄ō Edmundo
	Rob¹ᵘ le Mitenmaker	Joħes de Sc̄ā ffide	Roger' Abbot

From this it appears that seven of those who were serving in 1288 were still holding the same office in 1291. Two of these, Roger Abbot and Richard de Stalham are among those from whom tithings are named in 1286, so that they must have continued in office for at least six years. An examination of the Conesford lists would show a similar result. Individual instances of a very lengthened tenure of the office may perhaps be detected. The name of John Slabbard occurs in Conesford in 1288 and in 1290 and also in 1313, and he may be traced as an inhabitant of the district throughout the period. It is difficult also to doubt the identity of 'Joħes de Aschewell jun.' who is mentioned in Mancroft in 1288 and again in 1313, both times with the same descriptive affix.

This permanence of a fair proportion of the presenters of offences must have greatly facilitated the working of the system.

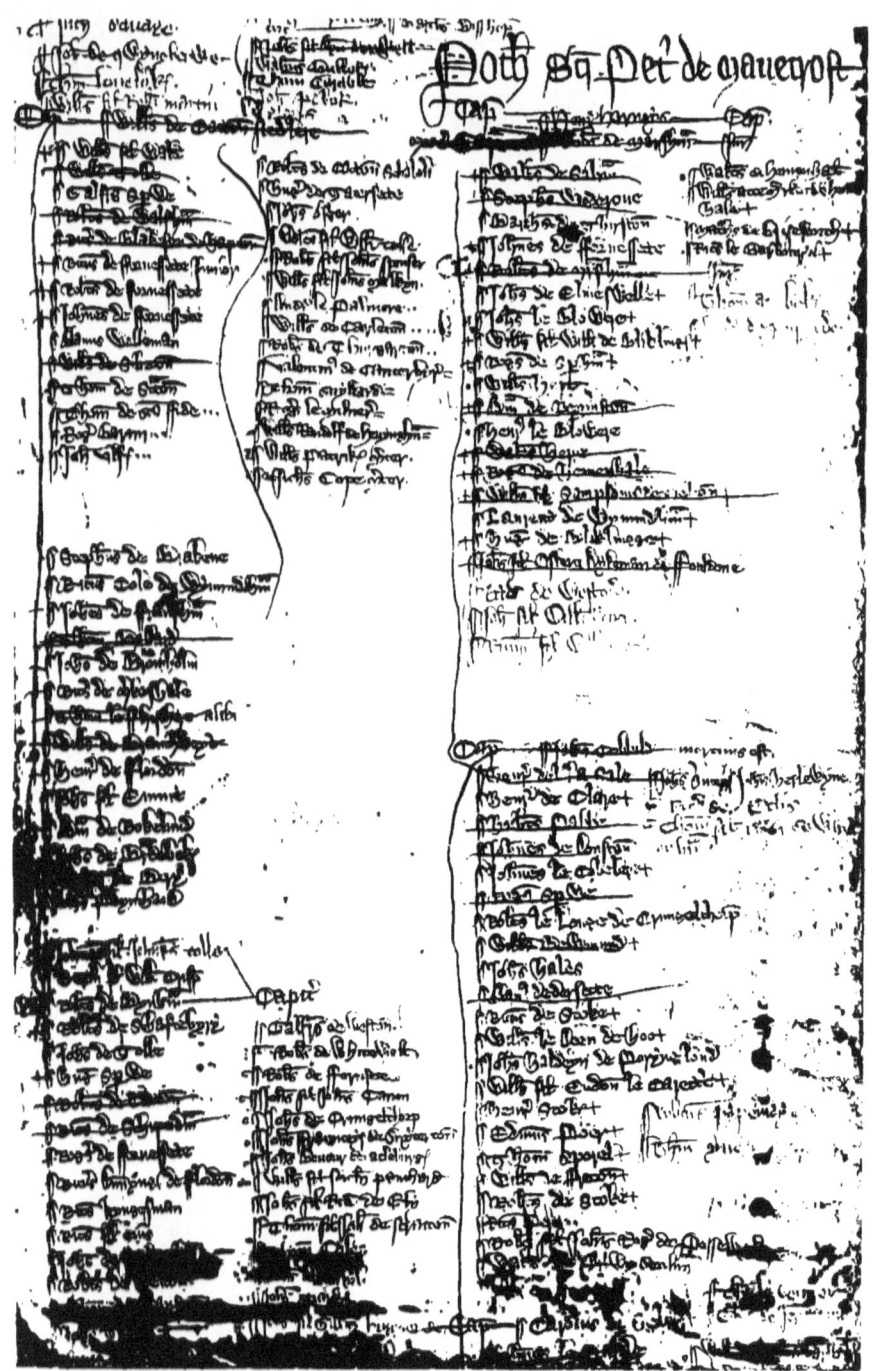

TITHING ROLL. ca 1311.

VIII. The Mancroft Tithing Roll.[1]

1. As it is impossible to separate the consideration of the Capital Pledges entirely from that of the tithings, we may now describe the Mancroft Tithing Roll which has already several times been referred to. *[The Mancroft Tithing Roll described]*

It is made up of four parchment membranes fastened together at the top, and consists entirely of sets of names. It has neither descriptive heading nor date, the only heading being 'Leta de Nedham et Manecroft et de Magna Newegate.' The mention of this last locality at once places the date of the roll as subsequent to 1304, when the Leet of Great Newgate, which had been recovered by the King from the Prior in 1291, was granted to the citizens.

An examination of the document shows that it is a list of all the persons enrolled in tithings in the Leet of Mancroft. The membranes are written on both sides, and each side contains two columns of names. The names are arranged in sets, a space being left between the end of one set and the beginning of another. At the head of most of the sets is a name placed a little out of line with the rest and marked 'Cāp,' the word being generally written after the name as well as before it. That these sets of names are those of the members of a tithing is plain of itself, and it is so stated. At the foot of one column occurs the note, 'Respice supra in eadem decenna;' and in another *[Contains sets of names]* *[which are tithings]*

---

[1] The portion of the Roll of which a Facsimile is here given is taken from the centre of the dorse of membrane 1. The sets of names, or tithings, in the column on the left belong to the parish or subleet of St. Stephen. Those on the right form the commencement of the parish or subleet of St. Peter Mancroft. The tithings and the Capital Pledges are clearly shown. The long coupling line on the left starting from the name of 'Wiłłs de Catton' and covering the two tithings following his own, neither of which has a Capital Pledge, shows that he answered for them all. The meaning of the long coupling line in St. Peter Mancroft covering a tithing which has its own Capital Pledge is not so apparent. It may have served for some special occasion. The short coupling lines on the left connect the last (original) name in one tithing with the first of the next, and seem to indicate that two tithings so connected were permanently combined for the purpose of representation. The wavy line marks the later addition of several names to two of these old tithings combined in one.

xlviii   THE MANCROFT TITHING ROLL.

place, 'Thomas de Colton alibi in decenna Ranulphi de Colneye.'

Frequently altered

2. After the original list has been made out and used it has been the subject of a great many alterations. In three membranes nearly the whole of the spaces originally left between the sets of names are filled in, and the fourth membrane is an additional one, added because there was no space left in the other membranes. It is headed ' Leta de Nedham et Manecroft,' and refers back to the former lists, as ' Adhuc Cap' pl' Joñes de Ely Lorymer,' and then come a few names to be added to his tithing.

The original list can, however, be recovered with a fair approach to certainty. It contains about 690 names.

Comparison between Capital Pledges in Tithing Roll and in Leet Roll of 1313

3. Perhaps the most useful feature which the Roll reveals is one which throws no little light on the date of the document, the working of the whole tithing system at that period, and especially on the original organisation of the subleets. It is found that the names of a large number of the Capital Pledges correspond in a most remarkable manner with those of the subleet of St. Peter Mancroft who were amerced at the Leet of 1313. In order to appreciate the full significance of this correspondence a little more explanation is necessary.

The whole list is divided into two parts: the first headed ' Parochia Sēī Stephani,' and the second ' Poch Sēī Petri de Manecroft.' The former we may dismiss at present. The list for St. Peter Mancroft contains either thirty-two or thirty-three sets of names. In one case it is doubtful whether a separate set is really intended. For convenience sake we may number these sets from 1 to 33. It is to be observed that many of these sets are not provided with a Capital Pledge at all. They are connected with others by coupling lines. The sets which may be numbered 5, 8, 14, 16, 18, 19, 22, 26, 31, and 32 are thus vacant. This leaves twenty-three with Capital Pledges. Now the number amerced in the Roll of 1313 is twenty-three, and almost the whole of these twenty-three correspond with names in the Tithing Roll and *occur in exactly*

Number of separate tithings in subleet of St. Peter Mancroft, with and without Capital Pledges

the same order, thus showing that the list of Capital Pledges who served at the Leet of 1313 must have been taken from the Tithing Roll, and moreover that these Capital Pledges represented not merely their own twenty-three tithings, but the whole of the thirty-three in the subleet.

The correspondence between the two sets of Capital Pledges will be seen more clearly by setting down in two parallel columns, first, the whole number of tithings on the Tithing Roll with the Capital Pledges where there are any, and secondly, the Capital Pledges as they are recorded in the Roll of Amercements of 1313. The *order* of the names in the latter column is not altered: they are only placed opposite to the corresponding names in the first column.

Tithing Roll	Capital Pledges amerced in 1313
1. Rob⁰ de Marsham	Rob⁰ Kep de Marsham
2. Joħes Cobbild	Joħes Cobbild
3. Carolus le Seler	Carolus le Seler
4. Rads le Blowar	Riĉus de Swayefeld
5. vacant	Hugo de Colvyston
6. David de Elingham	David de Helyngham
7. Wiħs de Brok	Wiħs de Brok
8. vacant	
9. Riĉus Rodlond	Riĉus Rodlond
10. Joħes Smelte de ffornesette	Joħes Smelte de ffornsete
11. Rob⁰ de Kyrkestedde	Rob⁰ de Kirksted
12. Joħes de Aschewelle jun'	Joħes Aschewell jun'
13. Nich de Walsham	Nich de Walsham
14. vacant	
15. Rob⁰ fil' Joħis le Verdonn	Rob⁰ le Verdon
16. vacant	
17. Wiħs Wade	Wiħs Wade
18. vacant	
19. vacant	
20. Joħes de Walsham	Joħes de Walsham
21. Joħes le hornere	Joħes le hornere
22. vacant	
23. Henricus de Bradefeld	Henricus de Bradefeld
24. Riĉus Swyn	Riĉus Swyn
25. Rog's fil' Wiħi de ffornesetto	Rog's fil' Wiħi de ffornseto
26. vacant	
27. Joħes de Cauntebrigg	Joħes de Cauntebrigg
28. Andreas de Besthorp	Andreas de Besthorp
29. Rog's le Pundermakere	Rog's le pundermaker
30. Joħes fil' Clem' [1]	Joħes Brundych [1]
31. vacant	
32. vacant	
33. Dyonisius le cobellere	

---

[1] I have not been able to identify these.

DATE OF THE TITHING ROLL.

The names in the Leet Roll not as in the original list of the Tithing Roll

4. In reference to the correspondence between these two documents I must observe that the names in the tithings numbered 4 or 5, 7, 17, 20, 21, and 25 are not the original names in the Tithing Roll; 5 is apparently vacant in the original list; 7 is also vacant. 'Witts de Brok' is entered among the members of the tithing with 'cap' before his name in very similar writing. In the other cases the names here given have been substituted for previous names crossed out. The original list in the Tithing Roll is therefore earlier than the Leet Roll of 1313. Two pieces of evidence seem to make the Tithing Roll a year earlier than the other. A certain 'Johes de Wroxham, taverner,' is entered in the Tithing Roll. One of the Conveyance Rolls contains an enrolment of his will by his executors in May, 5 Ed. II. (which year ended on July 8, 1312). The Leet to which the Amercement Roll refers was held in 6 Ed. II.—*i.e.* about March 1313. The will of Galfridus de Costessey, another name entered, was proved in Feb., 5 Ed. II. (1312).

5. The question, then, may now be considered, When and for what purpose was the Tithing Roll made? The natural answer would be, for the view of frankpledge. Then comes the further question, When was that held? On this point we have no local evidence to guide us. The legitimate time for holding it was at Michaelmas.[1] The facts of the case before us would harmonise with such a theory.

Tithing Roll perhaps made for view of frankpledge at Mich. 1311

If we may conjecture that this Tithing Roll was first drawn up at the view of frankpledge at Michaelmas 1311, and that the alterations were chiefly made at the view of frankpledge in 1312, that would seem to explain both the general correspondence and the comparatively few alterations. The view of frankpledge must have been held previously to the presentment of offences, for there are always a number of presentments of persons for not being in tithings, which must have been inquired into beforehand.

[1] Magna Carta, 25 Ed. I. c. xxxv.

6. It may further be taken for granted that when the Leet was coming on it was somebody's business to draw up a list of the Capital Pledges from the latest Frankpledge Roll, and probably to summon them. If when called upon they were absent without excuse, their names are marked with a +. This is rare. If they had a valid reason, it appears that some one was appointed to serve for them. In the Roll for 1288 it is more than once specified that a Capital Pledge is absent, and that some other person 'ponitur loco suo.' In this Tithing Roll it is not unfrequent to find 'cap' prefixed to the name of an ordinary member of a tithing, and the note added 'jur' ad diem.' If the last-entered Capital Pledge was dead, his name was crossed out, and 'mortuus est' added, and another name was entered on the list. Sometimes a Capital Pledge actually present would attempt to escape the burden by refusing to be sworn. He was immediately declared to be 'in miā pro maximo contemptu,' and the result is 'postea juravit.' *Capital Pledges for the Leet summoned from Tithing Roll*

There is no sort of hint to be found as to how or by whom a Capital Pledge was appointed. It can only be conjectured that the members of the tithing which had lost its Capital Pledge elected a new one. That he was frequently taken from among their own number is plain from the alterations in this Roll. It is true that not unfrequently a member of one tithing in this Roll became Capital Pledge of quite a different one. This may, however, have been the case only in St. Peter Mancroft, which was a peculiarly circumstanced parish. *Appointment of new Capital Pledges*

IX. The original Number of Tithings in the City and Formation of the Subleets.

1. I will now proceed to a still more interesting series of deductions which may be gathered out of a consideration of the numbers of the tithings and Capital Pledges in this Tithing Roll as compared with the numbers of the Capita Pledges in the Leet Rolls of 1288 and 1313.

lii ORIGINAL NUMBER OF CITY TITHINGS.

Number of tithings in the Roll corresponds with number represented in Mancroft subleet in 1288

I have numbered the separate tithings enrolled in the subleet of St. Peter as thirty-three. This is the full number of separate sets of names. Perhaps in one or two cases they were not really intended to be separate tithings. In any case, the number tallies in a remarkable way with the number of tithings represented by Capital Pledges in the Leet Roll of 1288. Then thirty Capital Pledges appeared for this subleet. In addition to this correspondence between the number of tithings at the two dates we may note the further facts that at the Leet of 1288 only twenty-three of the thirty Capital Pledges were sworn, that in the Tithing Roll twenty-three tithings only are provided with Capital Pledges, and that at the Leet of 1313 the number amerced is twenty-three.

Probably remained constant during the twenty-five years

May we assume, as a first inference from these facts, that about thirty was the constant number of tithings in this subleet throughout those twenty-five years? I think we may. If so, it does not seem unwarrantable to assume further that the number (allowing for some additions and diminutions easily accounted for) had remained constant

and from the beginning

from the beginning, and that, in fact, we have in the Roll of 1288 a fair approach to the number of tithings throughout the City at the original organisation of the subleets, presumably in 1223.

Apply this to whole city

2. On this basis the Tithing Roll will furnish us with evidence by which we may picture to ourselves the original process of grouping the tithings into districts, together with the changes which had taken place in their composition and their representation by Capital Pledges. For this purpose some further details with respect to this Roll are necessary.

Observe variations in the size of tithings in Roll, and frequent omission of a Capital Pledge

The Roll, as already stated, includes the two subleets of St. Stephen and St. Peter Mancroft. The list for St. Stephen's parish contains sixteen sets of names or tithings. Four of these, which are distinctly separate, are unprovided with a Capital Pledge. As to number of members, the third, with a Capital Pledge, has twenty-four names in the same handwriting without a break. No. 6,

with no Capital Pledge, has twenty-three. No. 16, the last, without a Capital Pledge, has twenty-six. In this case the fifteenth name is at the bottom of a column and a note, 'Respice supra in eadem decenna,' carries the reader to the top of another column, where eleven more names are found in the same handwriting. In contrast to these overgrown tithings No. 8, with its own Capital Pledge, contains only eight names, and No. 12, without a Capital Pledge, has the same number. No. 11 has a break after the eleventh name, leaving a small group of five persons, possibly representing the relics of an old tithing which had dwindled away. The same variations are found in the Parish of St. Peter Mancroft. The tithing I have numbered as 21 has twenty-one names and is immediately followed by a tithing, without any Capital Pledge, containing twenty-eight names. The break is here rather doubtful, so that it may be one tithing containing forty-nine members. On the other hand No. 11, with a Capital Pledge, has only nine members.

3. To go back now to the Roll of 1288, we find that there were 163 Capital Pledges present at all the sub-leets of the City in that year. The exact number of tithings thus represented should probably be taken as somewhat less than this, because in two or three cases a Capital Pledge appears to be mentioned and also another who served for him. We may therefore reckon the tithings at about 160. I have assumed, from the evidence just given, that this may be taken for the full number of the tithings in the City, and I have further assumed that the number of the City tithings had remained almost constant from the first establishment of the organisation. In support of this view one important fact may certainly be gathered from the Tithing Roll. The increase of population was not accompanied by a corresponding increase in the number of tithings. The tithings themselves were in many cases enlarged to double their normal size. In one way a few new tithings may have been added, in consequence of the increase of the City boundaries during the thirteenth century. *Original number of tithings in City, as judged from lists in 1288, about 160*

liv   ORIGINAL NUMBER OF THE CITY TITHINGS.

In the 'Historia Fundationis Ecclesie Cathedralis Norwicensis,'[1] the cathedral monks complain that in 37 Hen. III. (1253) 'the Commons of Norwich had licence to enclose the said town with ditches, which they could in no wise do without prejudice to others by enclosing lands of other fees and franchises and lying in divers hundreds.' They then go on to specify the lands so enclosed, all round the City. In this way a few tithings may have been added.

Points to an original organisation of twelve subdivisions with twelve tithings, at least, in each

Allowing for some slight uncertainty as to the original number arising from this and other causes, we may take it to have been about 160. I have a strong suspicion that this number, taken in conjunction with the number of eleven subleets in use at the close of the century, points to an original organisation of twelve subdivisions, each containing at least twelve tithings. We must not expect the exact number of tithings in a district, as a little consideration will show if we remember the known conditions which must have governed the original process of sub-

Exactness not to be expected, because the subdivisions were subject to the conditions of suiting (a) the four Great Leets, suggesting an arrangement of 4 × 3, as in first Leet, viz. Conesford; (b) the grouping, in sets with the requisite population, of forty-six parishes of variable size

dividing. In the first place the smaller divisions were subordinate to the four Great Leets. This of itself would suggest the arrangement of three subleets to each Leet. The organisers began, then, we may suppose, with Conesford, which always stands in the first place, and they appear to have found no difficulty in grouping the parishes of this Leet so as to form three sets of about twelve tithings each. But we must observe that the fact that the arrangement was made by grouping adjoining parishes of altogether unequal size makes it impossible that they could have included in a subdivision just exactly the required number of tithings. They were obliged to include the twelve but must sometimes have had to include more. The considerable number of the subleets, however, in which the number twelve is approximately realised in 1288 makes it probable that from the

Elasticity allowed in the size of the tithings

first this result was assisted by the elasticity allowed in the size of the tithings. In no other way can such a system have been carried out under the limitations and variations

---

[1] Dugdale, *Monasticon*, iv. 14; Book of Pleas, fol. lviii.

occasioned by the necessity of considering the boundaries of so many parishes, of which no less than forty-six are represented in 1288.

This opportunity may be taken of remarking on the connection of the parishes with the frankpledge system. It is evident that the tithing was in some way subordinate to the parish, otherwise the Capital Pledges would not have answered, as they did, for certain parishes. There is nothing in our existing Leet Rolls to further explain it. Perhaps the parochial organisation had been previously used for carrying out the view of frankpledge. It was the parish and not the tithing which was summoned to attend by its representatives when the Coroner held an inquiry; and perhaps these same representatives may have been charged with the duty of attending the Sheriff's Tourn before the citizens had their Leet in their own hands. *Connection of tithings with parishes*

4. After dealing with the Leet of Conesford the organisers of the subdivisions would come to the Leet of Mancroft. In it the parish of St. Stephen produced about the right number of tithings. But when they came to the parish of St. Peter Mancroft they must have found themselves in a difficulty. We have seen that in 1288 it contained no less than thirty tithings. At that time the Leet of Mancroft, judging by the number of persons fined annually for breaking the assize of beer, must have included more than a fourth part of the whole population of the City, while the comparative number of tithings in the two parishes which formed the Leet shows that quite two-thirds of the population in this Leet was in the parish of St. Peter Mancroft, which was then almost entirely occupied by the various branches of the market. There is evidence to be gathered from various sources to prove that the trade of the City developed considerably during the thirteenth century, and the population had constantly been converging to this district. In 1313 out of 250 amercements for breaches of the assize of ale no less than ninety-two, or more than one-third, are in the Leet of Mancroft. *The second Leet, Mancroft* *Peculiarity of subject of St. Peter Mancroft:*

lvi ORIGINAL NUMBER OF THE CITY TITHINGS.

Possibly, therefore, some new tithings may in consequence have been created in this parish. But in any case the population must from the first have largely exceeded that of any other parish and in all probability sufficed at first, as it did afterwards, to produce not one but two sets of twelve tithings. Yet there is no ground for supposing that the parish was ever divided so as to form two subleets and so make three for the Leet of Mancroft. The reason why a third subleet was not added may have been because, as it was, the Leet included one-fourth of the tithings of the whole city.

furnished double the requisite number of tithings; yet not divided into two subleets

Third Leet, Wymer, had four subleets of normal size

Passing to the third Great Leet, that of Westwyk or Wymer, we find it divided into four subleets not greatly differing from the normal arrangement of twelve tithings each. It may be surmised that the four subdivisions in this Leet were held to balance the two in the Mancroft Leet.

Fourth Leet, Ultra Aquam, had two subleets of abnormal size

Then we come to the Leet Over-the-Water, and here we have the greatest variation from the twelve tithings. Of the two subleets, one contains eighteen tithings and the other fifteen. How are we to account for this excess? Not certainly by the density of the population. I believe that we are here dealing, not with an increase, but with a decrease; that these two subleets are the relics of what had originally been three. It is evident that if a population which had once produced at least thirty-six tithings fell below that number it could no longer be divided into three subleets. We have already seen that at a later period two of the subleets of Conesford were combined into one (p. xix). The reason I suggested for the change in that case was the diminution of the available population by the settlement of the Grey Friars and the Austin Friars. The other two great bodies of Friars, the Black Friars and the Carmelites, similarly absorbed considerable portions of ground in the Leet Over-the-Water. The Black Friars settled in the centre of the district in 1226, and by 1250 had obtained possession of an old parochial church of St. John the Baptist, which parish accordingly is not mentioned in the 1288 Roll.

Reasons for thinking there were originally three

5. I consider, therefore, that we have some ground for supposing that the original number of subdivisions for Leet purposes in the City was twelve. But I would add that although this symmetrical arrangement may have been aimed at, there was no really practical advantage to be gained by preserving it. So long as the presentments required by the law were duly made and amercements were paid, to the replenishing of the City chest, the precise state of the organisation was of slight importance. There is evidence in the Mancroft Tithing Roll of a tendency which would tell strongly against too much precision. Evidently the supplying of tithings with Capital Pledges had become a matter of difficulty. The office could not have been a pleasant one, and we should not be surprised to find that no one would willingly hold it. I cannot in any other way account for so many of the tithings in the Roll being entered without any trace of their having a Capital Pledge at their head. If the thirty tithings or so which are entered on the Roll really correspond with the thirty tithings represented in the subleet of St. Peter in 1288, it is significant that in 1288 there should have been thirty Capital Pledges accounted for, whereas in the Tithing Roll there are apparently no more than twenty-three. It is also significant that the number of twenty-three at the later date, which is also the number amerced in 1313, corresponds (perhaps exactly) with the number actually sworn at the earlier date.[1] It looks as though in the

No advantage in keeping the arrangement symmetrical.

Difficulty of providing a full number of Capital Pledges.

Where need arose, tithings grouped together and Capital Pledges appointed for the day.

---

[1] The use of the number twenty-three at the two later dates must evidently have been derived from its use at the earlier. Why were only twenty-three out of thirty Capital Pledges sworn in 1288? It is stated (Tomline, *Law Dict.*, s.v. 'Court Leet') that a Leet Jury might not exceed twenty-three, the presumed object, as in a modern Grand Jury, being that a clear majority of at least twelve might be secured, which could not be guaranteed with a Jury of twenty-four. But it is doubtful whether such a refinement had originated so early as 1288. Moreover, the business of these Juries was not that of a Grand Jury, to decide upon presentments after being sworn. They were sworn for the purpose of making in due form presentments previously decided on amongst themselves. Jurors who were sworn for the day must have fallen in with the returns already prepared by the permanent Capital Pledges. It is plain, however, that whatever had been the original object of the limitation, twenty-three was the prescriptive number of the sworn Jury in the Mancroft subleet. And it can hardly be doubted that, because

interval a practice had been allowed to grow up of not insisting upon the appointment of more Capital Pledges than were actually necessary. For the purpose of presentments tithings were grouped together, and if need arose tithingmen were sworn as Capital Pledges 'for the day.'

X. Various questions affecting Capital Pledges and Tithingmen: their Social Position, Residence etc.

Various questions about Capital Pledges and tithings

1. We may now pass to a branch of our investigation which includes several kindred subjects of inquiry: What social position did the Capital Pledges hold? What sort of persons were enrolled in the tithings? How far can it be shown that a tithing coincided with a limited district? Did a Capital Pledge live in the midst of the members of his tithing? and lastly, Who were outside the system, and how far was a tithing responsible for their doings? On all these points some information may be obtained, though neither so full nor so definite as we should wish.

Assistance to be derived from contemporary Conveyance Rolls

I may here observe that much help is derived in this part of our subject from a series of documents preserved in the Guildhall, and catalogued in the 'Repertory' as 'Court Rolls.' The title is strictly correct, for they were Rolls of the City Court, but its association with the Rolls of a Manor Court makes it misleading. The real title is 'Rotulus Cartarum recognitarum in plena Curia Norwici.' I have referred to them as Conveyance Rolls, for they are almost exclusively enrolments of Conveyances of messuages, lands etc. in the City. They begin in 1285, and contain on an average about seventy enrolments in each year. From them it is possible to identify, in many cases, a definite person's occupation, social position, and even residence.

2. An examination of the list of Capital Pledges in the Leet of Conesford in the year 1288 will furnish fair evidence both of their social standing and of their local distribution in the matter of residence.

no more than that number were actually required, therefore the number of permanent Capital Pledges of tithings was allowed to drop to twenty-three.

The subleet of (South) Conesford was represented by thirteen Capital Pledges. I can find no special information about four of these. The remaining nine, judging from the occurrence of their names in the Conveyance Rolls, were fairly distributed throughout the district. The district contained six parishes. In the first of them, St. Peter de Suthgate, three of the Capital Pledges, Wm. King, Wm. Lippard, and Silvester Siger, held messuages between the street of Conesford and the river. Here, probably, the bulk of the population of that parish lived. A fourth, Ralph de Suthgate, resided on the hill side on the opposite side of the street. Next came a parish of St. Edward on the hill side. Here Richard le Botman lived. In the next parish of St. Etheldreda Henry Attewro is found between the street and the river. Then Hugo de Bromholm similarly in the adjoining parish of St. Clement. In the parish of St. Julian, Thomas de Surlingham lived on the hill side on the south of the street of Sandgate, which joined Conesford Street to Berstrete. Just beyond Sandgate in Conesford Street John Slabbard resided for a long time in the parish of St. Michael.

The Capital Pledges in the Subleet of (South) Conesford in 1288 distributed through the different parishes

Thus it appears that each of the parishes contained at least one Capital Pledge besides the four not accounted for. There is little actual evidence to show whether they lived in the midst of their tithings, but the fact of their being so equally distributed throughout the district is certainly in favour of such an assumption. If, as appears to have been the case, the Capital Pledges were (as a rule) attached to a locality, we may surely conclude that their tithings were also, especially as it is clear that a tithing was included within the boundary of a parish. Our only evidence on this point must be gathered from the Leet of Mancroft.

3. With regard to the social position of these persons our information is somewhat meagre. The best known is Hugo de Bromholm, who was a man of good standing. After his death his property was the subject of more than one lawsuit and was evidently of considerable value. He was Constable of the Leet of Conesford at this time. He is

Their social position

The title civis Norwici' as used in the Conveyance Rolls

also described as a 'citizen of Norwich.' This title is very sparingly and distinctively used in the Conveyance Rolls. Although it is occasionally applied to traders of various kinds, yet in a majority of instances it is confined to 'merchants,' 'lyndrapers,' and 'drapers' who dealt in foreign goods, and presumably were men of the greatest substance. It is also used as a distinctive appellation without any occupation or trade being given; and it is to be understood that in the case of a person who is so described the title is given to him almost as often as his name occurs. It may therefore be taken for granted that those who had it were the leading citizens. Besides Hugo de Bromholm, Thomas de Surlingham is so described, but not any of the others. Ralph de Suthgate is once fined among the 'piscenarii.' Richard le Botman may have been a boat-owner. Many of these names already descended from father to son as surnames. In many cases no doubt the occupation descended also.

Capital Pledges of (North) Conesford, their residences and occupations

4. Passing to the Subleet of (North) Conesford we find the same features. There were here four parishes. To the first parish, St. Peter de Parmentergate, there is only one name to be assigned, John le Lindraper. He lived on the same side of the street as the church, and was certainly not a man of so much importance as several others who were living in the immediate neighbourhood at the time. In the adjoining parish of St. Vedast was Hugo de Rokelund, a 'citizen of Norwich' of unknown occupation. He held a messuage near the church. Probably there were two others—Thomas, son of Nicholas de Coventrie, and William, son of Walter le Tanur. This Walter and a Robert de Coventrie, both tanners, had lived in the street of Nether Conesford in this parish, but the names of Thomas and William do not occur in connection with the tenure of the property. The former was a householder somewhere in the district, for his wife was fined in the Leet of Conesford for breaking the assize of beer. Further up Conesford Street came the parish of St. Cuthbert where Roger le Mareschal lived on the east side of the street and John de Bedeford on the same side further on, while on the

west side of the street lived Nicholas le Mareschal close to the small parish of St. Mary the Little, in which, not far off, lived Alexander del Sarteryn. Of these latter persons, John de Bedeford was a painter; Roger and Nicholas le Mareschal were farriers, and they had a workshop where Nicholas lived. Roger is described as a 'citizen of Norwich.' So also is Alexander del Sarteryn, who was a 'pelliparius' and one of the very few known Capital Pledges who held the office of Bailiff, which he did in 1291. Of the remaining four names in this district I can find no trace.

5. In the third subleet of Conesford, Berstrete, five only of the twelve names can be identified with special localities. Two, William Calf and Robert Mendham, belonged to the parish of St. Sepulchre, the former to the west side of Berstrete, the latter to the east side. Simon le Prude belonged to St. Michael on the eastern side towards St. Julian, and John de Aschele to the same parish on the other side; and Thomas le Neve to St. John de Berstrete on the eastern side. Of four fresh names which occur in the following year, three fill up some of the missing portions of this district; Robert le Parcheminer being connected with the parish of St. Bartholomew, which lay between St. Sepulchre and St. Michael, Walter de Colton with the western portion of St. John de Berstrete towards St. Stephen, and John Canum with the adjoining parish of All Saints. *Capital Pledges of Berstrete*

William Calf was a butcher and a 'citizen,' and Robert le Parcheminer was also a butcher. The occupations of the rest are not mentioned.

6. Adjoining this subleet was that of St. Stephen in the Leet of Manecroft. Here the information to be obtained is fuller and quite confirmatory of that given with regard to Conesford. It will be enough to state that ten out of the twelve Capital Pledges may be localised in different portions of the parish as divided by its three main streets. One of them, Thomas Sparwe, was a merchant and 'citizen,' and a man of importance. John Curthose was a barber, Thomas de Elmham a smith, Laurence de Tacolston a *Of the subleet of St. Stephen*

'cissor,' Hugo de Wymondham a cordwainer, and Richard de Aylsham most likely a baker. One other, William de Attelburgh, 'clericus,' does not easily fall into his place. His name is entered last, and he is not marked as 'jur.,' though he is required to make up the number twelve. There were plenty of 'clerici,' who were to all intents laymen, being married and holding civic offices, and being styled 'citizen.' His name occurs three times in the Conveyance Rolls, and each time in connection with Hosyergate in the parish of St. Andrew in the Leet of Wymer.

<small>General distribution of the Capital Pledges throughout the City;</small>

7. The evidence produced with respect to these four subleets may be held to stand good for the rest. We may picture to ourselves the 160 Capital Pledges systematically scattered throughout the whole city, every one of the numerous, and in many cases very small, parishes containing at least one, and the larger and more populous containing more in proportion to their population.[1] As already remarked, it seems unreasonable to doubt that the members of the tithings were collected round their Capital Pledges. In the small parishes which contained only one or two tithings it must have been so.

<small>therefore probably of their tithings</small>

<small>General social position of the Capital Pledges, just below the highest official class</small>

The other conclusion which has been suggested, that the Capital Pledges were drawn from a class just below the highest, may seem to want more proof. It must be remembered that such a proof is very difficult to give. The relative importance of the various trades in the city at this time, the comparative frequency with which the names of persons occur in the Conveyance Rolls, the value of their holdings, and other details, can only be estimated by an intimate knowledge of those Rolls, and it is hardly possible to convey a right impression by a few isolated references. The general impression left by a study of the Conveyance Rolls is that among the lists of Capital Pledges there is a

---

[1] Cf. the statement in Seld. Soc. vol. iv. p. 80 : ' Et sciendum est quod quolibet vico burgi erit unus custos ad minus ad quem hutesium levatum possit presentari et ille idem illud presentabit in plena curia vel in pleno hundredo.' This system was exactly carried out at Nottingham. See below, p. lxxii. (n).

INTRODUCTION, X. 8. lxiii

marked absence of the names of those with whom the reader soon becomes familiar as the great holders of houses, lands, shops and stalls in all parts of the City.

8. We may now see what may be learned about the tithings from the case of the parish of St. Peter Mancroft and the Tithing Roll of the Leet of Mancroft. We will first return to the parish of St. Stephen, which was a parish of an ordinary kind. Considering that a large number of the members of the tithings were not even householders, we cannot expect to find many of whom we can learn much, and we must be satisfied if we can here and there find a few facts to rest on. Information about tithings in the Mancroft Roll

Of course we at once notice that very frequently members of the same family or household occur in the same tithing, not only persons bearing the same name, but described as 'son of' or 'servant of.' Not unfrequently, however, sons of the same father are found in different tithings, no doubt because they had left home and either set up for themselves or entered the household of some other trader.

The fifth tithing in St. Stephen's sublect contains several names which occur in the Conveyance Rolls. The Capital Pledge, William Bele, was a butcher and held a messuage on the west side of Nedham Street. First on his list comes Thomas Sparwe, who had formerly been a Capital Pledge. His messuage lay at the back of Nedham on the west side and near St. Stephen's church, which stood in the Horsemarket, a street which issued from Nedham at right angles running from east to west. The next person, Adam de Bliklingge, amongst several holdings had one on the west of Nedhamgate. Another, William de Causton, had a messuage at the corner of Nedham and the Horsemarket. Another, Henry de Brok, had a messuage on the west of Nedham, near Thomas Sparwe's; and another, Roger Schod, also had a messuage on the west side of Nedham. We may therefore fairly conclude that this tithing with its Capital Pledge occupied the angle between Nedhamgate and the Horsemarket. This tithing is remarkable for the character of its members. All the five just mentioned and Examination of a tithing in St Stephen's sublect

May be localised in a certain angle between two streets

another, Estannus de Horseford, are described as 'citizens.' Three were merchants and two drapers. This proves that these well-to-do citizens were not all above the obligation of belonging to tithings.

9. The subleet or parish of St. Peter de Manecroft presents unusual difficulty. It contained all the different portions of the market. Most of the traders, whose names can be identified as holders of property in it, held it in such various forms and places that it is hardly possible to localise them, and those who are unknown furnish little clue to go by. A more careful comparison with contemporary deeds might do something towards localising the tithings. So far as I can judge they must be arranged according to residence rather than occupation, for persons of one occupation occur mixed up with persons of another occupation carried on in a different part of the market.

There is, however, one group of tithings which offers a somewhat satisfactory result. The north side of the market towards its eastern end was called the 'Aurifabria,' which was also continued a little way along the north side of Hosyergate, a street which here issued from the market towards the east. At this time it was not occupied by hosiers, but by 'latoners' and 'furburs.' The tithing I have distinguished as No. 17 had in the Leet Roll of 1313 for Capital Pledge. William Wade. He held a shop in Hosyergate sold to him by a cutler. In the Tithing Roll the word 'Cap' is written, with no name. Wm. Wade (marked 'Cap') comes first on the list. He is followed by Stephen Wade, who also held a messuage in Hosyergate. Further on is Geoffrey, son of John de Attelburgh, mentioned presently. After twelve names comes a break, and then a new set without a Capital Pledge. In this set occurs Arnald de Flixton, who was a latoner and held a messuage by Wm. Wade's. Ralph le furbur is in this set. At the tenth name is a short coupler which bridges over another gap and joins on to a third set of names, again without a Capital Pledge. The second name here is 'Johes de Attelburgh, orfevre,' whose son is found in the first set. He also held a messuage in Hosyergate.

Further down is Robert de Flixton, and further still Alexander de Flixton. After this set comes another which introduces confusion. It is the one marked No. 20. In the Tithing Roll its Capital Pledge is John de Ingham, whose name I find nowhere else. In the Leet Roll of 1313 it is John de Walsham. His name is entered in this tithing in the Tithing Roll, and he is described as a taverner. His tavern appears to have been in St. Stephen's. At the top of the list, as if added afterwards, is John de Wroxham, taverner. He certainly lived in Sadelgate or the 'Sellaria,' a street at the south-east of the market. In the same tithing is Henry Braban, a goldsmith, who had several shops on the other side of Sadelgate. Yet, for at least one occasion, this tithing, which seems to have no connection with Hosyergate, is connected by a long coupler with the next, which brings us back to that locality. Its Capital Pledge in the Tithing Roll is Robert, son of Ralph le furbur. In 1313 it is John le Horner. Among the names are Peter le latoner, John de Essex, and Thomas le latoner, both the latter holding messuages or shops in Hosyergate. At the fifteenth name a short coupler connects it with the next set. In the gap is entered later Edmund le furbur. The next set, without a Capital Pledge, contains Richard, son of John de Essex, William and Richard, sons of Alan le latoner, and Thomas, son of Thomas le latoner, whose father was in the preceding tithing. This Alan and Thomas both came from York, and occupied adjoining messuages in Hosyergate. Thus a large number of the members of these tithings were metal-workers connected with one portion of Hosyergate.

10. The remaining questions, What sort of persons composed the tithings? Who was outside them? and, How far was the tithing responsible for everyone in its own neighbourhood? have partly been answered already and may be a little further answered together.

The tithings must have included persons of all classes except those who were legally exempt. We have just seen (p. lxiv) that this exemption did not include more than

Tithings included persons of all ranks

lxvi   EXTENSIVE OBLIGATION OF FRANKPLEDGE.

possibly a limited number of leading citizens, for many such were enrolled in the Tithing Roll. The chief question that suggests itself is in regard to a man's household—Who was reckoned in his 'mainpast'? It is remarkable that the word is hardly ever used in the earlier Rolls. It appears *A man's son or his 'serviens' not to be reckoned in manupastu'* that a man's son of legal age residing in his house was not allowed to be so counted. We find in Roll IV., 'De Johe filio Witti de Walsham quia non fuit in decenna, vj d. De Witto de Walsham pro recettamento eiusdem, xij d.' 'De Witto Erse pro receptamento filii sui extra decennam.' 'De Galfrido le Pasteman quia recepit filium suum extra decennam.' A 'serviens' also was in the same position. Thus in Roll V.: 'De Nicholao Elsingg quia receptat quendam servientem suum extra decennam.' A 'serviens' may sometimes have been in a more or less independent position, for persons are fined for defrauding the Bailiffs by acting in partnership with a 'serviens' who is not 'de libertate.'

Even one who was rightly described as a person's mainpast was not always exempt, as the following entries from Roll VII. (p. 52) show: 'De Galfrido de Brandon man' Riči de Snoringg quia non est in decenna, xij d. De eodem Riĉo pro receptamento eiusdem, xij d.' 'De Johe serviente Galfridi le taverner et manup' quia non est in decenna, xij d. De Galfrido le taverner pro receptamento eiusdem Johis, xij d.' The anxiety of the authorities to bring all they could within the responsibility of a tithing may be explained by the 43rd Chapter of Customs. There were, it seems, in the City a large number of journeymen labourers who from their combined independence and poverty eluded all control. When complaints were made against these 'servientes operantes ad unum denarium pro diurno' etc. they could not be attached 'quia nihil habent'; the offences did not warrant their arrest; their masters were not responsible, 'eo quod non sunt de manupastu eorum quia recipiunt denarium diurnum ut predicitur.' Therefore, it is directed that when such a servant is complained of, no master shall receive him until he has stood to his law. If he refuses to do so, he is to be expelled from the city.

11. The persons who were legally outside frankpledge were 'clerks' and 'strangers.' In the inquiry before the Itinerant Justices in 1286 the constantly recurring entries are 'non in decenna quia clericus,' or 'quia extraneus.' It must be understood, however, that the exemption of 'clerici' did not extend to all who went by that name. There were many clerks in the City, like the clerks of the Bailiffs, who can hardly have been in ecclesiastical orders at all. They were married, held civic offices, and lived and traded as citizens. All such were bound by the law of frankpledge. This is strikingly illustrated by an entry in Roll IV; in the subleet of North Conesford: 'De Ričo clerico ecclesie Sc̄i Petri de Parmentergate quia non est in decenna, xij d.' The clerk was not the parson, but some sort of servant or attendant. People in their wills leave xij d. to the 'persona,' and ij d. to the 'clericus.'[1]

Exemptions

Clerks

An 'extraneus' was one who was not admitted to the 'libertas' of the City. He might remain in the city unmolested for a year unless he became a 'suspectus.' After that time he was bound to enroll himself in a tithing. Roll VII. (p. 50) begins ' De Witto filio Bartholomei de Redham quia stetit in Civitate Norwici per annum et diem et non est in decenna, xij d.' 'De Galfrido de Matishale pro eodem, xii d.—De Robert Ivri pro eodem, xij d.'

Strangers

12. One other case of exemption connected with the City may be considered. In the Iter of 1286, Reginald, son of Reyner de Erlham, is reported to have killed Robert de Crek with a sword in Norwich. He fled. He was not 'in decenna, quia liber.' He had no chattels, but had land, viz. a messuage in Norwich, land at Earlham etc.[2] I feel sure this must refer to Reginald's status at Earlham (a country village in the immediate neighbourhood), not at Norwich. The term 'liber' was not in use in the City and could only be equivalent to 'de libertate,' which would exempt

'Liber',' not exempt in City, perhaps in country

---

[1] See Glossary, s. v. *Clericus parochialis.*
[2] Plac. Coron. 4 } 2 m. 39.

every City trader. Another case[1] in the same Iter confirms this view. John de Vallibus of Schotesham (a neighbouring village) claims Henry Fischel de Schotesham as his 'nativus.' He says he is seized of him as his villain, and that he has withdrawn himself and married in Norwich without his licence. Henry says he is in tithing with other villains of the said lord in Schotesham, and that he gives to his lord each year 'chevagium.' He acknowledges his obligation, and offers to pay two shillings for the fault of marrying without his licence.

These two cases seem to imply the exemption of a man who is 'liber,' and to identify being in a tithing with being in villainage—this, however, in the country, not in the City.

This consideration may explain the insulting remark of Robert Fish of Oulton (near Lowestoft) in Roll III. (p. 34), where he is reported to have said 'quod non veniret ad villanos de Conesford.' If he were a freeholder at Oulton and accustomed to associate the obligation of frankpledge with villainage, he might call the tithingmen and Capital Pledges of the City no better than 'villani.' He appears, however, to have been enrolled, as a citizen, in the tithing of William King, who was ordered to produce him and reported the remark.

13. As to responsibility, the Capital Pledges were bound as we have seen, to know and present all offences committed within their Leets or subleets. The Rolls do not give any information as to the responsibility of tithings. Amercements are not laid on them except in one instance. In Roll IV. in the Leet of Wymer occurs, 'De Waltero de Berningham et tota decenna sua quia non venit, xij d.' Then follow four others for the same. What this refers to is not explained. A tithing might be amerced for not producing one of its members, but beyond keeping a watch over strangers and reporting not only their offences but anything suspicious in their conduct, they could hardly be held responsible for those who did not belong to them.

[1] m. 92, dors.

XI. Frankpledge in Norwich and London.

1. As a fitting conclusion to the subject of the frank- Frankpledge in East Anglia
pledge system in its original form of administration it
would be interesting, if the materials exist, to compare the
highly developed organisation of the Norwich Leets with
the system in operation with similar objects in other
towns. At present the materials for such a comparison
are very scanty. There was plainly a close resemblance
between the Norwich system and that of a *country manor*
where the Leet presentments were made by the Capital
Pledges of the tithings to the lord's steward. Even there,
however, it is doubtful whether the obligation of being in
frankpledge extended to persons of free condition as in
Norwich. With regard to *towns* it is most probable that
in the East Anglian towns of Ipswich and Yarmouth,
where the headship of the community was vested in *Bailiffs*
and the divisions of the town were called *Leets*, some
organisation similar to that of Norwich would be found to
have existed. The case of Lynn might be different, for its
constitution differed from that of Norwich, it having had
a mayor as early as 1204. Yet there were Capital Pledges
there making presentments at the Leet, in the beginning
of the fifteenth century,[1] and a system of presentments by
a Leet jury of Head-boroughs still maintained a lingering
existence there in 1835. The 'capital pledges, anglice, the
Head-borowes,' are mentioned at the town of Dereham in
Norfolk in 1684.[2] We may almost safely conclude, therefore,
that the Norwich organisation and procedure were only
highly developed forms of a type of local government widely
spread at least in this part of the country.

It is perhaps of more importance to observe how materi- In London
ally it differed from that which obtained contemporaneously
in the City of London. From the offences mentioned in
the 'Inquisitiones Wardemotarum' as given in the London
Liber Albus (vol. i. p. 337, Riley) it appears that the

---

[1] *Norfolk Archæology*, VI. 228.   [2] Carthew, *The Town we Live in*, p. 67.

chief part of the jurisdiction exercised in Norwich by the Leet courts was in London within the cognisance of the Wardmotes. As the Leets of Norwich corresponded to the Wards in many other towns, and the London Wards, like the four Great Leets of Norwich, occupied the position of a Hundred, this might seem to indicate a similarity of system. But a closer consideration of the procedure at the Wardmotes and the language used of frankpledge in London shows that the similarity went no further. On p. 37 (*ibid.*) we learn that a Wardmote consisted of all the male householders of the Ward with their servants. Their names were entered on two Rolls, one containing only freemen, the other servants and non-freemen. The absentees were amerced. At this assembly the Bedel of the Ward presented to the presiding Alderman a panel of the substantial men of the Ward who were to form a jury. This panel the Alderman might correct. The jurors then had the Articles of Inquiry read to them and a day named to make their presentments. On that day they presented their verdict indented to the Alderman, who afterwards presented his part to the Mayor and from him received sanction to carry out the amercements.

2. The mention of the verdict being indented would give the date of this description as subsequent to the statute of 1 Ed. III. c. 17, and the mention in one of the last of the Articles of Inquiry of masters paying workmen more than the ordained wage, would date those Articles as later than the Statute of Labourers in 1349. But the compiler of the Liber Albus evidently knew of no other mode of presentment of this class of offences as having been in operation at an earlier time.

<small>Different meaning of frankpledge in London</small>

The essential difference thus revealed between London and Norwich during the thirteenth and fourteenth centuries in respect of the character of the presenting jurors is equally marked in the language used from time to time of frankpledge. No mention is made of tithings or of Capital Pledges. Where the Norwich documents would say that a man is 'in decenna,' the London documents say 'in

francoplegio' (*ibid.* pp. 87, 99 *bis*), and by that expression seems to be meant no more than providing himself with a few pledges or sureties. No man may abide in the city like a citizen more than three nights 'nisi inveniat duos plegios et sic est in franco plegio' (p. 90). The expression is also used to signify such a surety: 'Ideo francus plegius in misericordia' (p. 99). 'Nihil de francis plegiis quia extraneus' (p. 97). It appears also that the obligation was not imposed on freemen. In the description of a Wardmote it is said (p. 38), 'Ad hoc Wardemotum debent hii qui non sunt liberi civitatis, et qui prius jurati non fuerunt ibidem, mitti [? admitti] in francum plegium . . . et jurabunt sacramentum quod habetur de admittendis in francum plegium.' The oath is an oath of allegiance given on p. 315.

All this is very different to the Leet system in Norwich up to the fifteenth century, but is very similar to the procedure at the Sheriffs' Tourns as described in the Statutum Walliæ and elsewhere, and as conducted at a later time by the City Sheriffs in Norwich. It can hardly be doubted that the Norwich Leets rather than the London Wardmotes were the truer representatives of the ancient spirit of local self-government. And this reflection cast no little doubt on the assumption so often put forward, that the London municipality was the model which other towns set before themselves in the struggle for freedom from the grasp of Norman feudalism. In the end, it is true, the London, or magisterial, system prevailed in Norwich, but it was the triumph of a principle altogether antagonistic to that which had found one form of embodiment in the earlier Leet organisation. The more popular system lived long in Norwich, but in the presence of stronger influences it died out, as will be shown in the next section.[1]

[1] Some valuable information on this subject may be gathered from the published *Records of the Borough of Nottingham*. That borough had a Mayor in 1284 and two Bailiffs. This form of government lasted till 1448, when the borough became a county, and, as in Norwich in 1403, the place of the two Bailiffs was taken by two Sheriffs. The Mayor, apparently from at least 1308 (vol. i. p. 67), held a Court called 'Magnum Turnum' or 'Mickletorn' at which presentments

XII. The Decadence and later History of the Leets.

1. Before proceeding with the later history of the Leets under altered conditions it will be well briefly to recall what has been learned of this branch of local jurisdiction in the City to the end of the fourteenth century. So far as we are able to make reliable inferences from ascertained facts, we may surmise that in the twelfth century the view of frankpledge for the City would be held by the Sheriff of the County in his own court, the burgesses being organised on the basis of the four previously existing divisions of the borough. Judging from the fact that even under the more highly organised Leet system the tithings were included within parishes, it seems probable that in the twelfth century the representatives of parishes rather than of tithings appeared before the Sheriff. The Borough Court[1] or Husting, the successor of the Folkmote, was meanwhile presided over by a Provost appointed by the king. In 1194 King Richard I. granted the City to the citizens with leave to choose their own Provost. This may have included the right to hold their own view of frankpledge, and in that case the four

Recapitulation

View of frankpledge in the twelfth century

Under Charter of Richard I.

were made partly by large juries of (p. 268: Oct. 1395) twenty-three or even (p. 312: Ap. 1396) twenty-five persons, and partly by officials called 'Decennarii.' Two of these officials were attached to every 'vicus' [see above p. lxii, n] or street and to other places, and were described by the name of their 'decennaria,' as 'disenarii de Foro Cotidiano' (1308: p. 68), 'decennarii de Fleshewergate, de Bergesgate, de eodem vico, ad finem Pontis' etc. (p. 298 et seq.) In one case two persons described as 'decennarii de Bridilsmythgate' (pp. 307, 308) are immediately afterwards called 'constabularii de Bridilsmythgate.' This was in 1396. These persons acted as Petty Constables, presenting offenders, attaching them (p. 211) and conducting them to prison (p. 160). Their name 'decennarii,' if not of foreign importation, would imply that they had once been heads of tithings. But neither capital pledges, tithings, frankpledge nor leets are mentioned in the published extracts. In the Glossary, however (p. 448, s. v. *Magnum Turnum*), occurs the statement 'The Leet Jury is still called the Mickletorn Jury.' The system seems to mark a transition stage between those of Norwich and London, approximating rather to the latter. In Norwich 'decennarius' described a member, not the head, of a tithing.

The Court Leet of Manchester, the Records of which have been published by the Cheetham Society, followed the ordinary form of a Manorial Court Leet in its later development, and presents none of the features which owe their origin to the frankpledge or the tithing system.

[1] See below, Note G.

divisions may have come to be called from that time the four Leets. In 1223 King Henry III. granted them four Bailiffs instead of a Provost. No charter exists conveying this privilege, and no particular notice is taken of it in later documents. Yet it cannot be doubted that its significance lay in the fact that the citizens at that time obtained the control of the criminal jurisdiction which was then attached to the Hundred Court, and especially to the Sheriff's Tourn. In a franchised Hundred the Bailiff took the place of the Sheriff. As will be seen presently, when the Hundred jurisdiction in Norwich was subordinated to that of the 'County of the City,' Bailiffs ceased to be the chief executive officials, and the new Sheriffs of the City resumed the place formerly held by the Sheriff of the County.   *Appointment of Bailiffs and establishment of Leet presentments in 1223*

At this time, then, in 1223, the criminal presentments ordered by the Assize of Clarendon, which might previously have been made to the Sheriff by twelve representatives from each of the four divisions, were transferred to the court of the City under the presidency of the Bailiffs. Then began the fully developed organisation of Leets and subleets with their annual courts of presentment and amercement, of which a detailed picture, especially at the close of the thirteenth century, has been attempted to be produced in the foregoing pages.

The Leet Rolls of 1375 and 1391 show us this jurisdiction being exercised still on the same lines. Some differences may be detected. There is more systematic arrangement of offences, and some are more fully described. Fewer persons are amerced for breaking the assize of ale; many more for 'not coming to the Leet' and for forestalling, with occasionally very heavy amercements; English words become more frequent, and 'aliens' or 'Duchemen' appear on the scene. But on the whole, the proceedings are much the same as in 1288.   *Continued through fourteenth century*

2. Great changes, however, were at hand, and the Leet jurisdiction was vitally affected by them. It is hardly a matter of surprise that it ceased to retain its hold. Although admirably adapted for the *detection* of crime or of breaches   *Weak points of the system*

of the City custom, it is impossible not to be struck with its inefficiency in the way of *repression* and penalty. The amercements in many cases seem altogether inadequate as due punishments for the offence, and even so it is doubtful whether many of them were ever obtained. Moreover, what has been observed with regard to the assize of ale may be shown to hold good of most other trade offences. The annual amercement was nothing else than annually paying for a licence to continue the offence. The offenders are entered on a list, originally according to their residences, and the same lists are copied year after year with only slight changes such as would naturally occur. To take, for instance, the supply of fish: in 1289 (p. 31) Ranulph le pessuner is fined the paltry sum of 2 s. for forestalling and forbarring of fish, and for buying before the lawful time. His name is followed by those of 83 other persons fined various sums for the same offence. In 1292 he appears in a similar entry with an amercement of 4 s.; in 1296 with one mark, and again in 1300 in a like entry repeated in the same words, with a fine of half a mark. On all these occasions the names which follow are to a great extent the same. So with the tanners, poulterers and others. Yet forestalling was reckoned so grievous an injury to the community that according to the 37th Chapter of Customs the offender was for the first offence to be heavily amerced, for the second to lose his merchandise and be put in the pillory, and for the third to be deprived of the freedom of the City. It is just possible that this enactment might have been incorporated in the Customs subsequently to the Roll of 1300. But the 'Customs' must certainly have been anterior to the Rolls of 1375 and 1391, and even then, although the fines are occasionally heavy, there is no trace of any punishment of a severer kind being inflicted.

This inherent weakness of the frankpledge system in the exercise of repressive authority would naturally tend to become exaggerated in a large and prosperous community where the conditions of life and government were growing more complex with each generation. And other forces were

at work to discredit it. The soul of the system consisted in the universal obligation of every member of a tithing (that is, in theory, every adult male) to disclose and bring to punishment every breach of the laws and customs by which the community was bound. But from at least the thirteenth century onwards, other ways of effecting the same object had gradually been coming into operation. Private gilds had been endeavouring to get control over individual crafts; supervisors were appointed in the name of the community to inquire into trade practices; twenty-four citizens were chosen and, in 1374, authorised by charter to assist the Bailiffs in the general administration of City affairs, and finally the crown was set to the complete revolution both of the civil and judicial organisation of the City by the establishment of a Municipal Assembly and by the conferring of magisterial authority on the twenty-four Aldermen. All these changes were effected before the middle of the fifteenth century, and there was plainly no longer need or room for tithing responsibility. How long the tithings were even nominally kept up I have no means of judging. The system of leet presentments did indeed continue, but somewhat as an anachronism. It tended to fall more and more into the background, and its very existence has only been saved from oblivion by the fortunate preservation of a few isolated Rolls. *Adverse influences*

Decay of the old Frank-pledge System from 1403

3. The change which principally concerns our subject is that in 1403 the City was constituted a County, and this led to the substitution of Sheriffs for Bailiffs. King Henry IV.'s charter directs the Sheriffs of the City to exercise every duty belonging to the office of a Sheriff, and they therefore proceeded to hold their Tourns twice a year, in October and in the following April or May. They also took the place of the Bailiffs in receiving the presentments of the Leets, which was done as of old in the early part of Lent. This stage in the history of the Leets may be gathered from some bundles of miscellaneous Rolls in the Guildhall, not catalogued, but labelled as 'Rolls of Presentments.' There is one set for the fifth year of Edward VI., another for 1 & 2 Philip and *Sheriffs appointed; they hold Tourns*

Mary, and then nothing until the last quarter of the seventeenth century, at which period there are several. These Rolls all refer to the Tourns and Leets. There are other Rolls of the seventeenth century and later, recording similar presentments made by other Inquests to the Justices at Quarter Sessions.

<small>The Tourns of the City Sheriffs; held for the four Great Wards</small>

4. The Tourns and Leets differed from each other chiefly in respect of the juries who made the presentments. At the Tourns there were four juries, one for each of the four Great Wards which still retained the old names of Conesford, Mancroft, Wymer, and Ultra Aquam. In the Roll of 1 & 2 Philip and Mary (p. 92) the jurors are described as 'Milites Turni,' or 'Knights of the Turn.' The expression was doubtless merely an adaptation of the county practice. The juries would be chosen from a similar class to that which furnished the juries at the Tourn of the County Sheriff. That they were appointed by the Sheriffs themselves appears from the oath which the city sheriffs were required to take when they entered on their office:[1] 'Ye schal holden your schrevis-turnes opynly, in the gyldehalle, as the schreve of Norfolk and other schreves doon in her countees wyth inne the reme of Inglond, upon the fourme of statute, and ye schall no men putten upon the enquestis, that xall be taken for the schrevis-turn, but good men and sufficient; that ben men of good name and good fame' etc. Their presentments must have been the result of reports received from parochial officials.

In 5 Edward VI., the Sheriff's second Tourn held on April 21 (p. 88) is called 'The turne with the residue of the Lete.' 'Residuum lete' is said by Spelman[2] to have been a name given to the Leet held in the spring as a completion of the other Leet held in the foregoing autumn. This hardly suits the use of the expression here. The term 'Leet' is never applied even in the later Rolls to anything but the courts held before Easter. The court held in October is called the 'first *turne*.' 'Residue of the Leete' appears to

<small>[1] Norwich Liber Albus, fol. 183.
[2] *Glossarium*, s. v. 'Lete.'</small>

mean here that the Tourn held after Easter picked up some of the unaccomplished business of the Leets which had just been held before Easter.[1] In one respect the spring Tourn certainly did refer back to the Leet. In three of the seventeenth century Rolls (pp. 94, 97, 100) there are long lists of persons amerced at that Tourn for not having attended at the previous Leets. In the Roll for 1 & 2 Philip and Mary the two Tourns and the Leet are very clearly distinguished. In the Tourn held on October 23 in that year for the Ward of Mancroft thirty-seven persons are amerced for trading without being 'freemen.' Of these two are marked in the margin (p. 91) 'ult' turn' (meaning, I suppose, that they had been already presented at the last tourn after the previous Easter); one is marked 'prim' turn' (that held in the previous October); and twenty-three are marked 'let' (i.e. the Leets held in the foregoing Lent). These numbers seem to show that at this date the greater proportion of the presentments, at least for some offences, were still made through the Leet juries.

5. Our information about the later history of the Leets as distinguished from the Tourns is almost exclusively derived from one Roll of 5 Edward VI., 155$\frac{2}{3}$, and three of 1682, 1693, and 1698. Only the first of these and one little fragment of a later one contain any record of their proceedings. Still, although the evidence is meagre, it is quite conclusive as to the continued existence of the old Leets in the City till at least the beginning of the eighteenth century. From the earlier of these Rolls we learn that in 155$\frac{2}{3}$, while the Tourns were held for each of the four great divisions of the city, the Leets were held as of old for the small divisions. The Roll is only a fragment and contains a record of only five of the divisions for which separate juries made presentments. On 26 Febr. in that year Leets were held before the Sheriffs in the Guildhall for the districts of 'St. Gregory within the Ward of Wymer,' 'the Warde of West Wymer,' and a third, of which the name is lost (p. 85). It was probably called either 'St. Andrew' or 'Middle

The Leets down to 1700 retained their old districts

[1] See Scriven, *Law of Copyholds*, p. 352.

Wymer.' On 2 March two more were held for 'Est Wymer' and 'Berstret.' It will be remembered that in the fifteenth century the City had for general municipal purposes been divided into four Great Wards, each subdivided into three Small Wards. The occurrence in this Roll of the names of the *Wards* of East and West Wymer would seem to indicate, at first sight, that the Leets had accommodated themselves to the new organisation and that a Leet jury made presentments for each Small Ward. That must not, however, be hastily assumed, for, on the other hand, the name of ' St. Gregory ' was that of an old subleet and never of a Small Ward. And if (as internal evidence suggests) the third Leet held on February 26 was for St. Andrew's district, that would make four juries for the Wymer great division, in accordance with the old system and not the new. Still after finding the Leet districts in 1551 called, at least in some cases, by the names of the Small Wards, we are hardly prepared for the very interesting revelation made by the three Rolls alluded to at the close of the seventeenth century. These are Rolls of the Sheriffs' Tourns, but in each case there is a membrane added containing the names of persons amerced for non-attendance at the 'several Courts of the View of Frankpledge of the Lord King' held in the Guildhall before the Sheriffs 'in their several Leets on the several days' specified. The names of the defaulters are arranged in Leets and with each Leet is specified the day on which it had been held. From these lists it appears that the Leets were being held, not for the twelve Small Wards, but for the ten old subleets, just exactly as they had been held 300 years before at the time of the Rolls of 1375 and 1391. The revised municipality had long ago reorganised the ten old Leet divisions for its own purposes into twelve, but the Leet system continued to work upon the old divisions as long as it is possible to trace it. What is equally remarkable is that in 168$\frac{1}{2}$ and again in 169$\frac{3}{4}$ the Leet of Conesford was held on Monday, 6 March, which in each case was the first Monday in Lent, the normal day for commencing the

courts in the thirteenth century. So inveterate is custom when there is nothing to alter its course.

6. In 1551 the presentments at the Leets still included many of the offences dealt with in earlier days. They are, however, greatly diminished in number. The most numerous class is that of persons amerced for trading without being freemen. There is also forestalling and regrating, drawing a dagger, using defective weights and measures, 'noyeing the highway with stokks and blokks,' 'typplers,' 'houses of ill rule,' 'corrupt vittal,' 'muk,' 'encrochyng.' The small fragment for the Leet of Coslany on 16 March, 169$\frac{3}{4}$, appears to be a complete return for that Leet. There are only seven amercements, three for unsealed flagons, one for drawing beer without licence, one for a defective measure, one for not paving a street, and the City Chamberlain in the good round sum of £20 for not repairing the city walls. *Presentments at the later Leets*

7. On one important matter connected with the later Leets these few Rolls give us no information, viz. the composition of the Leet Juries. How long did they continue to be the Capital Pledges of tithings, and how were they appointed afterwards? In the Roll of 1551 there are five sets of jurors given. One is composed of thirteen persons, the other four of fourteen each. In four of them they are not in any way described. In the fifth, that for St. Gregory, they are called in the margin 'Capitales Plegii' (p. 85). It is impossible to say whether this was a strictly correct description or only an old name handed down to times when its real meaning was lost. There is no mention of any one being amerced for not being 'in decenna.' It seems hardly likely that the tithing system was kept in working order. The numerous presentments of 'foreigners' made by the juries rather suggest that they represented the freemen of their districts, a sufficient jury being either specially summoned or sworn in at the time. *The later Leet Juries*

8. There can be little doubt that after the municipal reorganisation of 1403 the Leet presentments were superfluous. The Sheriffs in their Tourns made precisely similar inquiries and amerced similar offences, the amercements (in *Rival authorities which supplanted the Leet Juries*

accordance with the statute of 1 Ed. IV.) being sanctioned at the Quarter Sessions by the Mayor and two other Justices of the peace, who certify at the foot of every membrane that they have 'perused these estreates and do affeare the same.' The Municipal Assembly also took cognisance of many matters with which the Leets claimed to deal, and did not hesitate to overrule the weaker authority. On one occasion, having ordered a certain lane leading to a staith in Conesford to be stopped, they add: 'If any amercement shall happen to be made on that account by the Capital Pledges, such amercement shall be pardoned, the customs of the Comon Stath being prejudiced by Landing of goods there.'[1] Besides the Tourns and the Assembly there was also in operation as far back as 1629 an inquiry called the 'Quest of Wards.' One for that year is headed 'The presentment of the Quest of Wards for the Great Ward of Wymer as followeth holden at the Sessions in the Guyldhall, Norwich, being the 15th day of December 1629.' In the margin the presentments are divided into 'East Wymer,' 'Middle Wymer,' and 'West Wymer.' A similar inquest for Mancroft, subdivided into three Small Wards, had been held the previous day. Plainly, therefore, these inquests had nothing to do with the Leet districts. The offences presented are 'not paving streets,' 'unlicensed tiplers' etc., as at the Leets.

With these several authorities concurrently dealing with the same offences, the Leet juries probably found their business passing bit by bit out of their hands till at last nothing was left but the presentment of defective weights and measures and of the sale of unwholesome food.

Obscurity of our last view of the old system

9. Although the continued existence of the old Leet organisation in Norwich so late as the close of the seventeenth century is clear, the character of its vitality is not so apparent. The small return from the Leet of Coslany in 1693 shows that presentments were still made in the old form. With this exception our information is entirely derived from

[1] Quoted by Kirkpatrick (*Streets and Lanes*, p. 7) as 10 Hen. VII. The reference is not to be found in the Assembly Book of that year.

the lists already mentioned of persons amerced for non-attendance at the Leets. On those three occasions defaulters are amerced from every one of the Leets, and it is observable that the numbers vary in only a comparatively small degree. The lowest for any Leet is eleven, the highest twenty. This fact would certainly lead to the supposition that the defaulters were the several Leet juries and that the word 'jur' by which they are described is intended for 'juratores.' But if from eleven to twenty jurors were absent in each Leet, we fail to see who were left to make presentments.[1] The language quoted from Kitchin on p. 94 suggests the solution that 'jur' might be 'jurati' in the sense of 'sworn lieges' and that the defaulters were amerced for neglecting the suit they owed to the court. But this explanation fails to account for the similarity in the numbers in each Leet. On the whole, the most probable solution of the difficulty is that we have here a view of the Leet system when it had become a barren skeleton of outward forms from which the life had almost passed away. From the fourteenth century we may mark the process of degradation slowly but surely going on. With the growth of a local magistracy having powers of criminal jurisdiction, tithings became an antiquated instrument for the preservation of social order. In course of time the view of frankpledge[2] seems to have ceased to serve any other purpose than that of making presentments to the Sheriffs. Still there remained the obligation of making certain presentments at the Leets, and it was doubtless the duty of some official to summon the persons on whom the burden was supposed to rest. But by the end of the seventeenth century it had come to

---

[1] It is unfortunate that in the case of Coslany in 1693, where the names of a presenting jury of twelve persons have survived, the names of the corresponding defaulters have perished.

[2] The old names long survived the institutions which originally gave them their meaning. The Leet Court (or Court Leet) continued universally to be called the 'view of frankpledge'; the presenting juries were still called 'Capital Pledges'; and at least in some places the persons who owed suit to the court were called 'decennarii,' as in Kitchin (*ubi supra*). The expression 'decennarii Domini Regis' occurs in a Norfolk manor in 1489 and 1584. (Chandler, *Court Rolls of Cressingham*, pp. 54, 98). So completely had the local responsibility become lost in the public obligation.

this, that the greater number of the persons summoned preferred to suffer amercement rather than take the trouble to answer the summons.

Final extinction in 1835

10. This is not altogether a satisfactory explanation of these lists of defaulters. But something of this sort must most probably have been taking place at this time in reference to the old Leets. No further trace of them has survived. At some time during the eighteenth century they practically ceased to exist, and such of their duties as still remained were committed to a very unworthy heir of their name. The Commissioners who visited Norwich in 1833, prior to the Municipal Reform Act of 1835, state in their Report (vol. iv. 2466) : ' The Leet performs the duties of inspectors of weights and measures, and receives fines on convictions of persons for using defective weights etc.' They do not state what the Leet consisted of, but fortunately a published ' Digest' of the evidence given on 25 November, 1833, informs us what it was the Commissioners found. 'The Leet,' says the then Town Clerk, 'consists of four persons appointed by the Mayor ; they have no salary, but have fines on conviction ; has heard of Bradberry's case ; he is one of the Leet ; heard he was apprehended for felony a short time ago.' Bradberry was a constable for North Conesford Ward. He had stolen a pair of shears, but the owner declined to prosecute, out of pity for his wife and children. Nevertheless he 'continued to be on the Leet.' The number four probably means one person from each of the four Great Wards. At Lynn, where an inquiry had been held the previous week, and where things had not sunk quite so low, the Leet consisted of twenty persons, two for each of ten wards. They were appointed by the Alderman of each ward and were called Headboroughs, their duties being to inspect weights and measures and to look into the wholesomeness of food.

With this degenerate travesty of the 160 Capital Pledges of the thirteenth century the last stage in the history of Leet presentments in Norwich came to an end.

In concluding this Introduction the Editor wishes to offer some apology for its length. The present volume differs from those which have preceded it in the exclusively local character of its information. While this gives an Editor acquainted with the locality and having free use of local documents the opportunity of examining more closely into his subject than would otherwise be possible, it places the general reader at a certain disadvantage. The Editor has desired to redress, as far as possible, the balance between himself and his less favourably circumstanced readers, as well as to justify the statements which his local knowledge has led him to make. This will, it is hoped, furnish a valid reason for the fulness of detail with which he has endeavoured to draw out a picture of the organisation and working of internal police administration in the City of Norwich in early times through the agency of the frankpledge system and through Leet presentments and amercements. In doing so he has confined himself entirely to the elucidation of the documents here given, that so the reader may test the truth of the picture presented.

All the documents which have been dealt with are the property of the Corporation of the City of Norwich, and the thanks of the Selden Society are due to the City Committee of the Town Council for permission to publish them. The Editor also gratefully acknowledges his personal obligation to G. B. Kennett, Esq., Town Clerk of Norwich, for his courtesy in granting him constant access to them, and to others who have in various ways given him generous assistance, especially Professor Maitland, Dr. Bensly, Chapter Clerk of Norwich, and Mr. T. R. Tallack of Norwich, whose intimate acquaintance with the contents of the City Record Room and skill in deciphering them he has constantly found of the greatest service.

lxxxiv   LOCAL DOCUMENTS.

LOCAL MANUSCRIPTS AND BOOKS REFERRED TO IN THIS VOLUME.

A. Manuscripts in the possession of the Corporation of Norwich.

1. 'Repertory.' A Catalogue of the Muniments in the City Record Room, made in 1848 by Mr. Goddard Johnson.
2. 'Conveyance Rolls.' Enrolments of Deeds acknowledged in the City Court. They commence in 13 Edward I. (July 1285). Catalogued in the 'Repertory' as 'Court Rolls.'
3. 'Leet Rolls.' Edited in this volume. Catalogued as 'Court Leet Rolls.' Some other documents are mixed with them in the 'Repertory.'
4. 'Presentment Rolls.' Here edited. See p. lxxv. They have been omitted in the 'Repertory.'
5. 'Book of Pleas.' A bound volume containing copies of ancient Pleas, Charters, and miscellaneous documents. The Series was compiled probably soon after 33 Hen. VI. (1453). In this Book, commencing on fol. 89, are copied fifty-one 'Chapters of Customs' ('Leges et Consuetudines antiquitus in civitate Norwiconsi usitate'). Internal evidence would assign a date somewhat earlier than 1340 as that when the customs were reduced to this form.
6. 'City Domesday.' A bound volume chiefly relating to the lands, shops, stalls and other common property of the city in the time of Richard II.
7. 'Old Free Book.' A bound volume containing the earliest lists of Admissions to the Freedom of the City from 11 Edward II., with some other miscellaneous entries. It was purchased in 1844.
8. 'Liber Albus.' A bound volume of copies of miscellaneous documents, begun in 1426.

B. Printed Books.

1. 'Blomefield's History of Norwich.' Volume II. of Blomefield's *History of Norfolk*: orig. edit. in five folio volumes (1745).
2. 'Streets and Lanes of the City of Norwich.' A MS. by John Kirkpatrick (c. 1720): published by the Norfolk and Norwich Archæological Society in 1889.

C. Numbers of the Rolls here edited as catalogued in the 'Repertory':—

Roll	I.	Court Leet Roll	2	Roll	VIII.	Court Leet Roll	21
,,	II.	,, ,,	3	,,	IX.	,, ,,	19
,,	III.	,, ,,	4	,,	X.	,, ,,	17
,,	IV.	,, ,,	5	,,	XI.	,, ,,	18
,,	V.	,, ,,	6	,,	XII.	,, ,,	15
,,	VI.	,, ,,	7	,,	XIII.	,, ,,	9
,,	VII.	,, ,,	8	,,	XIV.	,, ,,	12

The remaining Rolls are not entered in the 'Repertory.'

Note A.—*Citizenship in the Thirteenth Century.*

1. The Leet Courts dealt with citizenship only in respect of its exercise; a 'stranger' was presented for wrongfully exercising the privileges of a 'civis'; a citizen was amerced for exercising his privileges to the injury of the whole 'communitas.' The question as to whether a man had a right to call himself a citizen must have been decided by reference to an official Roll. No list of admissions to citizenship earlier than 1317 has survived. It is probable that in the disturbed years at the close of the reign of Henry III. many earlier lists may have been lost; otherwise it is difficult to account for the fact that the 'citizenship' of even some leading traders is sometimes questioned. The only form in which a man's status is objected to is that he has never 'made his entrance.' The meaning of this is explained in the Chapter of Customs quoted below. It does not appear that any questions were raised in the case of an applicant as to his previous status or origin, except that a serf had to produce his lord's licence.[1] What was inquired into was his substantial credit—when the City was tallaged or fined, or called upon to make any other payment, would he be likely to meet his personal liability? Would he be able to bear the burden of being 'at lot and scot' with his fellow-citizens?

2. '*Non pares*' (Leet Roll X. p. 63).—The name by which a citizen is described throughout these rolls is either 'civis' or 'concivis.' Only in one case, in the Roll for 1375, a different expression is used: the persons who are presented are called in the margin 'non pares,' the expression being equivalent to ' non cives ' in other places in the same Roll. The word 'par' has a special interest from its use in the Chapters of Customs. It is there of constant occurrence and always as the equivalent of 'civis.' It is plainly an assertion of the original equality of all citizens, and the equality consists in the possession of the 'libertas' by which the status of a citizen is always described in these Rolls. He

[1] In London and elsewhere servile origin was a bar to admission into citizenship: Lib. Alb. p. 33. Gross, *Gild Merchant*, i. 30.

alone is 'de libertate civitatis.' The original significance of the term 'libertas' in its application to citizenship is not quite so easy to decide. In the early Leet Rolls it refers exclusively to trade. One who is 'de libertate' may freely trade; no one else may. But the word 'pares' introduces a further consideration, and suggests that 'libertas' originally meant freedom from feudal servitude, and this I believe to be the meaning of 'liberi et non servi alicujus' in the 36th Chapter of Customs. The only difficulty in the way of this interpretation is the comparatively late date at which the word 'par' occurs in the Norwich documents. The date of the compilation of the Chapters of Customs is uncertain, but several indications point to about 1340. Outside of these the word occurs, so far as I know, only in the Leet Roll of 1375 and in an entry in the 'Old Free Book'[1] where two persons whose citizenship was questioned were declared to be 'cives et pares civitatis Norwici.' This was in 19 Edward III. (1346). Still, although these references are of late date, the Customs profess to have been 'antiquitus usitate,' and this expression 'pares' may be a relic of a far earlier epoch. An instance of its use at the Fair of St. Ives in 1276 is to be found in Selden Society, vol. ii. p. 152; and several in the Domesday of Ipswich[2] compiled in 19 Edward I, and said to be a re-compilation of a lost set of Customs written in 1291. The 36th Chapter of Norwich Customs throws such valuable light on this subject of early admission to citizenship that I give it in full :—

Item nullus mercandizet in ciuitate qui in eadem facit residentiam nisi sit ad lottum & scottum illius ciuitatis & ad communia eiusdem auxilia contribuat Et quia omnes qui recipientur in parem ciuitatis sint liberi et non servi alicuius bene inquiratur antequam recipiantur Et illi qui admittentur graviter & solempniter faciant introitum suum coram illis qui ad hoc assignantur per totam communitatem singulis annis quater in anno ad terminos usuales Ita quod ad minus in talibus introitibus quandocunque contigerit sint duodecim de assignatis presentes & sine minore numero nullus admittatur quod si cecus [sic] fiat irritum sit & vanum Et quia omnes qui sic admittentur diligenter admittentur examinentur per sacramentum proprium ante eorum receptionem de quantitate bonorum suorum secrete per illos duodecim & per alios qui noticiam habent ipsius [sic] & facultatum suarum per sacramentum in hac parte prestandum Et si ille forinsecus [sit] & non extiterit apprenticius in ciuitate non minus recipiatur quam pro viginti solidis communitati solvendis Et ulterius det secundum quod sue suppetant facultates Et nullus apprenticius admittatur ad parem ciuitatis nisi bonum habeat testimonium de domino suo & visneto illius & nullo modo pro minore precio quam una marca Et si huiusmodi

[1] Fol. xii.
[2] *Black Book of the Admiralty* (Rolls Series), vol. ii. 136.

INTRODUCTION : NOTE A. 3.   lxxxvii

apprenticii facultates ulterius possint sufficere illa vice plus det pro introitu suo secundum ordinacionem illorum duodecim Et nomina illorum duodecim ad quemlibet introitum irrotulentur et nomen illius intrantis in uno Rotulo indentato & duplicato & finis illius intrantis & plegii sui & terminus solutionis sue & annus & dies & nomen clerici iurati qui habebit unum rotulum penes se & alius remanebit in communi cista Et nullus alius irrotulet quam clericus iuratus Et quilibet ingrediens dabit clerico sex denarios pro labore suo Et ille novus par ciuitatis bonam securitatem faciet quod infra annum sue receptionis in parem impetrabit sibi certum habitaculum nisi prius habuerit in illa ciuitate ad morandum in eadem cum familia sua & bona sua mobilia ad dictam trahet ciuitatem Et si non fecerit post annum completum habeatur pro extraneo cum sequela sua sicut prius Et nullus ingrediens illo anno [in quo] facit introitum suum quicquam dabit lottum neque aliquid auxilium in eadem ciuitate nisi tantummodo ad muros eiusdem ciuitatis faciendos [et] si necesse fuerit reparandos Set propter hoc non erit quietus versus dominum regem si contingat ipsum aliquod auxilium vel tallagium in eadem imponere cum voluerit unde nullus se poterit excusare Et si servus velit ingredi primo querat licenciam domini sui per literas suas patentes.

The special use of the term 'civis' in the Conveyance Rolls at the close of the thirteenth century as a distinctive appellation of the upper class of citizens has been commented on already.[1]

3. *The case of William de Colton* (Roll I. p. 8).—The Coram Rege Roll 6 Ed. II. m. 26, contains a Plea of Villainage in which this William de Colton was concerned. At that date, twenty-six years later than this Leet Roll, he and seventeen others were claimed as villains by the lord of the manor of Costessey, near Norwich. William and three others claimed to be free as citizens of Norwich, and William stated that he had been for sixty years at scot and lot and tallages with the free citizens. First they proffered a charter of King William I. to the effect that 'servi' who remained unclaimed in one of the king's cities for a year and a day should be thenceforth free. This plea, however, was not thought sufficient, for three of them then produced deeds of King Edward I. relating to their holdings. William had obtained his as follows. In the twenty-first and twenty-second years of Edward's reign the stalls and sheds in the Nedler-row in the market were rebuilt. William, who owned three pieces of land there, obtained leave from the Bailiffs and Commonalty to build on them.[2] In the case of two of these pieces, which were perhaps chargeable with the payment of the king's landgable, he had to seek the sanction of an 'Inquisitio ad quod damnum,' which reported in his favour, and he obtained a royal grant of confirmation in 33 Ed. I. This deed and a similar one

[1] *Supra*, X. 3.   [2] Deed in Guildhall, May 1293.

granted to the father of the other two defendants, being granted by the king 'ut liberis hominibus,' 'contra quas [cartas] nulla inquisitio patrie est admittenda,' were held to justify their claim to freedom. The case of the fourth citizen, who had no such royal grant, was postponed for further discussion, in spite of his assertion that he had been in the City for thirty years.

If William's statement is correct he must have come to the City about 1253. It seems strange that in 1288 when he was a wealthy trader, he should be accused of never having 'made his entrance.' The loss of lists, as suggested above, might have made such an accusation rather difficult to disprove.

4. *De Ricardo de Knapeton . . . quia . . . non est ad lottum & scottum.* Roll VI. (Wymer, p. 48.)—This unusual expression cannot mean that Richard de Knapton was not a citizen. He is one of those distinguished in the Conveyance Rolls by the title 'civis Norwici.' He held property in the Leet of Wymer in Hosyergate, in the parish of St. Andrew. He is last mentioned there in the year preceding this entry. It may be surmised that in the interval he had given up his house and obtained a corrody in St. Giles's Hospital, which was an ecclesiastical foundation on the north side of the cathedral precinct, and within the exempt jurisdiction of the Prior. He was thus claiming the benefits of citizenship while escaping from the obligations. He was not fulfilling the condition of having a house on which, if need arose, distraint could be made.

NOTE B.—*Craft Gilds in Norwich.*

The statement made in Roll V. (p. 42) with regard to the Cobblers' Gild that it was 'contrary to the prohibition of our lord the King', might mean only 'contrary to the prohibition of the Bailiffs,' for the two expressions are frequently interchanged. But I do not think it would be used except of something forbidden either by a general statute or by a special charter. In the case of Norwich it almost certainly refers to a charter of 40 Henry III. which contains the words, 'Concessimus . . . quod nulla gilda de cetero teneatur in civitate predicta ad detrimentum eiusdem civitatis.' The clause has been interpreted of a merchant gild,[1] but there is no trace of a merchant gild having existed in Norwich, and the presentments in the Leet Rolls make it much more probable that

[1] Merewether and Stephens, *Eng. Boroughs*, p. 437.

it was aimed against associations of craftsmen. They were resented as interfering with the common interests of the City, and putting into private hands the control belonging to the central authority. In spite of discouragement, however, the trade gilds continued and grew stronger. Finally, though not till the middle of the fifteenth century, no one could become a citizen or freeman of the City except by joining a gild, and no one might follow an occupation except the members of that trade or craft.

Long after this time the clause of this charter was on one occasion turned to a curious use which may help to explain its original intention. In the reign of Henry VII. great complaints were made by the less wealthy members of some of the gilds (whether religious gilds or trade gilds does not appear) that the poorer brethren were constantly chosen to be 'feastmakers' at the annual feast. The governing Assembly being anxious to give the relief asked for by the petitioners, sheltered themselves under this clause as giving them authority to control the gilds. They say that 'King Henry III. among other grauntes prohibited that ther shuld no gyld not corporat that is to say the gyldes of craftys shuld be holden within the said cite to the hurte and empoveryshing of the same.'[1] They therefore proceed to lay down rules for the future appointment of feastmakers.

It may be presumed that the original object of the clause was to confirm the authority of the Bailiffs, as representing the whole Commonalty, over all trades and occupations.

NOTE C.—*The City Court of Norwich in the Thirteenth and Fourteenth Centuries.*

It is observable that none of the Leet Rolls in the thirteenth century, nor that of 1313 have any descriptive headings, not even 'Rotulus Presentationum' or 'Amerciamentorum.' The Rolls of 1375 and 1391 are headed 'Rotulus de Veredictis Letarum' etc. But it is not till we come to the sixteenth century Rolls and later that we find any such descriptions as 'Inquisitio in Leta Domini Regis' or 'Curia Visus Franciplegii Domini Regis' used to distinguish the proceedings as held at a special court for a special purpose. The absence of any descriptive heading to the

[1] Assembly Book, 9 Hen. VII., 18 July; 10 Hen. VII., 13 May.

Rolls, though they are evidently the final records copied up from the separate returns made for the Leets or subleets, may be explained by the assumption that the clerk copied just what he found, only modifying the form of the entries. The absence of any description of the proceedings as those of a special court is suggestive of a further explanation.

It probably occurred to no one at that time that the jurisdiction exercised by the Bailiffs in receiving and sanctioning the presentments made at the Leets was in any way of a different character to that which they exercised every day in reference to various other matters. So far as any clue is to be obtained from contemporary evidence, the one executive authority in the City during the thirteenth and at least half of the fourteenth centuries was that of the four Bailiffs in their corporate capacity, and the one court was that called the City Court, in which they presided. Whether they sat to deal with pleas, or to witness recognisances, or receive presentments, or administer any other City business, they were equally presidents of the court, and they did not stop to inquire from what particular sanction their authority was derived. The remarks made by Professor Maitland (vol. ii. p. xvi) on the absence of discrimination between the branches of jurisdiction in the Manorial Courts of this period would, *mutatis mutandis*, hold equally good of the City Court of Norwich.

On one name of this court an observation may be made. It is doubtless the same as the 'hustengum' mentioned in a clause of the charter of 5 Richard I., 'Concessimus . . . quod hustengum semel in ebdomada tantum teneatur.' The clause is found in other charters, as in one to London[1] in the same year. What the intention of the limitation may have been it is not necessary here to consider. That the court itself was no new institution originated by the charter is plain from the parallel case of the City of Lincoln.[2] In a contemporary and similar charter granted to the citizens of Lincoln the clause is thus varied, ' quod burwaramote semel tantum in hebdomada teneatur.' This variation makes it clear that the court was the old Boroughmote or Folkmote which previously to this charter had been presided over by a nominee of the king, but was now placed under the presidency of a Provost elected by the citizens. When the Provost was exchanged for four Bailiffs who became presidents of this court they would hardly consider themselves as forming a new court

---

[1] *Historical Charters of the City of London*, by W. De Gray Birch, p. 9. See also pp. 5 and 7, and a curious explanation on p. xvii.
[2] Rymer's *Foedera*, i. 52.

for the purpose of holding Leets. They would regard the Leet presentments as an accession of jurisdiction to the court already in existence.

The actual title 'husting' does not appear to have been used locally. It occurs a few times in thirteenth century documents, but only in such as have been drawn up in London or elsewhere.

NOTE D.—*The Dean of the City of Norwich.*

'*John, Dean of Norwich*' (Roll I. pp, 2, 15).—The office of Dean of the City of Norwich included the duties rather of an Archdeacon than a Rural Dean. He was the judge in the Court Christian. The 'Official Corrector' mentioned in Roll XI. (p. 71) was an official appointed by the Bishop, and appears to have been identical with the Commissary. In Bishop Tanner's 'MS. Collections for the Diocese of Norwich,' preserved in the Diocesan Registry, there is a list of the Deans till the sixteenth century. At the Reformation the office was merged in that of the Archdeacon.

The John here mentioned was not actually Dean but Subdean. The Dean was Henry Sampson, who on more than one occasion was called to account for his energetic vindication of his rights. One of these occasions may account for the act of violence here presented. In 1286 the Dean had been arrested at the Eyre on a charge of wrongfully exacting certain tolls collected by John the Subdean. He successfully defended himself, doubtless to the further irritation of the citizens. The persons here presented for stealing £40 from the Subdean's chest belonged to one of the leading families in the City, and both they and the Subdean lived in the same district. The money they summarily abstracted was very likely the proceeds of this obnoxious toll.

NOTE E.—*Surnames in the Thirteenth Century.*

The Editor who is required to translate such documents as those here presented to the reader is obliged to face the difficulty of rightly rendering the personal names. The present Editor, who can lay claim to a fairly intimate acquaintance with the citizens of Norwich at the close of the thirteenth century, can

only state his conviction that, while family names were certainly in use, they were not by any means in use as a general practice. Consequently the same person will figure sometimes with a name of origin, sometimes with a name of occupation, sometimes with a nickname, and to a casual reader his identity will be altogether unsuspected.

John the Subdean may furnish a fair illustration of the uncertainty of local practice and the difficulty of translation. His usual name is John de Berstrete, a name of course derived from the district so called. Yet to translate this 'John of Berstreet' would convey a wrong inpression that he himself lived in that district, whereas he lived on Tombland. Again, in a deed of 1290 occurs the name of a certain 'Hamo, son of Simon atte Hollegate.' Holgate was a street leading out of Berstreet, but no one would suspect this Simon to be a brother of John until he found his son Hamo called in another deed 'Hamo, son of Simon de Berstrete, and nephew and heir of John le Don.' The father of John and Simon was also called John de Berstrete, so that 'de Berstrete' had, to some extent, become the family name. But then in this first Roll, p. 15, we find mention of 'John le Mercer, Dean of Norwich,' who must be John de Berstrete. Now in the deeds of this period there occurs several times in the neighbourhood of Holgate a 'John, son of Simon le Mercer,' and although it cannot be proved, yet, considering the concurrence of 'John,' 'Simon,' 'le Mercer,' and 'Holgate,' it seems most probable that this was the elder John de Berstrete, and that the Subdean was called 'le Mercer' from his grandfather. Yet it would plainly be incorrect to take 'Mercer' for a settled family name and call him 'John Mercer, Dean of Norwich.'[1]

With regard to names descriptive of a trade or occupation: they unquestionably in a majority of cases describe the actual occupation of the person bearing them. But they also were used to describe other members of the family, even to two or three generations. The same is true of nicknames, as 'le Graunt.'

In this volume the Editor has felt it best to follow his own judgment in the rendering of names, having frequently been guided by collateral information which could not be given to the reader.

[1] The curious instance of Isabella Lucas has been noted on p. 71.

Note F.—*The Leet of the New Fee of the Castle.*

This was not one of the old Leet districts of the City. The ground round the Castle was enclosed within a bank and ditch, and exempt from the jurisdiction of the City. In 1344 the citizens petitioned the king to grant them the jurisdiction over this ground on the plea that it harboured evil-doers. The petition was granted, except that the Castle itself and the Shire-hall, which then stood on the highest or southern part of the enclosure, were reserved to the king. The ditch and bank were by degrees levelled and built over. Although for ecclesiastical and municipal purposes the new buildings were regarded as belonging to the nearest adjoining parish, they were not attached to the adjoining Leets. Either the Sheriff or the Constable of the Castle had held an annual court, and it was continued by the Bailiffs under the name of the 'Leet of the New Fee of the Castle.' It was not, however, held in Lent like the old Leets, but by itself at a later time in the year.

Note G.—*Some Words Explained.*

A few notes are here given on some words which require a little more lengthened explanation than can conveniently be comprised in a Glossary.

1. '*Curlevasche*,' Roll I. p. 18; '*curlevage*,' Roll VII. p. 51; '*curlevacher*,' Roll IX. p. 58.

This word occurs in the Domesday of Ipswich (*Black Book of the Admiralty*, ii. 104, 105), but Sir Travers Twiss, the Editor, could find no clue to its meaning. The three instances in which it occurs in these Rolls are not any more explicit. A fourth instance of its use at Norwich is of a singular character. It is in the 'Old Free Book' in an isolated entry on fol. xii d. : 'Presentatum est coram Ballivis et Communitate die Veneris proxima post festum Sc̄i Luce Evangeliste aⁿ r' regis Edwardi tertii a conquestu vicesimo quod Willelmus Harto de Habeton qui so dixit esse liber et civis Civitatis Norwyci est communis curlevache cum non liceat nec debeat, et cum quilibet ingrediens libertatem ad introitum suum juravit cōā cōitate [1] inter alios

[1] Sic in MS. There must be some error.

articulos incumbentes quod non erit curlevache communis nec pro tempore. Et idem Willelmus vocatus et inde allocutus, et non potest dedicere . per quod per totam Communitatem die predicto consideratum est quod idem Willelmus diutius libertate predicta non gaudeat pro contumacia sua set sit omnino forinsecus.' The earliest existing oath of admission is much later than this date and contains nothing to suggest the meaning of the word.

It seems to describe some form of violation of the trade regulations of the City and is probably an East-Anglian word. It must at one time have been in common use both at Norwich and Ipswich.

2. '*Dubbare veteres pannos cum trunco fullonis*,' p. 12 etc.—Halliwell (*Dict. of Archaic Words*) defines 'dub' as 'to strike cloth with teasels in order to raise the cloth or nap.' The cloth was also beaten for the same purpose in fulling mills. The 'truncus fullonis' of these Rolls seems to have served the purpose of a fulling mill. The word 'truncus' by itself is a 'block' (see Glossary). The 'truncus fullonis' was perhaps a hollowed-out block or trough which would hold water.¹ The frequent occurrence of this or similar entries in all the four Leets of the City is misleading, and gives an impression that these machines were in use in parts where water could not have been easily obtained. A comparison of the entries, however, shows that nearly all of them refer to only four persons, who, as usual, were duly fined over and over again, and openly continued the offence with the full connivance of the authorities. Four was probably the number of the 'trunci fullonis,' and they were very likely by the riverside.

The fraud consisted in making old clothes look like new, and according to the Statutum Wallie (c. iv.) there was a suspicion that the clothes so treated were stolen. To prevent recognition their shape was altered. The Sheriff in his Tourn is directed to inquire 'De redoboratoribus pannorum furatorum, eos in novam formam redigentibus et veterem mutantibus, ut de mantello tunicam vel supertunicam facientibus et similia.'

'*Omnes dubbatores qui dubbant correos vaccinos faciunt falsitatem in opere suo*' (p. 13).

---

¹ While this surmise was passing through the press the following notice appeared in the *Times*, Sept. 8, 1892: ' *Archæological Discoveries in Winchester*. . . . In another part of the city [was found] a massive oak block hollowed out in the form of a bowl. It weighs nearly 5 cwt., its diameter being 4 ft. and depth about 1 ft. It is conjectured that it may have been used by the tanners or cloth-workers who formerly carried on their trades in the street where it was found.'

The word 'dulbare' is frequently written for 'dubbare.' In this and several other entries the converse must, I think, be intended, and a further confusion must exist between 'dulbare' and 'dealbare,' which is correctly used in other cases. The former fraud (*dubbare pannos*) was perpetrated on cloth by the fripperers; the latter (*dealbare corea*, or *coreos*) on leather by the tanners or white-tawers, called in Norwich 'scowthers' or 'qwyttowers.' They dressed up old leather goods as the fripperers did the old clothes. See the offence described fully in the beginning of Roll IX. The Statutum Wallie also mentions it, 'De Whitauwariis, scilicet qui coria bovina vel equina furata scienter albificant ut sic non agnoscantur.'

3. '*Carnes Judaicas scilicet trepha.*' Roll I. p. 9; II. p. 28.

'Trefa' is the word still used by the Jews to describe meat rejected as not fulfilling their requirements. The Jewish butcher whose profits were thus interfered with would sell the rejected meat to a Christian butcher at a reduced price, and he would sell it to Christians for good meat. The offence was not that the meat was unwholesome—it is not so described—but that Christians were being put off with meat rejected by Jews. The offence is so named in the Judicium Pillorie and Statutum de Pistoribus (though the passage is said not to be in the original) : 'Si quis emat carnes de Judeis et eas vendat Christianis.'

This was only just before the expulsion of the Jews from the country, and a curious commentary on these presentments is furnished by Bishop Swinfield's excommunication of the citizens of Hereford who had accepted an invitation to a Jewish weddingfeast in 1286 (*Household Roll of Bishop Swinfield* [Camden Society], Introd. page c).

PRESENTATIONES ET AMERCIAMENTA AD LETAS
CORAM BALLIVIS CIVITATIS NORWICI.

PRESENTMENTS AND AMERCEMENTS AT THE
LEETS BEFORE THE BAILIFFS OF THE
CITY OF NORWICH.

1288 TO 1391.

I. [ROTULUS PRESENTATIONUM AD LETAS NORWICI A° R' REGIS EDWARDI XVI°.]

[1] LETA DE CUNISFORD DIE LUNE [2] PROXIMA POST CARNI-PRIVIUM ANNO REGNI REGIS E. SEXTO-DECIMO.

[3] Capitales plegii sc. Willelmus Lippard, Silvester Siger, Willelmus King, Ricardus Erych, Ricardus Undermel, Willelmus Inge, Henricus Attewro, Ricardus filius Alexandri Botman, Johannes Slabbard,[4] Radulphus de Suthgate, Hugo de Bromholm, Thomas de Surlingham, presentant per sacramentum suum quod Ernald de Castro wulneravit Hugonem de Bromholm et sanguinem ab eo extraxit contra pacem. Similiter presentant quod Nicholaus le Jay wulneravit quendam clericum extraneum et duos digitos ipsius clerici amputavit et hutesium ibi levatum fuit et idem Nicholaus captus fuit et imprisonatus ad sectam Hugonis de Bromholm constabularii de predicta leta et Ernald et alii evaserunt. Similiter presentant quod Johannes de Witton fuit verberatus per certos quorum nomina Ballivi habent penes se.

[1] Roll I.—This Roll is given in full as being the earliest, and also for its valuable details in respect to the grouping of parishes for the purpose of making presentments, and for its full list of the Capital Pledges of the Tithings. It consists of two membranes fastened at the top. The first is 20½ inches long by 7¼ broad, the second slightly shorter. They are written on both sides. The Roll is in the form of presentments without amercements.

[2] 15 February 128¾.

[3] For the parishes represented by these jurors see Roll III. (S. Conesford), p. 33.

[4] In MS. *et alii* is here struck out. The three following names are entered above the line.

I. [LEET ROLL OF 16 EDWARD I. (128⅞)].

LEET OF CUNISFORD ON MONDAY NEXT AFTER ASH WEDNESDAY IN THE 16TH YEAR OF THE REIGN OF KING EDWARD.

The Capital Pledges—that is to say, William Lippard, Silvester Siger, William King, Richard Erych, Richard Undermel, William Inge, Henry Attewro, Richard son of Alexander Boatman, John Slabbard, Ralph de Suthgate, Hugh de Bromholm, Thomas de Surlingham, present on their oath that Ernald de Castro wounded Hugh de Bromholm and drew blood from him contrary to the peace. Likewise they present that Nicholas le Jay wounded a certain clerk, a stranger,[2] and cut off two fingers of the said clerk, and the hue was raised there and the said Nicholas was taken and imprisoned at the suit of Hugh de Bromholm, constable of the aforesaid leet,[3] and Ernald and others escaped. Likewise they present that John de Witton was beaten by certain men whose names the Bailiffs have in their possession.

---

[1] The names by which the subleets were afterwards known are added in the margin for convenience of reference.

[2] One not yet admitted to the freedom of the city.

[2] This must mean the whole Leet of Conesford, not the subleet for which these presentments were made. The word is only used in the earlier Rolls for the four great divisions of the city.

De tesauro invento¹ sciunt set presentare contempnunt. De roberia presentant quod Robertus Scot et maritus Emme² Hauteyn roboraverunt servientem Roberti le parchiminer de iiij denariis et quadrante inter Norvicum et Brakendele.³ Presentant etiam quod Robertus de Lenn levavit hutesium super Walterum de Lenn etc. De hiis qui vendunt et emunt bladum presentant quod Robertus Gerveys omit bladum antequam venit ad forum per quod Ballivi⁴ etc. Presentant etiam quod omnes braciatrices vendunt ij galonas ad unum denarium et duas galonas ad denarium et obolum. Dicunt etiam quod Johannes de Berwyk vendit unam galonam ad denarium. Presentant etiam quod Johannes Spik et Ernald Pelse vendunt unam galonam cervisie ad unum denarium. Illii [sic] qui manent in redditu⁵ magistri Godefridi de Norton habent fenestram nocentem transeuntibus et itinerantibus in via Domini Regis.

Omnes in mīā pro concelamento. Presentat etiam Ricardus Erych quod Alanus de Catton invenit ix bidentes submersos et post vendicati fuerunt per quosdam extraneos. Presentant etiam quod Ricardus Schepeshe habet quoddam rete contra assissam. Presentant etiam quod serviens Roberti de Daleby invenit quandam vaccam et illam abduxit set nesciunt in quo loco.

⁶ Presentant etiam quod Johannes de Morle filius Rogeri de Morle et Hubertus frater eius fregerunt noctanter cistam Johannis quondam Decani Norwyci et asportaverunt de domo sua aurum et argentum ad valenciam xl ħ et amplius.

Dicunt etiam quod Willelmus Colyn traxit sanguinem de quadam muliere extranea cuius nomen ignoramus.⁷

¹ After *invento* is *presentant*, struck out.
² After *Emme* is *Pike*, crossed out.
³ A suburb of Norwich towards the south.
⁴ Supply *amittunt custumam* or *theolonium*.
⁵ This modern-sounding description of an inhabited tenement, which frequently occurs in these Rolls, must indicate a house or room for which the tenant paid a rent. I have not noticed the word in this sense in the Conveyance Rolls.
⁶ The next three entries have been interpolated in a vacant space. They belong to the next subleet.
⁷ The clerk has copied the exact word used in the return for North Conesford.

Concerning treasure trove they know but they refuse to present. Concerning robbery they present that Robert Scott and the husband of Emma Hauteyn robbed the servant of Robert the skinner of fourpence farthing between Norwich and Brakendele. They present also that Robert de Lenn raised the hue against Walter de Lenn etc. Concerning those who sell and buy corn, they present that Robert Gerveys buys corn before it comes to the market, whereby the Bailiffs [lose their custom or toll]. They present also that all the alewives sell two gallons at one penny and two gallons at one penny halfpenny. They say also that John de Berwyk sells a gallon at a penny. They present also that John Spike and Ernald Pese sell one gallon of ale at one penny. The people who are lodging in Master Godfrey de Norton's rent have a window which is a nuisance to passers-by and foot-passengers on the king's highway.

All [the jurors] are in mercy for concealment. Richard Erych also presents that Alan de Catton found nine drowned sheep, and they were afterwards claimed by some strangers. They present also that Richard Sheepseye has a net contrary to the assize. They present also that a servant of Robert de Daleby found a cow and led it away, but to what place they know not.

They present also that John de Morley, son of Roger de Morley, and Hubert his brother, by night broke open the chest of John, late Dean of Norwich,[1] and carried off from his house gold and silver to the value of £40 and more.

They say also that William Colyn drew blood from a certain woman, a stranger, whose name they do not know.

[1] See Introduction, Note D.

Galfridus de Sco̅ Edmundo capitalis plegius in mīa pro defalta.

¹ Thomas filius Nicholai de Coventre (jur.), Willelmus filius Walteri le tanur (jur.), Galfridus de Lingwode (jur.), Johannes le Lindraper (jur.), Rogerus le Marechal (jur.), Nicholaus le Marechal (jur.), Willelmus de Irstede (jur.), Willelmus Justice (jur.), Johannes de Surlingham (jur.), Alexander de Sarterin (jur.), Hugo de Rokelund (jur.), Johannes de Bedford peyntur (jur.), presentant quod Willelmus de Sessons fecit ampsokam ad domum Angnetis de Reddenhale unde dicta Angnes levavit utesium. De Johanne de Witton ut prius. De Nicholao le Jay ut prius.

Magister Rogerus de Gernemutha implacitavit Ricardum de Melton de placito debiti in curia Christianitatis contra defensionem domini Regis. Alexander le Machun non est in decenna et manet in parochia Sc̅i Vedasti. Simon carpentarius non est in decenna. Galfridus Craddok extraxit sanguinem de quodam homine de Erlham. Presentant etiam quod Nicholaus Godewyne de Irstedde fecit forstallum ² Ballivis. Magister Alanus de ffreton obstupavit aquam Regalem in Ripa cum fimis [et] cineribus contra defensionem domini Regis. Presentant etiam quod omnes Braciatrices vendunt cervisiam contra assissam. Johannes de Berwyk ad denarium contra assissam vendit. Dicunt etiam quod omnes piscatores et pulletarii emunt carnes et pisces ad cariorandum forum Norwyci. Dicunt quod Rogerus de Morle obstupavit viam regalem cum fimero suo. Dicunt etiam quod scelerarius ³ Norwyci habet fenestras impedientes equitantibus et itinerantibus in vico de ratunrowe.⁴ Willelmus Colyn extraxit sanguinem de Matilde serviente Willelmi filii Walteri le Tanur. Dicunt etiam quod Walterus filius Walteri le Barber ⁵ traxit sanguinem de Lucia sorore sua. Dicunt etiam quod Willelmus de Hemenhale

---

¹ For the parishes represented see Roll III. (North Conesford), p. 35.
² By forcible rescue of distraints. See Glossary.
³ The Cellarer of the Cathedral Monastery is intended; the spelling is hardly complimentary.
⁴ At the southern end of Tombland.
⁵ Sic. But read *Barker*, i.e. tanner, as in previous entry. He is often so called. *Barber* is spelled *barbur*.

Geoffrey de St. Edmund, a capital pledge, in mercy for default.

Thomas son of Nicholas de Coventry (sworn), William son of Walter the tanner (sworn), Geoffrey de Lingwode (sworn), John the linendraper (sworn), Roger the farrier (sworn), Nicholas the farrier (sworn), William de Irstead (sworn), William Justice (sworn), John de Surlingham (sworn), Alexander de Sarterin (sworn), Hugh de Rokelund (sworn), John de Bedford, painter (sworn), present that William de Sessons made hamsoken at the house of Agnes de Redenhall, whereof Agnes raised the hue. Concerning John de Witton as before. Concerning Nicholas le Jay as before.

Master Roger of Yarmouth impleaded Richard de Melton of a plea of debt in the Court Christian against the prohibition of the lord king. Alexander the Mason is not in tithing, and he lodges in the parish of St. Vedast. Simon the carpenter is not in tithing. Geoffrey Craddok drew blood from a man of Erlham. They present also that Nicholas Godwyn of Irstede made forestalment on the Bailiffs. Master Alan de Freton obstructed the king's water in the river with muck[1] and ashes against the king's prohibition. They present also that all the alewives sell beer contrary to the assize. John de Berwyk sells at 1d., contrary to the assize. They say also that all the fishermen and poulterers buy meat and fish in order to heighen[2] the Norwich market. They say that Roger de Morley obstructed the king's highway with his muck-heap. They say also that the Cellarer of Norwich has windows which are an impediment to riders and walkers in Ratonrowe. William Colyn drew blood of Matilda, servant of William son of Walter the tanner. They say also that Walter son of Walter the barker drew blood of his sister Lucy. They say also that William de Hemenhale and

[1] The word used afterwards in the English Rolls.
[2] The local word for raising the price; pronounced 'hain.' See Glossary.

et Johannes de Stoke indictati sunt de latrocinio eo quod furaverunt septem cumbas ordei et siliginis ad domum Alani de Baketon. Dicunt etiam quod Johannes Howard de Surlingham habet catalla sua ad domum Margarete Sumeres in parochia Sc̄i Petri de Suthgate et mercandizat in civitate et non est in decenna nec de libertate Norwyci. Johannes de Blakene non est in decenna et manet cum Roberto Warde. Thomas de Mouton manens cum Roberto Atteyates non est in decenna. Edmundus Middey mercandizat in civitate et non est de libertate. Radulphus Perconal invenit et habet unum plankum per iactum fluminis et non liberavit Ballivis. Hubertus Hunewine invenit aliud plankum et habet [et] non liberavit Ballivis. Walterus Baddyng seniore [1] invenit et habet unam percam [2] per iactum fluminis et non liberavit eam Ballivis.

Berstrette.[3]
  Galfridus de Howe receptavit Willelmum de Stirston qui fuit extra decennam.
  Willelmus Calf pro mangno contemptu facto Ballivis quia noluit prestare sacramentum in mīa, postea juravit. Willelmus de Denne receptavit Robertum de Howe filium Alexandri de Brakendenne per biennium. Ideo in mīa quia fuit extra decennam.

Robertus de Mendham (jur) Willelmus Godynou (jur) Henricus Pope (jur), Galfridus [4] de Ho (amotus [5]), Edmundus de Stafforth (jur), Galfridus filius Baldewini (jur), Johannes de Aschele (jur), Henricus de Hoylaund (jur), Simon le Prude (jur), Simon filius Ranulphi (jur), Eudo de Tybenham (jur), Willelmus Calf (jur), Thomas le Neve (jur), qui presentant per sacramentum suum quod Johannes serviens Roberti Cann extraxit sanguinem de Radulfo de Aslakton pistore. Dicunt quod Beatrix la Qwyte et Acilia socia eius assuete sunt evellere [6] bidentes et evelleraverunt

---

[1] Sic.
[2] Perhaps a measuring pole, or a wooden beam. The beam of a church rood-loft was called the *perk*.
[3] For the parishes contained in this sublect see Roll VIII.
[4] Struck out.
[5] Discharged from his office through incapacity or for some other reason.
[6] Cf. Statut. Walliæ, 'De tondentibus multones noctanter in ovilibus et eos excoriantibus.'

John de Stoke were indicted for larceny, for that they stole seven coombs of barley and rye at the house of Alan de Bacton. They say also that John Howard of Surlingham has his chattels at the house of Margaret Sumers, in the parish of St. Peter de Suthgate, and merchandises in the city, and is not in tithing nor of the freedom of Norwich. John de Blakeney is not in tithing, and lodges with Robert Ward. Thomas de Mouton, lodging with Robert Attegates, is not in tithing. Edmund Middey merchandises in the city and is not of the freedom. Ralph Perconal found and holds a plank cast up by the river, and has not delivered it to the Bailiffs. Hubert Hunwyn found another plank and holds it, and has not delivered it to the Bailiffs. Walter Badding the elder found and holds a perch cast up by the river, and has not delivered it to the Bailiffs.

[Berstrete] **Berstrete.**

Geoffrey de Howe has harboured William de Stirston, who was out of tithing.

William Calf, for great contempt done to the Bailiffs because he refused to proffer his oath. In mercy. Afterwards he took the oath. William de Denne has harboured Robert de Howe, son of Alexander de Brakendenne, for two years. Therefore in mercy because he was out of tithing.

Robert de Mendham (sworn), William Godynow (sworn), Henry Pope (sworn), Geoffrey de Ho (discharged), Edmund de Stafford (sworn), Geoffrey Baldwin's son (sworn), John de Ashill (sworn), Henry de Hoyland (sworn), Simon Proud (sworn), Simon Ralph's son (sworn), Eudo de Tybenham (sworn), William Calf (sworn), Thomas le Neve (sworn), who present on their oath that John, servant of Robert Cann, drew blood of Ralph de Aslacton, baker. They say that Beatrix White and Acilia her partner are wont to pull the fleeces of sheep, and they pulled the

cap.

vellera bidentium Johannis Molle capellani et furaverunt quandam supertunicam precii xl denariorum ad domum Henrici Gylur et predicta vellera et supertunicam detulerunt ad domum Galfridi Munne qui sciebat de predicta felonia et ipsas receptavit. Dicunt etiam quod Ricardus Cokard est fur et assuetus est furari aucas et galinas et stetit fur per septennium. Item presentant de Roberto Scot et marito Emme le Hauteyn ut supra. Presentant etiam quod Beatricia filia Roberti Beumund levavit hutesium et secuta fuit usque ad Teoloneum. Presentant etiam quod Henricus de Caumbys est fur et habent ipsum suspectum et quod est contra pacem et quod bene vestitur et nescitur unde et semper noctanter vacabundus est. Presentant etiam [quod] Priorissa de Carowe [1] et Robertus Gerveys de Brakendenne pascunt erbagium in fossatis Norwici et habent ibi porcos et bidentes sub custodia porcariorum et bercariorum. Presentant etiam quod Thomas le Schowthere [2] manens contra pontem de Trox emat bladum ad forbaramentum [2] fori per quod etc. Rogerus de Clakeston similiter. Robertus Gerveys de Brakendele similiter. Galfridus Ringolf similiter. Presentant quod omnes braciatores vendunt contra assissam. Dicunt etiam quod Adam de Barsham traxit sanguinem de Matilde le ledbettere. Idem Adam traxit sanguinem de Willelmo filio Ricardi de Goutorth. Johannes Gylur traxit sanguinem de Galfrido Munne. Dicunt quod omnes piscatores et pulletarii emerunt ante horam etc. Presentant etiam quod Vincentius et Adam de Saham foderunt viam Regiam apud Oldeswinemarket. Nicholaus de Reymerston fecit purpresturam per octodecim pedes in longitudine et per iij digitos in latitudine. Dicunt etiam quod Johannes de Ely lindraper vendit cervisiam ad denarium. Dicunt etiam quod Thomas Gerveys feloper et Walterus Hee habent truncos [2] fullonis ad operandum falso modo veteres pannos. Presentant etiam quod Walterus Hee habet quandam [3] mensuram non sigillatam ita quod ille mensure [3] faciunt

[1] A priory of nuns outside Conesford Gates.
[2] See Glossary.   [3] Sic.

fleeces of John Moll the chaplain's sheep, and they stole a surcoat of the price of 40 d. at the house of Henry Gylur, and the said fleeces and surcoat they took to the house of Geoffrey Munne, who knew of the felony and harboured

arrest   the parties. They say also that Richard Cokard is a thief and is wont to steal geese and fowls, and has been a thief for seven years. Also they present concerning Robert Scot and the husband of Emma le Hauteyn as above. They present also that Beatrice, daughter of Robert Beumund, raised the hue and pursued it up to the Tolhouse. They present also that Henry de Campesse is a thief and they hold him in suspicion and [say] that he is against the peace and clothes himself well and nobody knows what from, and is always roving about by night. They present also [that] the Prioress of Carrow and Robert Gerveys of Brakendenne make feed of the herbage in the city ditches and have pigs and sheep there in charge of swineherds and shepherds. They present also that Thomas the leather-dresser, lodging over against Trowse bridge, buys corn to the forbarring of the market, whereby etc. Roger de Clakeston likewise. Robert Gerveys of Brakendole likewise. Geoffrey Ringolf likewise. They present that all the brewers sell contrary to the assize. They say also that Adam de Barsham drew blood of Matilda the leadbeater. Adam also drew blood of William son of Richard de Gunthorp. John Gylur drew blood of Geoffrey Munne. They say that all the fishermen and poulterers have bought before the hour etc. They present also that Vincent and Adam de Saham have dug the highway at the Oldswinemarket. Nicholas de Reymerston has made a purpresture of eighteen feet in length and three inches in breadth. They say also that John de Ely, linendraper, sells beer at 1 d. They say also that Thomas Gerveys, fripperer, and Walter Hee have fullers' blocks for working up old clothes in a fraudulent manner. They present also that Walter Hee has a measure not sealed so that those

unam galonam. Dicunt etiam quod Rogerus Burgeys fregit hostium Simonis le prude. Dicunt etiam quod Johannes Qwyt, Johannes Hert de Trows senior, Walterus Hunne et Stephanus le carecter et Johannes Croke et Walterus Bely [et] Johannes Strike vendunt carnes infirmas et goggos.[1] Johannes Pekok furniens [2] ad pistrinam Petri de Wyleby traxit sanguinem de Radulpho serviente Ricardi de Alisham. Dicunt etiam quod anacorita Omnium Sanctorum obstupavit Cokeyam [3] ita quod nemo potest ibi transire. Dicunt etiam quod Rogerus de Lakenham vendidit carnes Judaicas scilicet trepha.[4] Dicunt etiam quod Humfridus de Alderford traxit sanguinem de Alexandro Cully cum quodam baculo et Alexander levavit hutesium. Dicunt etiam quod Ranulphus de Mangrene obstruxit viam Regiam per vj pedes in latitudine ex opposito solde sue ita quod carecte non possunt ibidem transire. Rogerus Beumund habet fimarium pessime nocentem. Willelmus de Kesewyk similiter. Martinus le Rede manens cum Ricardo de Aylesham [est] extra decennam. Johannes Keye extra decennam. Rogerus filius Ricardi de Aylesham extra decennam. Henricus de Bekles capellanus levavit hutesium in parochia Sc̄i Martini super Willelmum de Lakenham. Mariona uxor Rogeri de Corston levavit hutesium super Reginaldum de Lakenham in eadem parochia. Gundreda le puddingwyf levavit hutesium super Willelmum le linnite.[5] Ricardus de Hemenhale . . .[6] et rapuit Hausyam Balle. Hamo faber de Trox emit bladum per quod Ballivi etc. Uxor Thome le cordewaner levavit hutesium super Reginaldum de Lakenham. Dicunt de pulletariis et piscatoribus ut supra.

Presentant etiam quod uxor Andree Skeppere manens in domo Willelmi de Buretoft est fur et furata fuit ad domum Willelmi de Lakenham carnificis unam supertunicam pretii xij denariorum. Et assueta est huiusmodi facere.

Presentant etiam quod Robertus Scot assuetus est tran-

[1] Calves. See Glossary.
[2] Doubtful.
[3] See Glossary.
[4] Introduction, Note G. 3.
[5] Reading doubtful.
[6] The middle of this word is defaced. It might be *stupravit*. It reads like *s . . . flavit*.

measures make one gallon. They say also that Roger Burgeys broke open Simon Proud's door. They say also that John White, John Hert the elder, of Trowse, Walter Hunne, and Stephen the carter and John Croke and Walter Bely and John Strike sell unsound meat and gogges. John Peacock, baker at Peter de Wilby's bakehouse, drew blood of Ralph, servant of Richard de Aylsham. They say also that the anchorite of All Saints has stopped up the Cockey so that no one can pass by there. They say also that Roger de Lakenham has sold Jewish meat—to wit, trepha. They say also that Humphrey de Alderford drew blood of Alexander Culley with a stick and Alexander raised the hue. They say also that Ranulph de Mangrene has obstructed the king's highway for six feet in breadth opposite his shed, so that carts cannot pass there. Roger Beumund has an extremely noxious muck-heap. William de Kesewyk likewise. Martin le Rede, lodging with Richard de Aylsham, is out of tithing. John Keye is out of tithing. Richard de Aylsham's son Roger is out of tithing. Henry de Beccles, chaplain, raised the hue in the parish of St. Martin on William de Lakenham. Marion, wife of Roger de Causton, raised the hue on Reginald de Lakenham in the same parish. Gundreda, the pudding-wife, raised the hue on William Linnet. Richard de Hemenhale . . . and raped[1] Hawise Balle. Hamo de Trowse, the smith, buys corn, whereby the Bailiffs etc. Thomas the cordwainer's wife raised the hue on Reginald de Lakenham. They say of the poulterers and fishermen as above.

They present also that Andrew Skepper's wife lodging in the house of William de Burtoft is a thief, and has stolen at the house of William de Lakenham, butcher, a surcoat of the value of 12 d. And she is wont to do the like.

They present also that Robert Scot is wont to climb

[1] This offence, not mentioned elsewhere in these Rolls, would, as a rule, form the subject of an 'appeal' and be carried to a higher court.

scendere muros noctanter et perforare parietes et alias
fellonias facere.

¹ MANECROFT.

Parochia Sc̄i Stephani.

Laurentius de Takelston capitalis plegius pro
mangno contemptu. In mīā. Postea fecit sacramentum.

Stephanus le Turnur (jur), Johannes de Keteringham
(jur), Thomas Sparwe (jur), Johannes Curthose (jur), Radulphus Muddok (jur), Thomas de Elmham (jur), Laurentius de
Tacolston (jur), Alanus Barlisel (jur), Paulus Benedicite
(jur), Hugo de Wymundham (jur), Ricardus de Alysham
(jur), et Willelmus de Attleburgh clericus, presentant super
sacramentum suum quod Rogerus de Lakenham traxit
sanguinem de Ricardo Warinhale et uxor Ricardi Warinhale levavit hutesium de quo non fecerunt sectam set clam
inter eos concordaverunt. Ricardus de Haylesham et
Radulphus Mudok et Matildis Hodys obstupaverunt viam
regiam cum fumariis ita quod aqua non potest ibi currere
nec carectas ² ibi transire sine impedimento. Humfridus
de Alderford traxit sanguinem ut supra. Ricardus Pette
traxit sanguinem de Thoma Carl cum cultello. Humfridus
de Alderford coartavit viam regiam cum truncis ad introitum
pistrini ita quod carecte non possint ibi transire. Johannes
de la Jurye taverner habet apenticiam ad parvam tabernam
suam ad nocumentum ibidem equitantium et itinerantium.
Robertus le Daubere manet cum Hamone de Hidirseto et
mansit in civitate per triennium et non est in decenna.
Rogerus de Markesale levavit hutesium et nescit super
quem. Walterus le Daubere dē Acre est extra decennam.
Johannes de Parys habet fumerum ad portam pistrini sui
valde nocentem omnibus itinerantibus. Presentant quod
omnes braciatrices fregerunt assissam ut supra. Dicunt
etiam quod omnes piscatores et pulletarii carioraverunt ³
forum ut supra. Presentant quod Radulphus de Mangrene
coartavit viam regalem prout presentaverunt in Conisford.

¹ This is the Leet of Mancroft, the subleet of St. Stephen.
² Sic.   ³ MS. *cariaverunt*.

over garden-walls by night and break through house-walls and do other felonies.

MANECROFT.

[St.Stephen] **Parish of St. Stephen.**

Laurence de Tacolston, capital pledge, for great contempt. In mercy. Afterwards he took the oath.

Stephen the turner (sworn), John de Keteringham (sw.), Thomas Sparrow (sw.), John Curthose (sw.), Ralph Muddok (sw.), Thomas de Elmham (sw.), Laurence de Tacolston (sw.), Alan Barlisel (sw.), Paul Benedicite (sw.), Hugh de Wymondham (sw.), Richard de Aylsham (sw.), and William de Attleburgh, clerk, present on their oath that Roger de Lakenham drew blood of Richard Warinhale, and Richard Warinhale's wife raised the hue, whereof they made no suit but secretly agreed among themselves. Richard de Aylsham and Ralph Muddok and Matilda Hodys have blocked the king's highway with muck-heaps so that the water cannot run there, nor carts pass there without hindrance. Humphrey de Alderford drew blood as above. Richard Pette drew blood of Thomas Carl with a knife. Humphrey de Alderford has straitened the king's highway with blocks at the entrance of his bakehouse, so that carts cannot pass there. John of the Jewry, taverner, has a lean-to at his little tavern, to the nuisance of riders and passers there. Robert the dauber lodges with Hamon de Hethersett, and has lodged in the city for three years, and is not in tithing. Roger de Markshall raised the hue and knows not upon whom. Walter de Acre the dauber is out of tithing. John de Parys has a muck-heap at the door of his bakehouse very noisome to all the passers-by. They present that all the alewives have broken the assize as above. They say also that all the fishermen and poulterers have heightened the market as above. They present that Ralph de Mangrene has straitened the king's highway, as they presented in Conisford.

Presentant etiam quod omnes illi de Sproxton vendunt hillas et pudinges, emunt scienter porcos superseminatos et vendunt in foro Norwyci predictas hillas et pundinges, non necessarias corporibus hominum. Dicunt etiam quod Rogerus faber de Nedham assuetus [est] levare hutesium super servos suos noctanter et de die et hoc fecit sepissime post ultimam letam. Dicunt etiam quod Gylbertus de Elingham manens in redditu Ricardi prior vendit et emit mercimonia ad talliam [1] et non est de libertate. Dicunt etiam quod Priorissa de Carehowe subharravit viam Regiam a portis de Swynemarket usque ad portas Sc̄i Egidii et de portis de Swynemarket usque ad risgate. Dicunt etiam quod Walterus Jolyf et uxor eius emunt bladum antequam venit ad forum per quod Ballivi etc. De Johanne Towyt et Stephano le carecter ut supra in Berstrette. Dicunt etiam quod Thomas le Agullier de Stratton et Willelmus de Colton habent Cronys [2] in Nedelerowe et emunt et vendunt mercimonia sua ad talliam et non sunt de libertate et nunquam fecerunt ingressus. Willelmus Storm qui manet et mansit cum Rogero fabro de Nedham per annum et amplius est extra decennam. Walterus Jolyf fecit cursum cuiusdam aque super Willelmum Bele ubi nunquam fuit prius cursus aque et hoc ad nocumentum predicti Willelmi vicini sui. Rogerus Schod habet duos servientes qui ambo vocantur Stephani et non sunt in decenna.

Parochia Sc̄i Petri de Manecroft.

Petrus Drahesverd [3] (jur), Roger de Wymondham (jur), Robertus de Postwyk (jur), Roger de Biltham (jur), Robertus de Swathefeld (+), Johannes Woderowe (jur), Walterus de Pulham (jur), [4] Hernald Pese, Petrus le mustarder (jur), Rolandus de Colneye (jur), Andreas de Biltham (jur), Galfridus de Kyrkeby (jur), Walterus de Edy-

[1] See Glossary.
[2] I do not understand this word, unless it is a clerical error for *Tronys*; the presentment being that these merchants weighed their goods with their own balances instead of using the Trona Domini Regis according to the custom of the city.
[3] Substituted above the line in place of *Willelmus de Brok*, struck out.
[4] Here *Hermann le Gaunter* is inserted and struck out.

They present also that all those Sprowston men sell sausages and puddings, they knowingly buy measly pigs, and they sell the said sausages and puddings, unfit for human bodies, in Norwich market. They say that Roger de Nedham the smith is wont to raise the hue on his servants night and day, and has done it perpetually since the last leet. They say also that Gilbert de Elingham, lodging in Richard Prior's rent, sells and buys goods by tally, and is not of the freedom. They say also that the Prioress of Carrow has ploughed up the king's highway from Swinemarket Gates to St. Giles's Gates, and from Swinemarket Gates as far as risgate.[1] They say that Walter Jolyf and his wife buy corn before it comes to the market, whereby the Bailiffs etc. Concerning John Towyt and Stephen the carter, as above, in Berstrete. They say also that Thomas de Stratton the Needler and William de Colton[2] have crones [?] in the Nedler-row, and buy and sell their goods by tally, and are not of the freedom and have never made their entrance. William Storm, who lodges and has lodged for a year and more with Roger de Nedham the smith, is out of tithing. Walter Jolyf has made a certain watercourse over William Bele's [land], where there never was a watercourse before, and that to the nuisance of his neighbour,[3] the aforesaid William. Roger Shod has two servants who are both called Stephen, and are not in tithing.

[St. Peter de Manecroft] **Parish of St. Peter de Manecroft.**

Peter Drawsword (sworn), Roger de Wymondham (sw.), Robert de Postwick (sw.), Roger de Biltham (sw.), Robert de Swafield (+), John Woderowe (sw.), Walter de Pulham (sw.), Ernald Pese, Peter the mustardman (sw.), Roland de Colneye (sw.), Andrew de Biltham (sw.), Geoffrey de Kirkby (sw.), Walter de Edingthorp (sw.), John de Ashwell

---

[1] Some road outside the city not mentioned elsewhere.
[2] See Introduction, Note A, 3.
[3] Observe the presentment of nuisance to a single neighbour.

thorp (jur), Johannes de Aschewell (jur), Johannes Gamage (jur), Robertus de Knapeton (jur), Adam de Knapeton (jur), Adam de Donston (jur), Henricus de Senges (jur), Radulphus Sussam (jur), Thomas de Bauburgh (jur), Jordan de Rykynghale (jur), Johannes Raven (jur), Ricardus de Plumstede (jur), Rogerus de Ethil, Robertus de Poringlond, Rogerus Beniamyn, Johannes de Aschewelle junior, Robertus de Sc̄o Edmundo, Ricardus de Antyngham, presentant per sacramentum suum quod Ricardus serviens Jacobi de Weston traxit sanguinem de Johanne Gilur. Dicunt etiam quod Adam Cabel et Johannes le combistere emunt wylkes ad cariorandum forum. Dicunt de braciatoribus ut supra. Dicunt etiam quod Jacobus de Weston, Henricus de Costennoble, Sarra le Chapeller, Thomas le Pater, et Adam de Saham vendunt ad denarium. Dicunt etiam quod Willelmus le Blowere traxit sanguinem de quodam serviente suo. Dicunt etiam quod Simon de Belache fecit quoddam [*sic*] stallum contra seldam suam nocentem [*sic*] itinerantibus et illud locat extraneis. Dicunt etiam quod Johannes Janne vendidit carnes putridas et male salsatas Waltero de Edythorp et Ricardo le turnur similiter. Dicunt quod Isak filius Deuelcreys Judeus fecit quendam cursum aque ubi prius non erat cursus. Erlnald Pese vendit lagenam cervisie ad denarium. Dicunt etiam quod Roykyntle Ju traxit sanguinem de Waltero de Swathynge. Robertus de Hecham et Johannes Spik vendunt lagenam cervisie ad denarium.

Dicunt etiam quod Thomas Spik vendit correos male tannatos et assuetus est talia facere. Bartholomeus le blynde habuit duos servientes et uterque eorum traxit sanguinem ab alio. Johannes le Redeprest obstupavit aquam currentem cum quadam cloaca. Dicunt etiam quod Matheus Tuschenys traxit sanguinem de Henrico de Cknapeton capellano. Et quod idem Matheus cum serviente Johannis Beumund et alii quorum nomina sunt in rotulo placitorum ceperunt et asportaverunt colobium Rogeri de Rokhathe et annelacum suum et bursam suam et adhuc seysiti sunt. Dicunt etiam quod Johannes Geggard, Reginaldus de Lakenham, et Willelmus filius Thome Stan-

(sw.), John Gamage (sw.), Robert de Knapton (sw.), Adam de Knapton (sw.), Adam de Dunston (sw.), Henry de Senges (sw.), Ralph Sussam (sw.), Thomas de Bawburgh (sw.), Jordan de Rickinghall (sw.), John Raven (sw.), Richard de Plumstead (sw.), Roger de Hethel, Robert de Poringland, Roger Benjamin, John de Ashwell junior, Robert de St. Edmund, Richard de Antingham, present on their oath that James de Weston's servant Richard drew blood of John Gilur. They say also that Adam Cabel and John the combster buy whelks to heighen the market. They say concerning the brewers as above. They say also that James de Weston, Henry de Costinoble, Sarah the hatter, Thomas le Pater, and Adam de Saham sell at 1 d. They say also that William le Blower drew blood of a servant of his. They say also that Simon de Belaugh has made a stall over against his shed to the nuisance of passers-by, and lets it to strangers. They say also that John Janne sold putrid and ill-salted meat to Walter de Edingthorp and likewise to Richard the turner. They say that Isaac son of Deulecres, the Jew, has made a watercourse where there was not one before. Ernald Pese sells a gallon of beer for 1 d. They say also that Reykynt the Jew drew blood of Walter de Swathing. Robert de Heacham and John Spik sell a gallon of beer for 1 d.

They say also that Thomas Spik sells ill-tanned hides and is wont so to do. Bartholomew the blind had two servants, and each of them drew blood of the other. John the Redepriest has blocked a running water with a drain. They say also that Matthew Tusceynz drew blood of Henry de Knapton, chaplain. And that the same Matthew, with John Beumund's servant, and others whose names are in the roll [1] of pleas took and carried off a cloak of Roger de Rockhagh, and his dagger and his purse, and are still in possession of them. They say also that John Geggard, Reginald de Lakenham, and William, son of Thomas Stanhard,

---

[1] Only one very fragmentary bundle of these Rolls has survived. It is of later date—temp. E. III

hard vendunt baconem superseminatam. Dicunt etiam quod Johannes Geggard emit quandam vaccam mortuam apud Erlham et illam vendidit pro bona et sana carne in Norwico. Dicunt quod omnes pulletarii et piscatores vendunt ante horam et emunt ad cariorandum forum et extra civitatem ut supra. Dicunt etiam quod Adam Cabel vendit wylcos mixtos de bonis et malis et assuetus est talia facere. Dicunt etiam quod ad domum Roberti de Rakheythe est qualibet nocte clamor et hutesium levatum. Dicunt etiam quod Egydius serviens Simonis de Sparham depredasse voluit Johannem de Stoke de denario noctanter in venella juxta tabernam Galfridi le taverner. Dicunt etiam quod Galfridus de Lenn vendidit Ricardo de Knapeton juniori quendam coreum male tannatum et assuetus est talia facere et Thomas Spik vendidit eidem similiter. Robertus Wenge vendidit Rogero de Wytton correum male tannatum et assuetus est talia facere. Item Peyte serviens Cassandri de Hecham vendit coreos male tannatos et assuetus est talia facere communiter. Gregorius le letherkervere traxit sanguinem de serviente suo et ipse serviens de ipso. Dicunt etiam quod Radulphus Bullok vendit carnes porcarias superseminatas. Dicunt etiam quod Henricus le Barbur habet quendam Robertum servientem suum extra decennam. Johannes le Hauberger est extra decennam. Magister Radulphus de Colton manens in civitate non est in decenna. Dicunt etiam quod filia Johannis de Scolthorp furabat noctanter ad domum Hugonis de Castre quendam bukettum et cordam et posuit ea in Judeismo et Radulphus Brid et Lucas de Brunne obviaverunt ei itinerando versus Judeismum et ceperunt cordam et Bukettum de manibus eius et detinuerunt penes se quousque Hugo de Castre dedit quinque denarios et dixerunt quod inveniebant ea in Judeismo invadiata in Judeismo. Dicunt etiam quod Robertus Pikot est vacabundus noctanter et habent ipsum suspectum et quod est contra pacem. Dicunt etiam quod Richerus de Antingham levavit hutesium super Galfridum de Bungeye. Dicunt etiam quod Johannes de Burgh vendit lagenam cervisie ad denarium. Estrelda de Loppam similiter.

sell measly bacon. They say also that John Geggard bought a dead cow at Earlham, and sold it for good sound meat in Norwich. They say that all the poulterers and fishermen sell before the hour and buy to heighen the market and outside the city as above. They say also that Adam Cabel sells whelks with good and bad mixed together, and is wont so to do. They say also that at the house of Robert de Rackheath hue and cry is raised every night. They say also that Giles, servant of Simon de Sparham, attempted to rob John de Stoke of 1 d. by night in the lane near the tavern of Geoffrey the taverner. They say also that Geoffrey de Lenn sold an ill-tanned hide to Richard de Knapton junior, and is wont so to do, and Thomas Spik sold him one likewise. Robert Wenge sold to Roger de Witton an ill-tanned hide, and is wont so to do. Also Peyte, servant of Cassander de Heacham, sells ill-tanned hides, and is wont so to do commonly. Gregory, the leather-cutter, drew blood of his servant, and his servant drew blood of him. They say also that Ralph Bullock sells measly pork. They say also that Henry the barber has a servant of his, Robert, out of tithing. John the innkeeper is out of tithing. Master Ralph de Colton, lodging in the city, is not in tithing. They say also that John de Sculthorpe's daughter stole by night at Hugh de Caister's house a bucket and cord, and [? was going to] put them in the Jewry,[1] and Ralph Bird and Luke de Brune met her going towards the Jewry and seized the cord and bucket out of her hands and kept them in their possession until Hugh de Caister gave them five pence, and they said they found them in the Jewry, pawned there. They say also that Robert Pikot is a night-rover, and they hold him in suspicion and to be contrary to the peace. They say also that Richer de Antingham raised the hue on Geoffrey de Bungay. They say also that John de Burgh sells a gallon of beer for 1 d. Estrilda de Lopham likewise.

[1] The Jewry was at the southern end of the east side of the Market.

Dicunt etiam quod Willelmus le espenser du Chastele[1] cepit Willelmum de Brok et proiecit eum in profundo de gayole. Robertus de . . . fecit stillicidum in venella iuxta domum suam et apposuit fumarium super illud stillicidium ita quod carecte non possunt transire. Dicunt etiam de pulletariis et piscatoribus ut supra.

Omnes jurati pro concelamento eo quod non presentaverunt quod Jacobus de Weston fuit extra decennam . . .[2]

[WYMER.] **Parochia Sc̄i Egidii,[3] Sc̄i Swithuni, Sc̄e Margarete, et Sc̄i Benedicti.**

Walterus de Tasburg tannator pro contemptu, in mīā ij s.

Robertus de Tweyt (jur) Henricus filius Willelmi de Eston (jur), Galfridus de Derham (jur), Johannes de Disce (jur), Renerus de Wreningham (jur), Stephanus de Brakne (jur), Thomas fflaxman (jur), Johannes Ive (jur), Walterus de Tasburgh (jur), Johannes Hem (jur), Nicholaus de Kyningham (jur), Radulphus de Ludham (jur), presentant per sacramentum suum quod Ricardus le Skynnere fecit ampsoken Radulpho Gyn et traxit cultellum suum unde uxor Radulphi levavit hutesium et non secuta fuit et Ricardus le Skynnere est extra decennam et Radulphus Gyn hospitavit eam.[4] Presentant etiam quod Johannes Beumund subfodit fossatos. Dicunt quod molendinarius[5] Prioris de Bukenham subfodit fossatos et fecit purpresturam submuralem.[6] Dicunt de braciatoribus ut supra. Dicunt de pulletariis et piscatoribus ut supra. Dicunt quod Jacobus Nade vendit ad denarium. Dicunt quod Emma de Asschewelle emit de serviente persone de Pulham vj cumbas bladi et quia non habuit mensuram cumulatam detinuit ei unum obolum. Dicunt etiam quod uxor Ricardi Hidys

---

[1] ?=Dispensarius Castelli. Steward or Sewer of the Castle.
[2] The last few entries are at the foot of a membrane which has been much rubbed. The last entry is illegible.
[3] 'Sc̄i Egidii' is written in larger letters as the principal parish in the district. 'Leta de Wymer et Westwyk' has been omitted here.
[4] The Latin word is written 'eam,' in full. Surely Ralph harboured Richard.
[5] The Prior's Mill was on Chapel Field, a wind (not a water) mill. 'Streets and Lanes,' p. 19.
[6] MS. *submur*.

They say also that William, the Steward of the Castle, seized William de Brok and cast him into the dungeon of the gaol. Robert de . . . has made a gutter in the lane near his house and· placed a muck-heap on the gutter, so that carts cannot pass by. They say concerning the poulterers and fishermen as above.

All the jurors [are in mercy] for concealment, for that they have not presented that James de Weston was out of tithing . . .

[St. Giles] [WYMER.] **Parishes of St. Giles, St. Swithun, St. Margaret, and St. Benedict.**

Walter de Tasburgh, tanner, for contempt, in mercy, 2 s.

Robert de Thwaite (sworn), Henry, son of William de Easton (sw.), Geoffrey de Dereham (sw.), John de Diss (sw.), Reginald de Wreningham (sw.), Stephen de Bracon (sw.), Thomas Flaxman (sw.), John Ive (sw.), Walter de Tasburgh (sw.), John Hem (sw.), Nicholas de Kenningham (sw.), Ralph de Ludham (sw.), present on their oath that Richard the Skinner made hamsoken on Ralph Gyn and drew his knife, whereof Ralph's wife raised the hue and pursued it not, and Richard the Skinner is out of tithing and Ralph Gyn harboured her. They present also that John Beumund undermines the banks of the city ditch. They say that the miller of the Prior of Buckenham undermines the banks and has made a purpresture under the walls. They say concerning the brewers as above. They say concerning the poulterers and fishermen as above. They say that James Nade sells at 1 d. They say that Emma de Ashwell bought of the servant of the Parson of Pulham six coombs of corn, and because she did not get heaped-up measure she kept back a halfpenny from him. They say also that the wife of Richard Hides, who lodges

manentis (in vico) de ffibriggate emit bladum de quodam homine de Bernam et quia non habuit mensuram cumulatam detinuit ei unum quadrantem. Dicunt etiam quod Emma de Aschewelle et uxor Martini Qwytside refutant communiter mensuras bladi et brasei rasas. De pistoribus quod non observant assissam. Dicunt etiam quod Milicentia de Melton uxor Henrici le carpenter Sucling emit occulte bladum antequam venit ad forum per quod etc. et assueta est talia facere. Dicunt quod Alanus de Ringgelonde habet truncos fullonis et dubbat[1] pannos. Dicunt etiam quod Oliva uxor Henrici Costinoble assueta est emere blada ita quod Dominus Rex amittat bladum.[2] Dicunt quod Willelmus ffchis et uxor eius capiunt[3] [bladum] occulte in foro et illud latitant et deducunt extra forum in schoppis suis per quod dominus Rex amittit etc. Dicunt quod Willelmus de Colney scowthere obstupavit quoddam fossatum commune in via Domini Regis. Omnes capitales plegii in mīā pro concelamento quia Johannes Swinesheved levavit hutesium super Milicentiam Attegates et non presentaverunt. Postea presentant quod Johannes Swynesheved levavit hutesium super Milicentiam Attegates et Johannem le Graunt et Ricardum servientem Milicentie Attegates. Dicunt etiam quod Margareta Hoyn emebat in foro Norwyci unum bussellum frumenti et portavit ad domum suam occulte per [quod] Dominus Rex amisit theolonium. Dicunt etiam quod Thomas de Berth levavit quandam barreram in via Norwici nocentem itinerantibus.

Parochia Sēi Laurentii et Sēi Gregorii.

Herveus Milkegos (jur), Ranulphus le Blekstere (jur), Ricardus le Dormur (jur), Hugo Bene (jur), Galfridus de Jelverton (jur), Willelmus de Bukenham (jur), Johannes de Erlham (jur), Galfridus de Smaleberthe (jur), Martinus de Tudenham (jur), Willelmus Crisp de Ameringhale (jur), Ricardus de Ling Evesinger (jur), Ricardus Coleman (jur),

---

[1] See Introd. Note G. 2.
[2] Sic. Corr. *theolonium*.
[3] Substituted for *emunt* crossed out.

[in the street] of Fibriggate, bought corn of a man of Burnham, and because she did not get heaped-up measure she kept back from him one farthing. They say also that Emma de Ashwell and Martin Whiteside's wife commonly decline bare measures of corn and malt. Concerning the bakers [they say] that they observe not the assize. They say also that Milicent de Melton, wife of Henry Suckling the carpenter, secretly bought corn before it came to the market, whereby etc., and that she is wont so to do. They say that Alan de Ringland has fuller's blocks and dubs clothes. They say also that Oliva, wife of Henry Costinoble, is wont to buy corn in such wise that the lord king loses his custom. They say that William Fish and his wife secretly take [? corn] in the market and hide it and carry it down out of the market into their shops, whereby the lord king loses etc. They say that William de Colney, leather-dresser, has blocked a public ditch in the lord king's highway. All the capital pledges are in mercy for concealment, because John Swineshead raised the hue on Melicent Attegates and they have not presented it. Afterwards they present that John Swineshead raised the hue on Melicent Attegates and John le Graunt and Richard the servant of Melicent Attegates. They say also that Margaret Hoyn bought a bushel of wheat in Norwich market and secretly carried it to her house, whereby the lord king has lost his toll. They say also that Thomas de Burgh has set up a bar in the highway of the city, to the nuisance of the passers.

[St. Gregory] **Parishes of St. Laurence and St. Gregory.**

Hervey Milkgoose (sworn), Ranulph the Bleacher (sw.), Richard le Dormur (sw.), Hugh Bene (sw.), Geoffrey de Yelverton (sw.), William de Buckenham (sw.), John de Earlham (sw.), Geoffrey de Smalburgh (sw.), Martin de Tudenham (sw.), William Crisp of Arminghall (sw.), Richard de Ling, evesinger, (sw.), Richard Coleman (sw.),

presentant super sacramentum suum quod braciatores fregerunt assissam ut supra. Dicunt quod Henricus le

cap. Dauber manens iuxta domum Willelmi Popy est suspectus contra pacem eo quod vacabundus de nocte et circa horam mediam noctis sepissime [? redit¹] domum cum octo vel decem sociis ingnotis. Dicunt quod Angnes Gossibe manens in Pottergate emit per majorem et vendit per minorem.

cap. Dicunt etiam quod Johannes Bogris obviavit Willelmo servienti Henrici de Weston itineranti versus molendinum de Lakenham² et cum quodam gladio extracto ipsum insultavit et verberavit et petit ab eo si habuit aliquod argentum propter quod dicunt quod habent ipsum suspectum et quod male creditur. Dicunt quod Nicholaus de Merkesale levavit hutesium super Nicholaum de Merkesale.³ Dicunt etiam quod Walterus de Aswardeby super Johannem clericum levavit hutesium. Dicunt etiam quod Willelmus le schesemongere levavit hutesium super uxorem suam. Dicunt etiam quod uxor Johannis de Tweyt senioris levavit hutesium et uxor Johannis junioris de eadem videlicet utraque super aliam. Dicunt quod Gocelin de flordon et Thomas Ollebeche emunt bladum ad molendinum de Herford² per quod Dominus Rex etc. Dicunt etiam quod Adam ffrend habet quendam servientem nomine Adam qui stetit secum per biennium. Dicunt quod Reginaldus le barbur levavit hutesium iniuste set nesciunt super quem. Dicunt de pulletariis regratariis caseorum et piscatoribus ut supra. Dicunt quod Hugo Bateman est quidam curlevasche. Dicunt de Thoma de Berth ut supra. Dicunt etiam quod omnes dubbatores de corco vaccino faciunt falsitatem in opere suo. Dicunt etiam quod tannatores habent quandam gildam inter se quod si aliquis confratrum forisfecerit alii conquereretur Aldermano per quod Ballivi etc. Dicunt quod omnes cocii³ et pastiliarii calefaciunt pastilios et carnes per biduum et per triduum. Dicunt quod Stephanus le Turnur habet quendam trunkum apud Qwete-

¹ A word is omitted here in MS.
² Lakenham Mill and Hertford Mill were on the Yare, to the south of Norwich. The latter is thought to be a corruption of Yarford.
³ Sic.

LEET ROLL OF 128¾. 13

arrest present on their oath that the brewers have broken the assize as above. They say that Henry the dauber, who lodges near the house of William Popy, is suspected and is contrary to the peace, for that he roves about by night, and very often comes home about midnight with eight or ten unknown companions. They say that Agnes Gossip, lodging in Pottergate, buys by the greater and sells by the
arrest less. They say also that John Bogris met William, the servant of Henry de Weston, going towards Lakenham Mill and drew a sword and assaulted and beat him, and demanded of him whether he had any money, wherefore they say that they hold him in suspicion, and that he is ill thought of. They say that Nicholas de Markshall raised the hue on Nicholas de Markshall. They say also that Walter de Aswardby raised the hue upon John the clerk. They say also that William the cheesemonger raised the hue on his wife. They say also that the wife of John de Thwaite the elder and the wife of John de Thwaite the younger both raised the hue, to wit, the one upon the other. They say that Goscelin de Flordon and Thomas Oldbeech buy corn at Hartford Mill, whereby the lord king etc. They say also that Adam Friend has a servant, by name Adam, who has been with him for two years. They say that Reginald the barber raised the hue wrongfully, but they know not on whom. They say concerning the poulterers, regraters of cheese, and fishermen as above. They say that Hugh Bateman is a curlevasche.[1] They say concerning Thomas de Burgh as above. They say also that all the dubbers of cowhide do fraudulently in their work. They say also that the tanners have a gild[2] amongst themselves, to the end that if one of the brethren forfeits to another he should make plaint to the Alderman,[3] whereby the Bailiffs etc. They say that all the cooks and pasty-makers warm up pasties and meat on the second and third day. They say that Stephen the Turner

[1] See Introd. Note G. 1.
[2] Introduction, Note B.
[3] Alderman here means the chief officer of the gild. There were no city aldermen till 1415.

markette valde nocentem equitantibus et itinerantibus vie Domini Regis. Dicunt etiam quod Johannes le Blekestere et Ranulphus le Pessoner equitaverunt usque Brundale[1] et ad obviandum cuidam navi cariate de ostriis et illa emerunt per quod forum Norwicy carioratur. Dicunt etiam quod uxor Jacoby Nade per totum annum vendit ad denarium. Dicunt etiam quod Margareta Isak emit wilkos et alia mercimonia per quod forum carioratur. Dicunt quod Robertus persona habet quandam mensuram cervisie falsam et non sigillatam. Dicunt etiam quod Gocelin le Graunt non est in decenna. Omnes juratores in mīa eo quod concelaverunt hutesium quod Henricus de Ravele levavit.

Parochia Sc̄i Johannis de Madelmarket, Sc̄ē Crucis, Sc̄i Andree, Sc̄i Michaelis de Motstowe, et Sc̄i Petri.

Galfridus[2] ffaderman, Willelmus de Ludham (jur), Semanus de Blithburth (jur), Robert le persone (jur), Thomas March (+ in mīa[3]) (quia non venit[4]), Robertus de Holveston (jur), Johannes de Schotesham (jur), Rogerus de fframingham (jur), Johannes de Pulham (jur), Nicholaus Attebothe (jur), Thomas de Saxlingham (jur), Reginaldus le Grey (jur), Willelmus de Bedingham (jur), Johannes de Rolesby (jur), Thomas de ffeltewelle.

Johannes de Coutesale stetit in civitate per biennium et non fuit in decenna usque in hunc diem. Presentant etiam quod Alexander de Sparham taylur qui stetit in civitate per annum et amplius non fuit in decenna. Dicunt quod Ricardus le Taylur levavit hutesium super Robertum de Rakehetheythe. Dicunt etiam quod Laurentius Cokysschanke levavit hutesium[5]. . . . Dicunt etiam quod Galfridus de Alverthate traxit sanguinem de Waltero filio Iseude. Dicunt quod Walterus le Monner levavit hutesium. Dicunt etiam quod quedam mulier manens in domo

---

[1] About eight miles down the river on the way to Yarmouth.
[2] Struck out.
[3] Inserted above.
[4] Added at end of line.
[5] A word fairly written but unintelligible follows here. It reads Tp'rut or Tp'riū.

has a block in the Wheatmarket, to the great nuisance of the riders and passers on the lord king's highway. They say also that John the Bleacher and Ranulph the Fishmonger rode out to Brundall to meet a vessel laden with oysters and bought them, whereby the Norwich market is heighened. They say also that James Nade's wife for a whole year has been selling at 1 d. They say also that Margaret Isaac buys whelks and other goods whereby the market is heighened. They say that Robert the parson has a measure of ale false and not sealed. They say also that Goscelin le Graunt is not in tithing. All the jurors are in mercy for that they have concealed the hue which Henry de Raveley raised.

[St. Andrew] **Parishes of St. John de Maddermarket, St. Cross, St. Andrew, St. Michael de Motstowe, and St. Peter.**

Geoffrey Fatherman, William de Ludham (sworn), Seman de Blythburgh (sw.), Robert the parson (sw.), Thomas March (+ in mercy because he did not come), Robert de Holveston (sw.), John de Shotesham (sw.), Roger de Framingham (sw.), John de Pulham (sw.), Nicholas Attebooth (sw.), Thomas de Saxlingham (sw.), Reginald the Grey (sw.), William de Bedingham (sw.), John de Rollesby (sw.), Thomas de Feltwell.

John de Coltishall has been in the city for two years, and has not been in tithing to this day. They present also that Alexander de Sparham, tailor, who has been in the city for a year and more, has not been in tithing. They say that Richard the tailor raised the hue upon Robert de Rackheath. They say also that Laurence Cookshank raised the hue . . . They say also that Geoffrey de Alverthwaite drew blood of Isold's son Walter. They say that Walter the Minter raised the hue. They say also that a

Johannis de Lopham est receptatrix latronum et maximam suspicionem habent de ipsa. Dicunt etiam quod Thomas de Happesburch pistor traxit sanguinem de Ricardo le Taylur et Ricardus levavit hutesium et non secutus est. Dicunt etiam quod Galfridus le forestre fecit forstallum servientibus Ballivorum. De braciatoribus ut supra. Dicunt quod Adam de Saham et Odo de la Bothe vendunt lagenam cervisie ad denarium. De cocis regratariis piscatoribus et pulletariis de eisdem ut supra. Dicunt etiam quod Isabella manens iuxta Cokeye in redditu Galfridi Costinoble receptat quandam mulierem latronam ut credunt et habent ipsam suspectam ut pro receptario. Dicunt quod Rogerus de Penteneye habet fenestras nocentes quas emit de Margareta sorore Johannis le Mercer [1] Decani Norwyci. Dicunt quod Alanus de Costeseye manens in Cosclanic assuetus est ducere mercandizas extraneorum extra civitatem et advocat eas pro suis bonis ita quod Dominus Rex amittat custumam.

Omnes juratores in mīa pro concelamento eo quod concelaverunt quod Willelmus de Risinge fecit purpresturam per quendam murum lapideum. Similiter quod predictus Willelmus non est in decenna et quod Robertus nepos prioris non est in decenna, de eodem Roberto quia non est in assissam.[2] Dicunt quod Benedictus de Brakne fecit purpresturam Domino Regi per quandam parietem. Dicunt etiam quod Willelmus Sparwe non est in assissa. Galfridus qui desponsavit filiam Alexandri de Sarteryn non est in decenna. Dicunt etiam quod Johannes de Horsseford manens super feodum [3] castri traxit sanguinem de Roberto Tripet. Robertus de Lodne in mīa quia non est in assissa.

---

[1] See Introduction, Note E.
[2] This ordinarily is equivalent to 'in decenna.' I cannot say what distinction is here intended between the two.
[3] The exempt district to the south and east of the Castle.

woman lodging in John de Lopham's house is a harbourer of thieves, and they have very great suspicion of her. They say also that Thomas de Happisburgh the baker drew blood of Richard the tailor, and Richard raised the hue and did not pursue it. They say also that Geoffrey the forester made forestalment on the serjeants of the Bailiffs. Concerning the brewers, as above. They say also that Adam de Saham and Odo de la Bothe sell a gallon of beer at 1 d. Concerning the cooks, regraters, fishermen, and poulterers, as above. They say also that Isabella, who lodges by the Cockey in the rent of Geoffrey Costinoble, harbours a certain woman, a thief as they believe, and they hold her in suspicion as a harbourer of thieves. They say that Roger de Pentney has some windows which are a nuisance, and he bought them from Margaret, sister of John le Mercer, Dean of Norwich. They say that Alan de Costessey, lodging in Coslany, is wont to get the merchandise of strangers outside the city, and avows them for his own goods, whereby the lord king loses his custom.

All the jurors are in mercy for concealment for that they concealed that William de Rising has made a purpresture by a stone wall; likewise that the said William is not in tithing, and that Robert, the Prior's nephew, is not in tithing. Concerning the same Robert [they say] that he is not in assize. They say that Benedict de Bracon has made a purpresture on the lord king by a house-wall. They say also that William Sparrow is not in assize. Geoffrey, who married the daughter of Alexander de Sarterin, is not in tithing. They say also that John de Horsford, lodging in the Castle Fee, drew blood of Robert Tripet. Robert de Loddon is in mercy because he is not in assize.

Parochia Sc̄ōrum Simonis et Jude, Sc̄ī Georgii¹ ante portas Sc̄ē Trinitatis, Sc̄ī Martini ante portas Episcopi.

Willelmus Pirmund (jur), Adam Tiffanye (jur), Henricus Fourloves (jur), Henricus Cubyt (jur), Willelmus Galiz (jur), Ricardus de Wytton (jur), Johannes Bullok (jur), Robertus le Mey (jur), Henricus Buk (jur), Willelmus de Norton (jur), Radulphus de Stiberd (jur), Johannes Chilman (jur), presentant super sacramentum suum quod.² Thomas ffulflod quia non est in decenna et stetit per triennium et stat in civitate. Johannes filius Gerardi similiter. Dicunt quod Thomas serviens quondam Willelmi de Intewodde est assuetus recettare bona furata apud Gernemutham et ea adducere apud Norwicum ad vendendum et aliquando dicit quod ea bona sunt penne. Dicunt etiam quod Robertus Litecope levavit hutesium et non secutus fuit illud. Dicunt etiam quod Johannes Godesman levavit hutesium super filium suum in lege. Dicunt etiam quod persona de Jakesham obstupavit quandam venellam prope domum Galfridi le Mercer. Dicunt etiam de braciatoribus ut supra et de pistoribus quod non servant assissam, exceptis Thoma de Hiningham, Godefrido de Weston, Alano Bateman, Simone de Ling, Adam ffrend, Galfridus³ de Blofield et Johannes³ filius capellani. Dicunt etiam quod Clemens Herlewyne habet quandam porkariam extra metas domus sue nocentem vie Domini Regis. Dicunt etiam quod Petrus Pirmund vendit et emit de catallis Nicholay le Monner et dat sibi medietatem lucri. Dicunt etiam quod omnes cocii² calefaciunt carnes per biduum seu triduum. Dicunt quod Johannes Janne emit de Alano de Catton octo bidentes submersos et eos vendidit pro bonis carnibus. Dicunt de eodem Johanne quod vendit per servientes suos bacones superseminatos. Dicunt etiam quod Robertus le ffuler multa expendit et non habet unde et est vacabundus de nocte et male creditur de ipso de eo quod furari debuit bona Johan-

¹ Written in large letters. ² Sic. ³ Sic—in nominative.

[St. George] **Parishes of St. Simon and St. Jude, St. George before the Gates of the Holy Trinity,[1] St. Martin before the Gates of the Bishop.**

William Pirmund (sworn), Adam Tiffany (sw.), Henry Fourloves (sw.), Henry Cubit (sw.), William Galiz (sw.), Richard de Witton (sw.), John Bullock (sw.), Robert le Mey (sw.), Henry Buck (sw.), William de Norton (sw.), Ralph de Stibbard (sw.), John Chilman (sw.), present on their oath that Thomas Fulford is not in tithing and has been in the city for three years and is still in it. John, son of Gerard, likewise. They say that Thomas, sometime servant of William de Intwood, is wont to receive goods stolen at Yarmouth and to bring them into Norwich to sell, and sometimes he says that the goods are feathers. They say also that Robert Littlecope raised the hue and did not pursue it. They say also that John Godesman raised the hue on his son-in-law. They say also that the parson of Yaxham has blocked a certain lane by the house of Geoffrey the mercer. They say also concerning the brewers as above, and concerning the bakers that they do not observe the assize, except Thomas de Honingham, Geoffrey de Weston, Alan Bateman, Simon de Ling, Adam Friend, Geoffrey de Blofield, and John the son of the chaplain. They say also that Clement Herlwin has a pigsty outside the bounds of his house to the nuisance of the lord king's highway. They say also that Peter Pirmund sells and buys of the chattels of Nicholas the Minter and shares half the profits with him. They say also that all the cooks warm up meat on the second or third day. They say also that John Janne bought from Alan de Catton eight drowned sheep and sold them for good meat. They say of the same John that he sells measly pigs through his servants. They say also that Robert the fowler spends much and has nothing to spend from and roves about by night, and he is ill thought of for that it must have been he that stole John de Ing-

[1] The Cathedral.

nis de Ingham ad tabernam suam in Cookrowe¹. Dicunt etiam de Benedicto Berd [quod] traxit sanguinem de Adam fratre suo. Katerina Gele emit bladum per quod etc. Dicunt etiam quod Johannes et Thomas Walres non sunt in decenna. Dicunt quod Ricardus qui desponsavit filiam Ranulphi le pessoner non est in decenna. Dicunt quod Galfridus le skeppere receptat duos homines extra decennam. Dicunt quod Alicia Bele levavit sepissime hutesium et non secuta fuit. Dicunt etiam quod Alexander nepos Alexandri Wyndel emit et vendit per quod Ballivi amittunt theollonium. Dicunt quod Rogerus le Caly, Gerard le especer, Johannes et Willelmus filii eiusdem Gerardi tenent forum ad ² portam Scē Trinitatis per quod forum commune deterioratur. Omnes juratores in miā eo quod non presentaverunt quod Johannes Ringerose implacitavit Margaretam felipps in Curia Christianitatis de placitis que non tangunt matrimonium neque testamenta.

LETA ULTRA AQUAM. De parochiis Scī Michaelis de Coselanye, Scī Georgii, Scē Marie, et Scī Martini.

Philippus fraunceys (jur), Adam Cabel (jur), Ranulphus de Gonthorp (jur), Robertus Hasard (jur), Ricardus filius Hugonis de Melton (Hic³ deficit capitalis plegius Johannes faber, ponitur iste), Willelmus de Wymundham (jur), Willelmus Isoud (jur), Henricus de Hoveton (jur), Bartholomeus de Tassburth (jur), Thomas Thurbern junior (jur), Ricardus de Runham (jur), Simon de Hyndringham (jur), Ricardus de Lek (jur), Johannes de Bukenham (jur), Galfridus de Rokelund capitalis plegius quia non venit et ponitur loco suo Thomas de Melton³ (jur), Ricardus Beumund (jur), Willelmus de Attleburth (jur), Hugo de Bradefeld (jur), presentant per sacramentum suum quod omnes dubbatores qui dubbant correos vaccinos faciunt falsitatem in opere. Dicunt etiam quod Ranulphus Saluz traxit noctanter san-

¹ The street from Tombland to Fye Bridge.
² The Prior's claim to hold a market on Tombland on Sundays and holydays was a constant subject of contention between him and the citizens.
³ In the case of two Capital Pledges in this list, it is not easy to decide who served. Johannes faber,

LEET ROLL OF 128¾.   17

ham's goods at his tavern in the Cookrowe. They say also concerning Benedict Bird [that he] drew blood of his brother Adam. Katerine Gele bought corn, whereby etc. They say also that John and Thomas Walres are not in tithing. They say also that Richard, who married the daughter of Ranulph the fishmonger, is not in tithing. They say that Geoffrey the basketmaker harbours two men who are out of tithing. They say that Alice Bele has perpetually raised the hue and not pursued it. They say also that Alexander, nephew of Alexander Wyndel, buys and sells, whereby the Bailiffs lose their toll. They say that Roger le Caly, Gerard the spicer [and] John and William, Gerard's sons, hold a market at the gate of the Holy Trinity, whereby the common market is injured. All the jurors are in mercy for that they did not present that John Ringrose impleaded Margaret Philips in the Court Christian of pleas which touch not matrimony nor testaments.

[St.Michael] LEET OVER-THE-WATER. **Of the parishes of St. Michael de Coslany, St. George, St. Mary, and St. Martin.**

Philip Francis (sworn), Adam Cabel (sw.), Ranulph de Gunthorpe (sw.), Robert Hasard (sw.), Richard, son of Hugh de Melton (a capital pledge, John the smith, is here wanting: this one is appointed), William de Wymondham (sw.), William Isold (sw.), Henry de Hoveton (sw.), Bartholomew de Tasburgh (sw.), Thomas Thurbern the younger (sw.), Richard de Runham (sw.), Simon de Hindringham (sw.), Richard de Leek (sw.), John de Buckenham (sw.), Geoffrey de Rockland, capital pledge, did not come, and Thomas de Melton (sw.), is put in his place, Richard Beumund (sw.), William de Attleborough (sw.), Hugh de Bradfield (sw.), present on their oath that all the dubbers who dub cowhides make fraud in their work. They say also that Ranulph Saluz drew blood by night of Roger

the proper Capital Pledge, was absent, and Richard, son of Hugh de Melton, was substituted for him (*ponitur iste* being inserted above). Yet he is not marked as sworn. Just below, Galfridus de Rokelund is absent and Thomas de Melton, who is put in his place, is marked as sworn. Yet his name is struck out and Geoffrey's left.

guinem de Rogero Ruchballok quando venit circa horam mediam noctis cum blado. Dicunt quod omnes braciatores ffregerunt assissam ut supra. Dicunt etiam de piscatoribus regratariis et pulletariis ut supra. Dicunt etiam quod Rogerus Blackberd fecit Ampsok ad domum Alicie de Worstede. Galfridus frater Ricardi de Coslanye quia non est in decenna in mīa et stetit per triennium in civitate, postea [1] inventus est in decenna. De Simone de Melton pro maximo contemptu facto Ballivis quia noluit prestare sacramentum cum electus fuit subconstabularius per omnes juratores.

Sc̄i Augustini	Sc̄i Olavi	
	Sc̄i Bothulphi	Sc̄i Jacobi
Parochie	Sc̄i Clementis	Sc̄i Edmundi regis
	Sc̄ē Marie Combuste	Sc̄ē Margarete
	Omnium Sanctorum	Sc̄i Salvatoris a [2]

Rogerus de Hunworthe (jur), Robertus filius Gervasii (jur), Robertus de Donnewyco (jur), Johannes Knicht loksmicht (jur), Johannes de Brandon (jur), Henricus le Stotrere (jur), Henricus filius capellani (jur), Humfredus le Monjoye (jur), Reginaldus de Catton (jur), Adam ffegge (jur), Ricardus de Stalham (jur), Reynerus de Schuldham (jur), Warinus le Skynnere (jur), Rogerus Abbot (jur), Robertus le Mitenmaker (jur), presentant per sacramentum suum quod Galfridus de Wyleby coartavit viam Regiam cum trunko contra domum suam in fibriggate ita quod carecte impediuntur. Dicunt de braciatoribus ut supra. Dicunt etiam de Ranulpho Saluz ut supra quod traxit sanguinem. Dicunt etiam quod serviens Mabilie uxoris Henrici le Scriven ascendebat in quodam stillicidio Galfridi de Wyleby et cepit et abduxit [3] plumbum ibi positum pretii unius denarii. [4] Dicunt etiam de puletariis piscatoribus et regratariis ut supra. Dicunt etiam

---

[1] This insertion must have been put in after the presentments were made, though the writing is the same. This Roll may have been copied from separate Rolls presented from the subleets.

[2] A line with a at one end and b at the other intimates that this parish should have come after St. Mary Combust.

[3] Substituted for *furata fuit*, crossed out.

[4] The price is added above.

Ruchballok when he came with corn about midnight. They say that all the brewers have broken the assize as above. They say also concerning the fishmongers, regraters, and poulterers as above. They say also that Roger Blackbird made hamsoken at the house of Alice de Worstead. Geoffrey, brother of Richard de Coslany, is in mercy because he is not in tithing and has been in the city for three years; afterwards he was found to be in a tithing. Concerning Simon de Melton, [he is in mercy] for grievous contempt done to the Bailiffs because he declined to take the oath when he was elected sub-constable by all the jurors.

[St. Clement]

St. Augustine.	St. Olave.	St. James.
	St. Botolph.	St. Edmund the King.
Parishes of	St. Clement.	St. Margaret.
	St. Mary Combust.	
	St. Saviour.	
	All Saints.	

Roger de Hunworth (sworn), Robert, son of Gervase (sw.), Robert de Dunwich (sw.), John Knight the locksmith (sw.), John de Brandon (sw.), Henry the Stutterer (sw.), Henry, son of the chaplain (sw.), Humphry le Munjoy (sw.), Reginald de Catton (sw.), Adam Fegge (sw.), Richard de Stallham (sw.), Reyner de Shouldham (sw.), Warin the skinner (sw.), Roger Abbott (sw.), Robert the mitten-maker (sw.), present on their oath that Geoffrey de Wilby has straitened the king's highway with a block over against his house in Fibriggate, whereby carts are hindered. They say concerning the brewers as above. They say also concerning Ranulph Saluz as above, that he drew blood. They say also that the servant of Mabel, wife of Henry the scrivener climbed up a gutter of Geoffrey de Wilby and took and carried off lead placed there, of the value of 1 d. They say concerning the poulterers, fishmongers, and regraters as above. They say also that Hervey de Ware, who lodges in

quod Herveus de Ware manens in selda Anicii de Colneye emit et vendit mercandisas suas ad talliam et non est de libertate. Dicunt quod Robertus le ffulere congnoscit latrones et cissores bursarum et recipit de eis munera ne caperentur. Dicunt etiam quod Henricus de Dyvelin traxit sanguinem de Roberto capellano fratre suo. Dicunt etiam quod Henricus de Cantebrigge qui mansit in civitate per longum tempus non est in assissa. Dicunt etiam quod Nicholaus de Aylemerton invenit duos denarios[1] de auro et Johannes Chyrry emit eos pro tribus quadrantibus. Dicunt etiam quod Ranulphus Saluz emit bladum et tradit uxori sue ad faciendum braseum per quod Rex amittit etc. Dicunt etiam quod Willelmus de Wroxham, Johannes Gamen, Ricardus Grund capellanus assueti sunt facere fforestallum servientibus Ballivorum. Dicunt etiam de cocis ut supra. Dicunt etiam quod Alanus le Clerk est extra decennam et manet in parochia Sc̄i Olavy. Edmundus manens ex opposito fratrum Carmelitanorum[2] non est in decenna. Robertus Cote [et] Petrus atte gore non sunt in decenna. Dicunt quod Ricardus de Sweynsthorpe ffaber et serviens eius non sunt in decenna et manent in domo Ranulphi Godewyne. Dicunt quod Alicia uxor Rogeri Wrong traxit sanguinem de Matilde Litelcope. Johannes Kinggesman est in decenna Ricardi de Stalham, fecit defaltam ad hunc diem. Robertus de Donewyco receptat tres filios suos extra decennam.

cap

[1] 'A gold penny was struck in Henry III.'s reign which weighed two and was worth twenty silver pennies.'—*Bury Wills*, Camden Soc., vol. xlix. p. 239.
[2] Between the Church of St. James and the river.

the shed of Anice de Colney, buys and sells his goods by tally and is not of the freedom. They say that Robert the fowler knows of thieves and cutpurses, and receives gifts from them to save them from being taken. They say also that Henry of Dublin drew blood of Robert the chaplain his brother. They say also that Henry of Cambridge, who has lodged in the city for a long time, is not in assize. They say also that Nicholas de Aylmerton found two gold pennies, and John Cherry bought them for three farthings. They say also that Ranulph Saluz buys corn and gives it to his wife to make malt, whereby the king loses etc. They say also that William de Wroxham, John Gamen, and Richard Grund the chaplain are wont to make forestalment on the serjeants of the Bailiffs. They say also concerning the cooks as above. They say also that Alan the clerk is out of tithing and lodges in the parish of St. Olave. Edmund, who lodges opposite to the Friars Carmelites is not in tithing. Robert Cote [and] Peter Attegore are not in tithing. They say that Richard de Swainsthorp the smith and his servant are not in tithing, and lodge in the house of Ranulph Godwin. They say that Alice, wife of Roger Wrong, drew blood of Matilda Littlecope. John Kingsman is in the tithing of Richard de Stalham; he has made default to this day. Robert de Dunwich harbours three sons of his who are out of tithing.

II. [ROTULUS AMERCIAMENTORUM AD LETAS NORWICI A° R' REGIS EDWARDI XVII°.]

[1] AMERCIAMENTA AD LETAM DE CONESFORD ANNO XVII^{mo}.

Preceptum est {Michaeli / Radulpho

quietus est De Simone Carpentario de Eya quia stetit in civitate per unum annum et non fuit in decenna . . . xij d.
(Solvit iii d. residuum condonatur.)

d. De Roberto de Swafham de la fermerie qui vendit et emit in Civitate nec est de libertate . . . di. mar.

d. De Galfrido Sparwe pro eodem . . iiij s.

d. De Rogero de Senges tannatore quia traxit sanguinem de Willelmo de Sessons. . . . . . ij s.

q il' est De Johanne de Swafham manente ex opposito fratrum minorum quia non est in decenna . . . . ij s. }solv : vj d. / res : cond.

cond. De Johanne de Wytton manente ibidem pro eodem . . . ij s.
(Cond. ad instantiam fratrum minorum.)

[1] Roll II.—The first portion of this Roll, for the Leet of Conesford (with the exception of the amercements for breaking the Assize of Ale), is given in full on account of the fulness and precision with

II. [LEET ROLL OF 17 EDWARD I. 1288⁹⁄₉.]

AMERCEMENTS AT THE LEET OF CONESFORD IN THE 17TH YEAR.

Order given to Michael and Ralph.[1]

quit	Of Simon de Eye, the carpenter, because he has been in the city for a year and has not been in tithing	12 d. } paid 9d. rest excused.
owes[2]	Of Robert de Swaffham, of the Infirmary,[3] who sells and buys in the city, and is not of the freedom	half a mark.
o.	Of Geoffrey Sparrow for the same	4 s.
o.	Of Roger de Seething, tanner, because he drew blood of William de Sessons	2 s.
quit	Of John de Swaffham, lodging opposite to the Friars Minors, because he is not in tithing	2 s. } paid 6d. rest excused.
excused	Of John de Witton, lodging there, for the same	2 s.
	(Excused at the request of the Friars Minors.)	

which every amercement is recorded and accounted for. The Roll, which consists of membranes fastened lengthwise, must have been compiled from at least three returns—those of the Jury, the Affeerers, and the Collectors.

[1] These two, probably serjeants of the Bailiffs, were appointed to collect the amercements. See Introduction, IV. 6.

[2] The large number of names thus marked raises a suspicion that these persons were not present, and had to be proceeded against as defaulters.

[3] A servant of the Infirmarius of the Cathedral Monastery.

21 AMERCIAMENTA AD LETAS NORWICI.

d. De Agnete de Redenhale pro hutesio
levato . . . . . . xij d.
d. De Rogero le Carecter pro eodem . xij d.
d. De Lucia que fuit uxor Simonis le
paumer pro eodem . . . ij s.
vad. De Willelmo de Sessons quia subtraxit
barreras et eas detinet . . . ij s.
d. De Ricardo Somer quia vendit cervisiam flandrensem [1] occulte per quod
Ballivi perdiderunt custumam . ij s.
cond. De Magistro Johanne de Bures pro
duabus barreris subtractis . . ij s.
(Condonatur per Ballivos)
d. De fratribus de Gernedene [2] quia coar-
taverunt regiam ripam . . . ij s.
d. De Johanne le Scoudere manente in
Trows quia dealbat correa [3] extra
civitatem [4] . . . . . ij s.
d. De Radulpho le Scoudere manente
ibidem pro eodem . . . . ij s.
d. De Johanne de ffransham capellano
pro purprestura facta per quendam
murum . . . . . . iiij s.
d. De Thoma le Scoudere manente in
Brakendele quia dealbat correa [3]
extra civitatem . . . . ij s.
d. De Magistro Alano de ffriston Archi-
diacono Norfolk' quia coartavit
Regiam Ripam, pro truncis et
stapellis positis in Regali via et pro
quinque denariis de Landgabulo

---

[1] MS. *flandr'*.
[2] Garendon Abbey, Leicestershire. The holding was a small piece of ground between the street of Nether Conesford and the river. The term 'brethren' seems to imply that some of them lived there. They may have acted as agents for shipping Cistercian wool to foreign parts. The Cistercian Abbeys of Sibton, Woburn and Combe also held lands in Nether Conesford, the two former certainly by the riverside. 'Straitening the river' generally means making a landing-place.
[3] MS. *correa* — generally *correos*.
[4] This was forbidden outside the City, *i.e.* outside the control of a

o.	Of Agnes de Redenhall for raising the hue	12 d.
o.	Of Roger the carter for the same	12 d.
o.	Of Lucy, who was wife of Simon the palmer, for the same . . .	2 s.
gave gage	Of William de Sessons because he has withdrawn bars and keeps them	2 s.
o.	Of Richard Summer because he sells Flanders beer privily, whereby the Bailiffs have lost custom . .	2 s.
excused	Of Master John de Bures for withdrawing two bars . . . . (Excused by the bailiffs.)	2 s.
o.	Of the Brethren of Garendon because they have straitened the king's river	2 s.
o.	Of John the leatherdresser, lodging in Trowse, because he whitens hides outside the city	2 s.
o.	Of Ralph the leatherdresser, lodging there, for the same . . .	2 s.
o.	Of John de Fransham, chaplain, for making a purpresture with a wall .	4 s.
o.	Of Thomas the leatherdresser, lodging in Bracondale, because he whitens hides outside the city . . .	2 s.
o.	Of Master Alan de Freston, Archdeacon of Norfolk, because he has straitened the king's river, for blocks and stakes set in the highway, and for 5 d. of landgable [1] of	

constituted authority.—Statut. de Visu Franciplegii : ' Des dobbors des draps et correours des quirs aillors quen ville marchaunde.'

[1] A payment due annually to the king on certain tenements supposed to have been the original ' burgage ' tenements of the city. At this time these rents formed part of the Fee Farm Rent of the city, for which the bailiffs were personally responsible. In the ' City Domesday ' is a list of all the tenements so chargeable in the time of Richard II., and several later lists exist down to the seventeenth century.

	Domini Regis per unum annum iniuste detento [1]	dim̄. m̄.
d.	De Galfrido capellano nepote Magistri Godefridi de Norton quia habet fenestras nocentes	ij s.
qui' est	De Silvestro Siger pro purprestura facta super Regiam ripam . .	} solv: ij s. } totum.
	De Radulpho de Suthgate capitali plegio pro concelamento quia non presentaverunt quod Johannes et Hubertus filii Rogeri de Morle fuerunt extra decennam et aliis concelamentis	xij d.
quieti	De Silvestro Siger (xij d.), Willelmo King (xij d.), Ricardo Everich (xij d.), Ricardo Undermel (xij d.), Willelmo Inge (xij d.), Henrico atte wro (xij d.), Ricardo Botman (xij d.), Willelmo filio Walteri le tannur (xij d.), Hugone de Rokelund (xij d.), Willelmo de Irstede (xij d.), Galfrido de Lingwode (xij d.), Johanne de Surlingham (xii d.) . . . pro eodem . .	finem fecerunt per dim̄· marē. solverunt totum.
d.	De Johanne de Hemesby qui desponsavit Luciam que fuit uxor Simonis le paumer quia non est in decenna	ij s.
cond.	De Alano de Baketon pro defalta .	ij s. } cond: per
	De Bartholomeo de Acre pro eodem .	ij s. } Ballivos.
vad.	De Thoma de Hekyngham pro eodem	ij s.
d.	De Johanne de Berwyk tannur pro eodem	ij s.
d.	De Willelmo de Sessons pro eodem .	xij d.
	De Adam de Stirston clerico pro eodem	} cond: per ij s. } ballivos.
cond.	De Silvestro Siger quia subtraxit quandam bundam positam inter ipsum et Johannem de ffransham capellanum	ij s. cond.

[1] Sic, *detento*.

	the lord king wrongfully withheld for a year	half a mark.
o.	Of Geoffrey the chaplain, nephew of Master Godfrey de Norton, because he has windows that are a nuisance	2 s.
quit	Of Silvester Siger for making a purpresture on the king's river . .	2 s. paid the whole.
quit	¹ Of Ralph de Suthgate, capital pledge, for concealment because they have not presented that John and Hubert, sons of Roger de Morley, are out of tithing, and for other concealments	12 d.
	Of Silvester Siger, William King, Richard Erych, Richard Undermel, William Inge, Henry Atterow, Richard Boatman, William, son of Walter the tanner, Hugh de Rockland, William de Irsted, Geoffrey de Lingwood, John de Surlingham, for the same	12 d. [each] They made fine with half a mark. They paid the whole of it.
o.	Of John de Hemsby, who married Lucy that was wife of Simon the palmer, because he is not in tithing	2 s.
excused	Of Alan de Bacton for default . .	2 s. } excused by the Bailiffs.
	Of Bartholomew de Acre for the same	2 s.
gage	Of Thomas de Heckingham for the same	2 s.
o.	Of John de Berwick, tanner, for the same	2 s.
	Of William de Sessons for the same .	12 d.
excused	Of Adam de Sturston, clerk, for the same	2 s. } excused by the Bailiffs.
excused	Of Silvester Siger because he has withdrawn a bound set between himself and John de Fransham, chaplain	2 s. excused.

¹ The Capital Pledges for South and North Conesford combined. See Introduction, II. 12.

d.	De Johanne de ffransham capellano pro eodem	ij s.
qui' e'	De Willelmo de Irstede quia traxit sanguinem de quodam serviente suo cum quodam candelabro . . iij s.	} solv : ij s. res : cond :
d.	De Waltero de Hykeling et fratre eius quia non sunt in decenna . . xij d.	} pauperes.
d.	De Alicia la Norice pro recettamento eorundem . . . . . xij d.	
cond.	De Claricia de Gressenhall pro hutesio iniuste levato super Rogerum le pescur . . . . . . xij d.	} cond. quia pauper
d.	De Johanne Stannard capellano pro hutesio levato super Nicholaum de Reymerston	iiij s.
d.	De eodem Johanne quia subtraxit bundas positas inter ipsum et predictum N.	ij s.
d.	De eodem Johanne pro hutesio levato super Willelmum fratrem suum .	ij s.
	De Galfrido Munne quia traxit sanguinem de Cristiana de Bilneye .	pauper.
	De Katerina de Mendham quia traxit sanguinem de Agatha uxore Johannis le berere	—
d.	De Adam de Barsham quia traxit sanguinem de Matilde Munne .	ij s.
qui' e'	De Thoma fratre Willelmi de Carleton quia traxit sanguinem de Simone serviente Henrici Pope . . . xij d.	} solv : vj d. res : cond :
d.	De Johanne Gilur pro hutesio levato super Henricum Gilur . . .	xij d.
d.	De Thoma Herre de Kyrkeby pro hutesio levato super Johannem Gilur	xij d.
qui' e'	De Rogero Beniamin pro quodam fimario posito in via regali in quo sepellivit viscera animalium per quod aer pessime corrumpitur .	} solv' tot' ij s.

LEET ROLL OF 128⅚.   23

o.	Of John de Fransham, chaplain, for the same	2 s.
quit	Of William de Irstead because he drew blood of a servant of his with a candlestick. . . . . . 3 s.	} paid 2 s. rest excused.
o.	Of Walter de Hickling and his brother because they are not in tithing . 12 d.	
o.	Of Alice, the nurse, for harbouring them . . . . . . 12 d.	} poor.
excused	Of Claricia de Gressenhall for wrongfully raising the hue on Roger the fisher . . . . . . 12 d.	} excused because poor.
o.	Of John Stannard, chaplain, for raising the hue on Nicholas de Reymerston	4 s.
o.	Of the same John because he has withdrawn bounds set between himself and the said Nicholas . .	2 s.
o.	Of the same John for raising the hue on his brother William . . .	2 s.
	Of Geoffrey Munne because he drew blood of Christiana de Bilney . .	poor.
	Of Catherine de Mendham because she drew blood of Agatha, wife of John le berer	—
o.	Of Adam de Barsham because he drew blood of Matilda Munne . . .	2 s.
quit	Of Thomas, brother of William de Carlton, because he drew blood of Simon the servant of Henry Pope . 12 d.	} paid 6d. rest excused.
o.	Of John Gilur for raising the hue on Henry Gilur	12 d.
o.	Of Thomas Herre of Kirkby for raising the hue on John Gilur . . .	12 d.
quit	Of Roger Benjamin for setting a muckheap in the king's highway, in which he has buried the offal of beasts, whereby the air is abominably poisoned	2 s. paid the whole.

cond.	De eodem Rogero quia posuit quandam porcariam in via regia . . .	xij d. cond.
d.	De Reginaldo de Lakenham quia traxit sanguinem de Waltero Eye . .	ij s.
cond.	De Thoma de Ho quia pessime coartavit viam regiam cum fimario .	ij s. cond.
	De Ricardo de Schotisham pro cursu aque diverso	—
d.	De Johanne filio Johannis de Weston quia divertit cursum aque inter ipsum et Thomam le Waleys . .	xij d.
qui' e'	De Vincentio le Cuppere manente juxta domum Isabelle Salehar quia non est in decenna . . .	xij d. } solv: iij d. res: cond.
qui' c'	De Johanne Litel filio Emme le Cobelere manente ibidem pro eodem .	xij d. } solv vj d. res: cond.
d.	De Rogero de Claxton pro blado empto antequam venit ad forum per quod Ballivi perdunt theolonium . .	dī. m̄.
cond.	De Roberto Gerveys de Brakendel pro eodem	iiij s.
	(Condonatur ad instantiam Henrici Clerici.)	
d.	De Johanne de Bradefield pro eodem	ij s.
d.	De Thoma Vincent de Trows quia advocat bladum suum esse de feodo Prioris Norwyci cum non teneat de feodo suo nisi tres rodas et residuum terre sue de feodo Rikel quod creditur	iiij s.
d.	De Johanne de Brok de Brakendel quia vendit scienter carnes porcinas superseminatas	ij s.
?.	De Johanne Skrike de Trows pro eodem	ij s.

LEET ROLL OF 128⅜.

excused	Of the same Roger because he has set a pigsty in the king's highway .	12 d.	excused.
o.	Of Reginald de Lakenham because he drew blood of Walter Eye . .	2 s.	
excused	Of Thomas de Howe because he has abominably straitened the king's highway with a muck-heap . .	2 s.	excused.
	Of Richard de Shottisham for diverting a watercourse.		
o.	Of John, son of John de Weston, because he has diverted a watercourse between himself and Thomas le Waleys	12 d.	
quit	Of Vincent the cupper, lodging next the house of Isabella Salehar, because he is not in tithing . .	12 d.	paid 3 d. rest excused.
quit	Of John Little, son of Emma the cobbler, lodging there, for the same	12 d.	paid 6 d. rest excused.
o.	Of Roger de Claxton, for buying corn before it comes to the market, whereby the Bailiffs lose their toll .	half a mark.	
excused	Of Robert Gerveys of Bracondale for the same	4 s.	
	(Excused at the request of Henry the Clerk.)		
o.	Of John de Bradfield for the same .	2 s.	
o.	Of Thomas Vincent of Trowse because he avows his corn to be of the fee of the Prior of Norwich, whereas he holds of his [the Prior's] fee no more than three roods, and the rest of his land belongs to Rikel's fee, as is believed	4 s.	
o.	Of John de Brooke of Bracondale because he wittingly sells measly pork	2 s.	
o.	Of John Skrike of Trowse for the same	2 s.	

VOL. V.   E

AMERCIAMENTA AD LETAS NORWICI.

d. De Nicholao le Hirdler quia traxit sanguinem de Gilberto de London Gaunter . . . . . xij d.

d. De Johanne Giber pro hutesio levato super patrem suum . . . xij d.

qui' e' De Ricardo de Hemenhale carnifice quia traxit sanguinem de Waltero Pleye de Trows . . . . ij s. } solv : xij d. res : cond.

d. De Willelmo le Carecter Gaunter pro hutesio levato super Johannem de Castre . . . . . . xij d.

De Johanne clerico de Crostweyt quia non est in decenna . . . —

d. De Roberto le Bacur manente in redditu Willelmi de Burtoft pro eodem xij d.

d. De Willelmo de Burtoft pro recettamento eiusdem . . . . xij d.

d. De Galfrido le Bacur manente in redditu Thome le Man quia non est in decenna . . . . . xij d.

d. De Hugone le Gerthmakere pro eodem xij d.

cond. De Thoma le Man pro recettamento eorundem . . . . . iiij s. cond.

d. De Reginaldo de Lakenham pro purprestura facta super viam regiam per quoddam fossatum . . . xij d.

d. De Nicholao de Taverham quia traxit sanguinem de Rogero Liard . . xij d.

vad. De Stephano le Turnur pro eodem . xij d.

qui' c' { De Johanne le ledbetere capitali plegio [pro] concelamento quia non presentavit purpresturam quam Johannes de Parys fecit per quandam portam . . . . . xij d. De Willelmo Godynow (ij s.), Henrico Pope (xij d.), Radulpho de Stafford (ij s.), Galfrido Baldewyn (xij d.), Johanne de Aschele (xij d.), Henrico de } fecerunt finem pro dimidia

o.	Of Nicholas le hirdler because he drew blood of Gilbert de London, glover	12 d.
o.	Of John Giber for raising the hue on his father	12 d.
quit	Of Richard de Hemenhale, butcher, because he drew blood of Walter Pleye of Trowse . . . . . 2 s.	} paid 12 d. rest excused.
o.	Of William le Carter, glover, for raising the hue on John de Caister	12 d.
	Of John de Crostwight, clerk, because he is not in tithing . . .	—
o.	Of Robert the baker, lodging in the rent of William de Burtoft, for the same	12 d.
o.	Of William de Burtoft for harbouring him	12 d.
o.	Of Geoffrey the baker, lodging in the rent of Thomas le Man, because he is not in tithing	12 d.
o.	Of Hugh the girth-maker for the same	12 d.
excused	Of Thomas le Man for harbouring them	4 s. excused.
o.	Of Reginald de Lakenham for making a purpresture on the king's highway with a ditch	12 d.
o.	Of Nicholas de Taverham because he drew blood of Roger Liard . .	12 d.
gage	Of Stephen the turner for the same .	12 d.

[1] Of John the leadbeater, capital pledge, for concealment because he has not presented the purpresture which John de Parys made with a gate . 12 d.

quit { Of William Godynow (2 s.), Henry Pope (12 d.), Ralph de Stafford (2 s.), Geoffrey Baldwin, John de Ashill, Henry de Holland, Walter they made fine with half a

[1] The Capital Pledges for Berstrete district.

	Hoylaunde (xij d.), Waltero de Colton (xij d.), Eudone le carectere (xij d.), Thoma le Neve (xij d.), Roberto le Parcheminer (ij s.), Simone filio Ranulphi (ij s.), Johanne Canun (ij s.) pro eodem	marca. solverunt totum
Conesford qui' sunt	De Johanne le Ballye et uxore eius pro assissa cervisie non observata . De Johanne de Morle et uxore eius pro eodem	ij s. ij s. } solv : xij d. res : cond. } solv : xij d. res : cond.
qui' c'	De Laurentio clerico et uxore eius pro eodem	ij s. } solv : xij d. res : cond.
cond.	De Roberto de Dalby pro eodem . De Beatrice de Irstede pro eodem et pro fimario . . . . . (Solvit vi^d res : cond : ad instantiam Magistri Johannis Man pro amicitia carnali [1])	ij s. ij s. cond.
Berstrete	De Johanne de Sibeton et uxore eius pro eodem . (cond : quia janitor)	iij s.
cond.	De Johanne le Luminur et uxore eius pro eodem . . . . . (Cond : ad instantiam Johannis de Ely clerici)	iij s.
qui' e'	De Editha de Parys pro eodem . .	iiij s. solv : totum.
cond.	De Johanne le Newebrid et uxore eius pro eodem . (cond : per Ballivos)	ij s.
cond.	De Johanne de Bergh et uxore eius pro eodem . (cond : per Ballivos)	xij d.
cond.	De Eudone le carectere et uxore eius pro eodem . . . . . (Cond : quia causa non est vera.[2])	xij d.

[1] On 8 Dec. following this entry a stall in the Fishmarket was conveyed by 'John Man, clerk, and Beatrix his wife, daughter of Adam de Irstede ' (C. R. 18 E. 1).

[2] See Introduction, VI. 7.

	de Colton, Eudo the carter, Thomas le Neve (12 d. each), Robert the parchment dealer, Simon son of Ranulph, John Canun (2s. each), for the same	mark and paid the whole of it.
Conesford	[1] Of John the Bailiff and his wife for not observing the assize of ale . 2 s.	paid 12 d. rest excused.
quit	Of John de Morley and his wife for the same . . . . . 2 s.	paid 12 d. rest excused.
quit	Of Laurence the clerk and his wife for the same . . . . . 2 s.	paid 12 d. rest excused.
excused	Of Robert de Dalby for the same . 2 s. excused.	
quit	Of Beatrice de Irstead for the same and for a muck-heap . . . 2 s. (Paid 6 d., rest excused at request of Master John Man out of carnal friendship.)	
Berstrete	Of John de Sibton and his wife for the same . . . . . 3 s. (Excused because he is gate-keeper.)	
excused	Of John the limner and his wife for the same . . . . . 3 s. (Excused at request of John de Ely, clerk.)	
quit	Of Editha de Parys for the same . 4 s. paid the whole.	
excused	Of John le Newbird and his wife for the same (excused by the Bailiffs) 2 s.	
excused	Of John de Burgh and his wife for the same . (excused by the Bailiffs) 12 d.	
excused	Of Eudo the carter and his wife for the same . . . . . 12 d. (Excused because the charge is not true.)	

---

[1] The following amercements for breaches of the assize of ale are selected, chiefly for the causes of remission.

AMERCIAMENTA AD LETAS NORWICI.

cond. De [1] . . . . que fuit uxor Walteri le
Grey pro eodem . . . . . ij s.
(Cond: ad instantiam Michaelis)

cond. De Laurentio de Aula pro eodem . ij s.
(Cond : ad instantiam J. clerici)

cond. De Emma que fuit uxor Roberti ffabri
pro eodem . . . . . ij s.
(Cond: quia causa non est vera)

cond. De Roberto de Sancto Edmundo et
uxore eius pro eodem . . . ij s.
(Cond : per Ballivos)

cond. De Adam de Aldeby pro eodem . . ij s.
(cond: quia causa non est vera).

De Johanne franke quia posuit fimarium in via regia . . . ij s.
(Cond: quia causa non est vera.)

. . . .

Recepta per manum Michaelis xvj s.
die Sabbati proxima post festum
Sancti Gregorii Pape.
Item die sabbati proxima post festum
Annunciationis beate Marie per
manum eiusdem . . . . xxxvij s. xj d.
Item die Jovis prox. post festum Annunciationis beate Marie . . vij s. iiij d.
Item die sabbati in vigilia Dominice
Palmarum . . . . . v s.
Item die Jovis prox. post Dominicam
Palmarum . . . . . ij s.
Item die sabbati prox. ante Clausum
Pascha . . . . . . iij s.

[1] Name omitted.

LEET ROLL OF 128⅔.   27

excused   Of . . . , who was wife of Walter le
   Grey for the same . . . . 2 s.
   (Excused at request of Michael.)
excused   Of Laurence of the Hall for the same 2 s.
   (Excused at request of John the
   clerk.)
excused   Of Emma, who was wife of Robert the
   smith, for the same . . . 2 s.
   (Excused because the charge is
   not true.)
excused   Of Robert de St. Edmund and his
   wife for the same . . . . 2 s.
   (Excused by the Bailiffs.)
excused   Of Adam de Aldeby for the same . 2 s.
   (Excused because the charge is
   not true.)
   [57 persons amerced.]
   Of John Frank because he has set a
   muck-heap in the king's highway . 2 s.
   (Excused because the charge is
   not true.)
   . . . . .

Receipts by the hand of Michael. 16 s.
on Saturday[1] next after the feast of
St. Gregory the Pope . . . [16 s.]
Item on Saturday next after the feast
of the Annunciation of the Blessed
Mary, by the hand of the same . 37 s. 11 d.
Item on Thursday next after the feast
of the Annunciation of the Blessed
Mary . . . . . . 7 s. 4 d.
Item on Saturday being the Vigil of
Palm Sunday . . . . 5 s.
Item on Thursday next after Palm
Sunday. . .. . . . 2 s.
Item on Saturday next before the close
of Easter . . . . . 3 s.

[1] March 19, 26, 31 ; April 2, 7, 16.

Preceptum est {Makabe / Brid

[1] AMERCIAMENTA AD LETAM DE NEDHAM [2] ET MANE-
CROFT ANNO SUPRADICTO.

cond. De Roberto de Huntingfeud tyxtore pro contemptu (ij s., cond.) De Ricardo Lewin pistore quia emit bladum ad molendinum de Hertford per quod Ballivi perdunt theo-
qui' e' lonium (ij s., cond : per Ballivos) De Johanne Attegate-hend quia emit bladum in Civitate ad talliam nec est de
d. libertate (ij s., solv : vi d.) .... De Stephano le Carec-tere quia proiecit carnes bovinas putridas super terram Mathei Brun [3] (ij s.) .... De Willelmo serviente Rogeri Bele quia non est in decenna (ij s.) De Rogero Bele pro recettamento eiusdem (ij s., cond : quia causa non est vera). .... De Johanne Geggard quia vendidit Gogges (ij s.) De Johanne le Pastemakere quia vendidit Carnes quas Judei vocant trefa [4] (ij s.) .... De Radulpho de Castre et uxore eius quia braciant et non ponunt extra singnum (ij s., cond : quia pauperes) .... De Nicholao
vad. le Chapeller quia fregit barreras Civitatis (ij s.) .... De Adam Kabel pro forbarramento et forstallo facto in foro (ij s.) .... De Mauricio qui facit manubria ad
mortuus est cultellos pro hutesio levato (xij d.) .... De Ricardo de Stalham [5] pro falsitate facta in opere viz. eo quod tannat correos cum cortice fraxineo. .... De Willelmo balle quia advocat bona Ranulphi balle esse sua dominica per quod Ballivi perdunt custumam (di. mr̃.) .... De Matheo Tusceynz quia non est in decenna (di. mr̃.) De
cond. Willelmo Yntte pro eodem (xij d., cond : quia causa non
cond. est vera). De Hugone de London Regrater quia emit et vendit in Civitate nec est de libertate (xij d., cond : ad
vad. instantiam G. le Graunt). .... De Stephano de Erlham

[1] From this point only extracts of the Rolls are given.
[2] The original name of the district forming the parish of St. Stephen.
[3] A private nuisance.
[4] See Introduction, Note G. 3.
[5] Thirty-two others are presented 'pro eodem.' There are no amerce-ments, but in the amercement column is a list of twenty-three

Order given to Makabe and Bird.

AMERCEMENTS AT THE LEET OF NEDHAM AND MANE-CROFT IN THE AFORESAID YEAR.

excused Of Robert de Huntingfield, weaver, for contempt (2 s., ex-
excused cused). .... Of Richard Lewin, baker, because he buys
corn at Hertford mill, whereby the Bailiffs lose toll (2 s.,
quit excused by the Bailiffs). Of John Attegateend because
he buys corn in the city by tally and is not of the free-
o. dom (2 s.) .... Of Stephen the Carter because he cast
putrid ox-flesh on the land of Matthew Brown (2 s.)
excused .... Of William, servant of Roger Bele, because he is
not in tithing (2 s.) Of Roger Bele for harbouring him
(2 s., excused because the charge is not true). .... Of
John Geggard because he has sold gogges (2 s.) Of John
the pasty-maker because he has sold meat which the
Jews call trefa (2 s.) .... Of Ralph de Caister and his
wife because they brew and set no seal outside (2 s., ex-
gage cused because poor). .... Of Nicholas the hatter because he has broken the city bars (2 s.) .... Of Adam
Kabel for making forbarment and forestalment in the
market (2 s.) .... Of Maurice, who makes knife-handles,
for raising the hue (12 d.) .... Of Richard de Stalham for making fraud in his work, to wit for that he
tans hides with bark of ash.[1] .... Of William Ball because he avows the goods of Ranulph Ball to be his own
property, whereby the Bailiffs lose custom (half a mark).
.... Of Mathew Tusceynz because he is not in tithing
excused (half a mark). Of William Yntte, for the same (12 d.,
excused excused because the charge is not true). Of Hugh de
London, regrater, because he buys and sells in the city,
and is not of the freedom (12 d., excused at request of
gage Gervase le Graunt). .... Of Stephen de Erlham and

names, the object of which is uncertain. They might be a jury appointed to inquire into the practices of the tanners, but some of them are not of a position to warrant such a conclusion; *e.g.* 'Witts Spanie—Fil Witti Spanye—Socius eius.'

[1] Bark of oak should have been used.

AMERCIAMENTA AD LETAS NORWICI.

et Willelmo fratre eius quia bladum quod emunt in civitate vendunt extraneis nec sunt de libertate (iiij s.) De Nicholao de York quia non est in decenna (xij d. fugit).

qui' e' .... De Johanne del Stonhus et uxore eius pro assissa cervisie non observata (ij s. solv : vj d.) .... De Wil-
cond. lelmo le Skinnere et uxore eius pro eodem (xij d., cond :
ad'instantiam Is. de Tudenham ¹)..... De Petro de
cond. Wyleby et uxore eius pro eodem (iij s., cond : quia causa non est vera)..... De Johanne Ston et uxore eius pro
qui' e' eodem (ij s., solvit xij d. res : cond : per I. de Porringlond)..... De Rogero Bele quia posuit fimarium in via regali (xij d., cond : quia causa non est vera). ....

Recepta Radulphi Brid et Makabe et per eos liberata. xl s. die Sabbati prox. post festum Sc̄i Gregorii Pape. Item die sabbati prox. post festum Annunciationis beate Marie per manus eorundem (xxxiv s.) Item die sabbati in vigilia Dominice Palmarum (vij s.) Item die Jovis prox. post Dominicam Palmarum (ix d.) Item die Sabbati prox. ante clausum Pascha (xviij d.)

Preceptum est { Petro
 Kibel

AMERCIAMENTA AD LETAM DE WYMER ET WESTWYK ANNO SUPRADICTO.

vad. De Johanne le Carectere manente cum Johanne Yve quia non est in decenna, sicut idem Johannes le Carectere
vad. recognovit (xij d.) De Johanne Yve pro recettamento
d. eiusdem (ij s.).... De Willelmo le Skinnere quia proiecit cadavera murilegulorum in puteo Lothmere ² ita quod aer
d. corrumpitur (ij s.) De Johanne de Disce quia gratis ³ dat Theolonium et consuetudinem in mercatis et feriis

---

¹ Wife of Roger de Tudenham, one of the Bailiffs.
² A pit near the junction of the streets of Over and Nether Newport.
³ By Charter of 5 Richard I. the men of Norwich were free from toll

William his brother because the corn which they buy in the city they sell to strangers, and [because] they are not of the freedom (4 s.) Of Nicholas de York because he is not in tithing (12 d., fled). . . . . . Of John of the Stone-house and his wife for not observing the assize of ale (2 s. paid 6 d.) . . . . Of William the Skinner and his wife for the same (12 d., excused at request of Isabella de Tudenham). . . . . Of Peter de Wilby and his wife for the same (3 s., excused because the charge is not true). . . . . Of John Stone and his wife for the same (2 s., paid 12 d., rest excused by John de Poringland). [84 persons amerced for the same.] . . . . Of Roger Bele because he has set a muck-heap in the king's highway (12 d., excused because the charge is not true). . . . .

quit

Receipts of Ralph Bird and Makabe and by them delivered. 40 s. on the Saturday next after the feast of St. Gregory the Pope. Item on the Saturday next after the feast of the Annunciation of the Blessed Mary by the hands of the same (34 s.) Item on Saturday being the vigil of Palm Sunday (7 s.) Item on the Thursday next after Palm Sunday (9 d.) Item on the Saturday next before the close of Easter (18 d.)

Order given to Peter and Kibel.

AMERCEMENTS AT THE LEET OF WYMER AND WESTWICK IN THE AFORESAID YEAR.

gage

gage

o.

o.

Of John the Carter lodging with John Yve, because he is not in tithing, as the said John the Carter acknowledged (12 d.) Of John Yve for harbouring him (2 s.) . . . . Of William the Skinner because he has thrown the dead bodies of cats into the pit of Lothmere whereby the air is poisoned (2 s.) Of John de Diss because of his own accord he gives toll and custom in markets and fairs con-

in other towns. This privilege granted to one chartered borough was resented in another. John de Diss no doubt secured some private advantage by being complaisant at the cost of his patriotism, and is amerced as a traitor.

d.   contra libertatem civitatis (ij s.)   De Johanne de Poswyk quia subarravit divisas Mathei Brun (xij d.) .... De Willelmo Popy pro falsis ponderibus et quia emit per majus pondus et vendit per minus (ij s.) .... De Willelmo le luminur pro falsitate facta in pannis ponendo in iisdem filum de lino (—)   De Thoma Gosonthegrone quia forstallat forum de piscibus (ij s.) .... De Radulpho tixtore quia implacitavit Edmundum le Agulyer in curia Cristianitatis coram Magistro Adam de Wratham (ij s.) .... De Richero Alunday quia non fuit in decenna (ij s., cond : quia causa non est vera). De Johanne filio Ade de Stirston pro eodem (ij s.) .... De Johanne de Norwye pro recettamento duorum filiorum suorum qui non sunt in decenna (xij d.)   De Rogero de Penteneye quia habet fenestras nocentes equitantibus ad redditum suum super fossatum Castri (—).   De Johanne Janne quia forbarrat[1] homines de civitate de emptione cepe [*sic*] per quod forum deterioratur (dī. mř.) .... De Johanne Stabler et uxore eius (pro assissa cervisie non observata) (xij d., cond : quia causa non est vera). . . . De Estrilda de Lopham pro assissa cervisie non observata et pro fimario et truncis positis in via regia (iij s.) ....

Crispelok.[2]

Recepta per manum Petri Snago xxxviij s. die sabbati prox. post festum Scī Gregorii Pape.   Item per manum eiusdem die sabbati prox. post festum Annunciationis beate Marie (xvij s. vj d.)   Item die sabbati in vigilia Dominice Palmarum (xviiij d.)   Item die Jovis prox. post Dominicam Palmarum (xxxiij d.)   Eodem die extra summam (ij s.)

[1] This entry seems to define forbarring as buying up or storing goods to sell elsewhere, so diminishing the market supply. 'Cepe' is unusual for 'cepi,' or it may be a mistake for 'cere.'
[2] Perhaps a clerk with whom the collector settled his account.

trary to the liberty of the city (2 s.) Of John de Postwick because he has underploughed the bounds of Mathew Brown (12 d.) .... Of William Popy for false weights and because he buys by a greater weight and sells by a less (2 s.) .... Of William the limner for making fraud in cloths by putting linen thread in them (—) Of Thomas Gooseonthegreen because he forestalls the fish market (2 s.) .... Of Ralph the weaver because he impleaded Edmund the needler in the Court Christian before Master Adam de Wretham (2 s.) .... Of Richer Alunday because he was not in tithing (2 s., excused because the charge is not true). Of John, son of Adam de Sturston, for the same (2 s.) .... Of John de Norway for the harbouring of his two sons who are not in tithing (12 d.) Of Roger de Pentney because he has windows which are a nuisance to riders at his rent over the city dyke (—). Of John Janne, because he forbars the men of the city from the purchase of tallow, whereby the market is diminished (half a mark)..... Of John Stabler and his wife for not observing the assize of ale (12 d., excused because the charge is not true). [81 persons amerced.] Of Estrilda de Lopham for not observing the assize of ale and for a muck-heap and setting blocks in the king's highway (3 s.)

Crispelok.

Receipts by the hand of Peter Snago. 38 s. on the Saturday next after the feast of St. Gregory the Pope [38 s.] Item by the hand of the same on the Saturday next after the feast of the Annunciation of the Blessed Mary (17 s. 6 d.) Item on Saturday being the vigil of Palm Sunday (19 d.) Item on Thursday next after Palm Sunday (33 d.) On the same day, beyond the amount [1] (2 s.)

[1] Beyond the amount entered as collected in money on the roll of amercements for this Leet. The writing is the same as in the other entries.

Preceptum est {Swerdeston, Rogero

AMERCIAMENTA AD LETAM ULTRA AQUAM ANNO SEP-
TIMO DECIMO.

.... De Magistro Thoma de Depham pro uno denario de [1] landgabulo Domini Regis iniuste detento (ij s.) ....
qui' e' [2] De Rogero de Honeworth, Roberto filio Gervasii, Roberto de Donewico, Henrico filio capellani, Thoma Spik, Reginaldo de Catton, Adam ffegge, Ricardo de Stalham, Reynero de Schuldham, Johanne le Skinnere, Rogero Abbot, Radulpho de Hevingham, Roberto le Myteyn-maker, Henrico le Stotere, Johanne le Loksmith et Johanne de Sancta ffide, capitalibus plegiis [3] de fine pro concelamento (di. mr., solverunt totum)..... De Henrico But et uxore eius pro assissa cervisie non observata (ij s., cond: quia amens)..... De Willelmo de Wroxham et uxore eius pro eodem (iiij s., causa non est vera).....

Recepta per manum I. de Swerdeston. xxxvj s. die Sabbati prox. post festum Sc̄i Gregorii. Item die Sabbati prox. post festum Annunciationis beate Marie (xxx s.) Item die Jovis prox. post festum Annunciationis beate Marie (xj s.) Item die Sabbati in vigilia Dominice Palmarum (ij s. vj d.) Item die Jovis prox. post Dominicam Palmarum (ij s.) Item die Sabbati prox. ante clausum Pascha (xij d.)

Amerciamenta Piscenariorum pro forbarramento.

De Ranulpho le pessuner pro forstallo et forbarramento piscium in foro Norwyci et quia emit ante horam primam contra communem proclamacionem factam in Civitate (—, solv: ij s.) ....

---

[1] *uno denario de* is entered above the line.
[2] The Capital Pledges for the second sublect, Over-the-Water.
[3] *capitalibus plegiis* written in full.

Order given to Swerdeston and Roger.

AMERCEMENTS AT THE LEET OVER-THE-WATER IN THE 17TH YEAR.

.... Of Master Thomas de Deepham for wrongfully detaining one penny of landgable of the lord king (2 s.) .... Of Roger de Hunworth, Robert son of Gervase, Robert de Dunwich, Henry son of the Chaplain, Thomas Spik, Reginald de Catton, Adam Fegge, Richard de Stalham, Reyner de Shouldham, John the skinner, Roger Abbot, Ralph de Hevingham, Robert the mitten-maker, Henry the stutterer, John the locksmith, and John de St. Faith, capital pledges, for fine for concealment (half a mark, they paid it in full, quit). .... Of Henry But and his wife for not observing the assize of ale (2 s., excused because mad). .... Of William de Wroxham and his wife for the same (4 s., the charge is not true). [64 persons amerced.]

Receipts by the hand of John de Swerdeston. 36 s. on the Saturday next after the feast of St. Gregory. Item on the Saturday next after the Feast of the Annunciation of the Blessed Mary (30 s.) Item on the Thursday next after the feast of the Annunciation of the Blessed Mary (11 s.) Item on Saturday being the vigil of Palm Sunday (2 s. 6 d.) Item on the Thursday next after Palm Sunday (2 s.) Item on the Saturday next before the Close of Easter (12 d.)

Amercements of Fishmongers for Forbarment.

Of Ranulph the fishmonger for forestalment and forbarment of fish in Norwich market and because he buys before the hour of prime [1] contrary to the common proclamation made in the city (—, paid 2 s.) [84 amercements.]

---

[1] The 37th Chapter of Norwich Customs forbids purchases 'quousque ad missam beate Marie ad ecclesiam Sce Trinitatis pulsetur.'

Amerciamenta Cocorum pro Carnibus Piscibus et Pastellis recalefactis.

qui' c* De Adam Tiffanye quia recalefacit carnes pisces et pastillos post biduum seu triduum (ij s., solvit vi d. res: cond.) . . . .

Amerciamenta Puletariorum pro fforbarramento.

De Hugone Wichard pro forstallo et forbarramento puletarie ad deterioracionem fori (ij s.) . . . .

Recepta per manus Thome clerici et Ranulphi belle die Jovis prox. post Dominicam Palmarum (xxx s.) Item die Sabbati prox. ante festum Apostolorum Philippi & Jacobi (xj s. iiij d.)

Amercements of the Cooks for warming up meat, fish, and pasties.

quit Of Adam Tiffanye because he warms up meat and pasties after the second or third day (2 s., paid 6 d. rest excused). [18 amercements.]

Amercements of the Poulterers for forbarment.

quit Of Hugh Wichard for forestalment and forbarment of poultry to the detriment of the market (2 s., paid 12 d.) [12 amercements.]

Receipts by the hand of Thomas the clerk and Ranulph Bell on the Thursday next after Palm Sunday (30 s.) Item on the Saturday next before the feast of the Apostles Philip and James (11 s. 4 d.)

III. [ROTULUS PRESENTATIONUM AD LETAM DE CONESFORD IN CIVITATE NORWICI A° R' REGIS EDWARDI XVIII°]

[1] LETA DE CUNESFORD DIE LUNE [2] PROXIMA POST FESTUM SANCTI VALENTINI ANNO XVIIJ^MO.

Parochia Sēī Petri de Suthgate—Parochia Sēī Edwardi—Parochia Sēē Etheldrede—Parochia Sēī Clementis—Parochia Sēī Juliani—Parochia Sēī Michaelis de Cunesford.

Radulphus filius Henrici de Suthgate (jur')
Silvester Siger (jur') . Henricus de le Wro (jur')
Ricardus Hydhef fecit defaltam . postea venit et jur'.

Willelmus Kyng }
Ricardus Everich } jur'   Ricardus Botman }
                          Johannes Slabbard } jur'

Ricardus Undermel }   Alanus de }
Willelmus Ingge   } jur'   Baketon   } jur'   Ricardus de
                            Robertus de }   Honington
                            Aldeby   }

Juratores presentant per sacramentum suum quod Rogerus le Millere non est in decenna . . . Dicunt etiam quod uxor Ricardi Botman vendit cervisiam per unam ollam et tres olle non faciunt unam lagenam cervisie . . . Dicunt etiam

---

[1] Roll III.—A fragmentary Roll of two membranes, containing Presentments only for the Leet of Conesford. It is of value as specifying the parishes composing the two districts of Conesford. A line is drawn from top to bottom of each membrane as though the entries had been copied elsewhere.

[2] 20 February 12$\frac{89}{90}$, the first Monday in Lent.

III. [LEET ROLL OF 18 EDWARD I. 12 89/90.]

LEET OF CONESFORD ON THE MONDAY NEXT AFTER THE FEAST OF ST. VALENTINE IN THE 18TH YEAR.

[S. Cones-ford]
Parish of St. Peter de Southgate—Parish of St. Edward—Parish of St. Etheldreda—Parish of St. Clement—Parish of St. Julian—Parish of St. Michael de Conesford.

Ralph, son of Henry de Southgate, sworn; Silvester Siger, sworn; Henry Atterowe, sworn; Richard Hydhef made default; afterwards he came and was sworn—William King and Richard Everich, sworn; Richard Boatman and John Slabbard, sworn; Richard Undermel and William Inge, sworn; Alan de Bacton and Robert de Aldeby and Richard de Honington, sworn.

The Jurors present on their oath that Roger the miller is not in tithing. . . . They say also that the wife of Richard Boatman sells beer by the single pot and three pots [1] do not make one gallon of beer. . . . They say also that

---

[1] An 'olla' is said to be equal to a 'sextarius,' a pint and a half or a quart. Here it seems to be a quart and a third.

quod Thomas Everich et Ricardus Schepesheghee capiunt pisces in aqua rescenti cum retibus que non sunt de assissa . . . Semanus de Blitheburgh quia receptavit Johannem filium suum qui non fuit in decenna.

Defalte.
    Ricardus Sumer pro defalta . in mīā . et dictum est Radulpho de Suthgate quod habeat eum cras.
    Edmundus Middey pro eodem . in mīā . et dictum est Silvestro Siger quod eum habeat cras.
    Rogerus ffychs de Oulton . in mīā . et dictum est Willelmo King etc.
        (Testatur per capitalem [1] [plegium] quod ipse Rogerus dixit quod non veniret ad villanos de Conesford [2])
    Johannes Ko in mīā et dictum est Richero Erych etc.
    Radulphus Surmylk in mīā pro defalta et dictum est Henrico del Wro etc.
        (Johannes et Radulphus [sic] solverunt Radulpho [sic] vj d.)
    Paulus de Pagrave in mīā pro defalta et dictum est Ricardo le Botman etc.
    Bartholomeus de Acre pro eodem et dictum est predicto Ricardo etc.

Afferatores . Ricardus Botman . Willelmus King . Silvester Siger . Radulphus de Suthgate.

Silvester et Alanus indictaverunt Johannem de ffransham capellanum coram Episcopo de quodam annuo redditu.

  .   .   .   .

---

[1] MS. *capit'*.
[2] MS. *Coñ*, the contraction used throughout these Rolls for Conesford.

Thomas Everich and Richard Sheepseye catch fish in fresh
water with nets which are not according to the assize. . . .
Seman de Blythburgh because he harboured his son, John,
who was not in tithing. . . .

[1] Defaults.
>   Richard Summer for default, in mercy, and Ralph de
>   Southgate is ordered to produce him to-morrow.
>   Edmund Middey for the same, in mercy, and Silvester
>   Siger is ordered to produce him to-morrow.
>   Roger Fish of Oulton, in mercy, and William King is
>   ordered etc.
>> (It is testified [2] by the Capital Pledge that
>> Roger said that he would not come to the
>> villains of Conesford.)
>   John Ko, in mercy, and Richer Erych is ordered etc.
>   Ralph Sourmilk, in mercy for default, and Henry
>   Atterowe is ordered etc.
>>   (John and Ralph paid Ralph 6 d.)
>   Paul de Pagrave, in mercy for default, and Richard
>   the boatman is ordered &c.
>   Bartholomew de Acre, for the same, and the said Richard
>   is ordered etc.

[3] Affeerers : Richard Boatman, William King, Silvester
Siger, Ralph de Southgate.

Silvester and Alan indicted John de Fransham,
chaplain, before the Bishop, touching a certain
annual rent.

.   .   .   .

[1] These entries are in different handwriting. The default is probably non-appearance to answer some charge at the Leet. The Capital Pledges are ordered to produce the defaulters on the following day when the Court would be sitting for another district.

[2] For some remarks on this statement see Introduction, X. 12. Oulton is a village near Lowestoft.

[3] This again is in different handwriting.

Juratores presentant quod Johannes le Redeprest levavit hutesium super Henricum le Clerk iniuste. Item dicunt *capiatur* quod idem Johannes est culpabilis de murdro unius parvi procreati de concubina sua . . . . . Item dicunt quod Rogerus Wortes et uxor sua de consuetudine levant hutesium super vicinos suos iniuste ad terrorem omnium vicinorum suorum et magnum scandalum totius populi . . . . Item *cap'.* dicunt quod Cecilia uxor Johannis Lomb furata fuit de persona Sc̃i Michaelis octo marcas argenti . . . . Item *cap'.* dicunt quod Ricardus filius Alicie Bele furatus fuit. de Roberto de Hadesco xviij den. et ob. noctanter in crastino Sc̃i Petri ad vincula Anno regni regis nunc xvij . . . . Item dicunt quod Johannes de ffransham capellanus impedivit Dominum Regem de tolneto suo . quod dicunt quod emit bladum suum extra villam Norwici et facit illud bladum cariari noctanter ad domum suam per quod Ballivi amittunt tolnetum suum. Item dicunt quod predictus Johannes capellanus est usurarius maximus . . . . Item dicunt quod Johannes le Man appropriavit sibi viam communem per quandam schoppam quam fecit iniuste . .

ADHUC LETA [DE] CUNESFORD DIE MARTIS[1] PROXIME SEQUENTIS ANNO REGNI REGIS E. OTTAVODECIMO.

Parochie Sc̃i Vedasti—Sc̃i Petri de Cunesford—Sc̃e Marie parve—et Sc̃i Cuthberti.

Willelmus filius Walteri le Tanur
Willelmus de Irstede
Galfridus de Lingwode
Willelmus de Lok } jur'

Johannes le Lindraper
Rogerus le Marechal
Nicholaus le Marechal
Gregorius Croyde } jur'

Johannes filius Matildis de Surlingham
Alexander del Sartryn
Hugo de Rokelund
Johannes de Hakeford } jur'

[1] 21 Feb. 12$\frac{43}{50}$.

The Jurors present that John the Redepriest wrongfully raised the hue on Henry the Clerk. Also they say that the same John is guilty of the murder of a male child begotten of his concubine (let him be arrested). . . . Also they say that Roger Wortes and his wife of habit raise the hue wrongfully upon their neighbours to the terror of all their neighbours and to the great scandal of the whole people. . . . Also they say that Cecilia, the wife of John Lomb, has stolen from the parson of St. Michael eight silver marks (arrest). . . . Also they say that Richard, son of Alice Bele, stole from Robert de Hadiscoe 18½ d. by night on the morrow of St. Peter in chains in the seventeenth year of the reign of the King now (arrest). . . . Also they say that John de Fransham, chaplain, has hindered the lord king of his toll, for they say that he buys his corn outside the town of Norwich and has it carried by night to his house, whereby the Bailiffs lose their toll. Also they say that the said John, the chaplain, is an excessive usurer. . . . Also they say that John le Man has appropriated to himself a common way by a shop which he has wrongfully made. . . .

MORE OF THE LEET OF CONESFORD ON THE TUESDAY NEXT FOLLOWING IN THE 18TH YEAR OF THE REIGN OF KING EDWARD.

[N. Conesford]
Parishes of St. Vedast—St. Peter de Conesford—St. Mary the Less—and St. Cuthbert.

William, son of Walter the Tanner, and William de Irstead and Geoffrey de Lingwood and William de Leek, sworn; John the Linendraper and Roger the Farrier and Nicholas the Farrier and Gregory Croyde, sworn John, son of Matilda de Surlingham, and Alexander de Sarterin and Hugh de Rockland and John de Hackford, sworn.

Semanus le Agulyer pro maximo contemptu quia
noluit jurare ... in mīā ...   condon^r
Laurentius de Burlingham pro eodem ...   condon^r

Jurati[1] presentant per sacramentum suum quod ....
fratres minores appropriaverunt sibi plura tenementa que
solebant dare Domino Regi langabulum. Presentant quod
fratres Scī Augustini appropriaverunt eis similiter. Presentant etiam quod Nicholaus Tepede fecit quandam purpresturam cum quadam domo super Tepeystathe et cum
quodam calceto posito super Ripam Domini Regis bene per
octo pedes et amplius.

. . . .

[1] *Jurati* is here written in full. Elsewhere only the contraction *Jur'* is found.

Seman, the Needler for gross contempt because he refused to take the oath, in mercy, excused.

Laurence de Burlingham for the same, excused.

The Jurors present on their oath that . . . the Friars Minors have appropriated to themselves several tenements which were wont to pay landgable to the lord king. The Friars of St. Augustine likewise. They present also that Nicholas Tepede has made a purpresture with a house at Teppaystaith and with a causeway set full on to the river of the lord king by eight feet and more.

. . . .

IV. [1][ROTULUS AMERCIAMENTORUM AD
LETAS NORWICI A° R' REGIS ED-
WARDI XIX°.]

[2]AMERCIAMENTA AD LETAM ULTRA AQUAM ANNO REGNI
REGIS EDWARDI XIX°.

. . . .

De Rogero le bald quia furatus est tres pecias tannatas (cap). . . . . De Henrico Grund quia receptavit Adam fratrem eius qui non est in decenna (xij d.) . . . . De Priore Norwyci quia pascit porcos suos super murum [3] Domini Regis (dī. mr.) De Magistro del Spitellond pro eodem (dī. mr.) De Rogero de Stratton quia fecit quendam murum super terram Elemosinarii [4] (xij d.) De Ricardo de Wolterton capellano quia fecit quendam murum super terram Walteri de Scā ffide (ij s.) . . . . De Willelmo Bissop quia appropriavit sibi quandam ildam que debet esse communis apud Calkmilles (ij s.) . . . . [5] De Radulpho de Hevingham quia conclavit quod Ricardus de Wolterton capellanus traxit Willelmum le Lumynur in curiam Christianitatis de rebus etc. (vj d.)
. . . .

. . . .

[1] Roll IV.—A long Roll similar to No. II.
[2] The Leets in this Roll are entered in reverse order, which is very unusual.
[3] 'Murus' is here used for 'fossatum,' the earthen bank with a ditch which had been made in 1253. The stone wall afterwards built on it was not begun till 1294.
[4] Of the Cathedral Priory.
[5] The Capital Pledges for the first sublect Over-the-Water.

IV. [LEET ROLL OF 19 EDWARD I. 129⁰⁄₁].

AMERCEMENTS AT THE LEET OVER-THE-WATER IN THE 19TH YEAR OF THE REIGN OF KING EDWARD.

. . . .

Of Roger the bald because he stole three tanned pieces (arrest). . . . . Of Henry Grund because he has harboured Adam his brother who is not in tithing (12 d.) . . . . Of the Prior of Norwich because he feeds his pigs on the lord king's wall (half a mark). . . . . Of the Master of the Spital-land for the same (half a mark). Of Roger de Stratton because he has made a wall on the land of the Almoner (12 d.) Of Richard de Wolterton chaplain because he has made a wall on the land of Walter de St. Faith (2 s.) . . . . Of William Bishop because he has appropriated to himself a certain island which ought to be common, at Calkmills (2 s.) . . . . Of Ralph de Hevingham because he has concealed that Richard de Wolterton chaplain drew William the Limner into the Court Christian touching things etc. (6 d.) [13 other jurors amerced 6 d. each.]

38   AMERCIAMENTA AD LETAS NORWICI.

[1] Rescu le Jur de S. Winewalle par la mein ppers   xxvj s.
Item Petrus die Sabbati prox. sequentis   .   . xvij s.
Item Petrus die Sabbati prox. sequentis   .   . viij s.
Item per manum eiusdem Petri die Sabbati.   . iiij s.
Item per manum eiusdem .   .   .   .   . xxvj d.
        Item solvit   .   x d.

DE PRESENTATIONIBUS[2] DE WYMER ET WESTWYK—
        LETA DE WYMER.

De Willelmo Crysp quia recepit unum bussellum ordei quem filia sua furata fuit (ij s.) . . . . De Johanne de Causton quia permittit homines forinsecos mercandizare secrete infra seldam suam contra libertatem Civitatis Norwyci per quod Ballivi amittunt custumam (ij s.) . . . . De mercatoribus de Clakston[3] quia tendunt pannos suos contra libertatem etc. . . . . De Matilde de Blo quia receptat latrones (cap^r.) . . . . De Rogero de Lenn quia dubbat veteres pannos cum trunco fullonis faciendo falsitatem in opere (iij s.) . . . . De Hugone qui duxit in uxorem Aliciam quondam uxorem Richeri Alunday quia non est in decenna (ij s.) . . . . De Thoma de Dunham quia usurarius est (ij s.)

De Willelmo filio Ranulphi le pessoner quia non est in decenna (xij d.) De Huberto fratre eiusdem pro eodem (xij d.) De Coco eiusdem pro eodem (xij d.) De Tabernario eiusdem pro eodem (xij d.) De eodem Ranulpho pro recettamento eorundem (dī. mr̄.)

[1] March 3, 10, 17, 24. March 3rd was the Saturday before Lent. This is the only piece of French in the Rolls.
[2] No distinction is made in this and some other Rolls between presentments and amercements.
[3] A village seven miles east of Norwich. Part of the ground now called Chapel Field in the parish of

Received on St. Winwaloy's day by the hand of
Peter . . . . 26 s.
Item Peter [pays] on the Saturday next following . 17 s.
Item Peter [pays] on the Saturday next following . 8 s.
Item by the hand of the same Peter on Saturday . 4 s.
Item by the hand of the same . . . . 26 d.
      Item he pays . 10 d.

OF THE PRESENTMENTS OF WYMER AND WESTWICK—
LEET OF WYMER.

Of William Crisp because he received a bushel of barley which his daughter stole (2 s.) . . . . Of John de Causton because he permits foreigners to merchandise secretly within his shed contrary to the liberty of the city of Norwich, whereby the bailiffs lose their custom (2 s.) . . . . Of the merchants of Claxton because they stretch their cloths contrary to the liberty etc. . . . . Of Matilda de Blo for harbouring thieves (arrest). . . . . Of Roger de Lynn because he dubs old cloths with a fuller's block, so making fraud in his work (3 s.) . . . . Of Hugh who married Alice, formerly wife of Richer Alunday, because he is not in tithing (2 s.) . . . . Of Thomas de Dunham because he is a usurer (2 s.)

Of William, son of Ranulph the fishmonger, because he is not in tithing (12 d.) Of Hubert his brother for the same (12 d.) Of the cook of the said Ranulph for the same (12 d.) Of the taverner of the said Ranulph for the same (12 d.) Of the said Ranulph[1] for harbouring them (half a mark).

St. Giles was at this time occupied by owners of tenting frames (S. and L. p. 21).

[1] Observe the size of this fishmonger's household, including a cook-shop and a tavern.

Recepta per manum Luce die S̄c̄ī Wynewaloy de
Leta de Wymer . . . . x s.
Lucas solvit die Sabbati prox. ante festum S̄c̄ī
Gregorii . . . . xiiij s.
Item per manum Luce die Sabbati prox. sequentis j marc.
Item per manum eiusdem die Sabbati prox. se-
quentis . . . . v s.
Item per manum eiusdem . . . . . xxx d.
Item per manum eiusdem . . . . . xviij d.

. . . .

De Tannatoribus.

De Ricardo de Stalham quia facit falsitatem in opere tannando correos suos cum cortice fraxineo . et vocatur Stalsitelether . et quia habent Gildam [1] nocentem Domino Regi in emendis correis, et quia corigant [*sic*] transgressiones que debent placitari coram Ballivis (j marc.)

. . . .

. . . .

[LETA DE] MANECROFT.

. . . .

De Galfrido le Pasteman quia recepit filium suum extra decennam (xij d.) . . . . De Willelmo Hope quia manet extra civitatem Norwyci et est dealbator correorum (ij s.) . . . . De uxore Ricardi Puttok pro thesauro invento in foro Norwyci (xij d.) De Waltero Jolyf pro redemptione latrocinii (cap[r].) De eodem Waltero pro diversione cuiusdam aque (ij s.) . . . . De Rogero le ffevere pro transgressione facta Johanni de Swerdeston (xij d.) . . . . De uxore Henrici Costinoble quia vendit lagenam ad duos denarios (xx s.) [2] . . . .

. . . .

[1] See Introduction, Note B.
[2] No reason is given for this very heavy amercement. Henry Costinoble was a goldsmith. The surname is a corruption of 'de Constantinople.'

Receipts by the hand of Luke on St. Winwaloy's
day from the Leet of Wymer . . . . 10 s.
Luke pays on the Saturday next before the feast
of St. Gregory . . . . . . 14 s.
Item by the hand of Luke on the Saturday next
following . . . . 1 mark.
Item by the hand of the same on the Saturday
next following . . . . 5 s.
Item by the hand of the same . . . . 30 d.
Item by the hand of the same . . . . 18 d.

Of the Tanners.

Of Richard de Stalham because he makes fraud in his work by tanning his hides with bark of ash—and it is called Stalsitelether—and because they have a gild hurtful to the lord king in buying hides, and because they correct transgressions which ought to be pleaded before the bailiffs (1 mark). [42 others, half a mark each; 6 others, 4 s.; 1, 3 s.]

[LEET OF] MANECROFT.

Of Geoffrey the pastyman because he has harboured his son out of tithing (12 d.) . . . . Of William Hope because he lodges outside the city of Norwich and is a whitener of hides (2 s.) Of the wife of Richard Puttock for treasure found in Norwich Market (12 d.) Of Walter Jolyf for redemption of larceny (arrest). Of the same Walter for the diversion of a watercourse (2 s.) . . . . Of Roger the smith for making trespass on John de Swerdeston [1] (12 d.) . . . . Of the wife of Henry Costinoble because she sells a gallon for twopence (20 s.) . . . .

---

[1] A serjeant and collector. See next page.

Johannes de Swerdeston solvit die Sabbati ante
festum Scī Gregorii de leta de Manecroft . . xxj s.

. . . .

Amerciamenta Cocorum . . . . De fforstallatoribus . . . .
Soluta per manus Willelmi Stanhard et Walteri
Hibil die Sabbati in vigilia Annunciationis beate
Marie . . . . xv s.
Soluta per manum eiusdem die Sabbati prox. se-
quentis . . . . xjs.ixd.

LETA DE CONESFORD ET BERSTRETE.

. . . .

De Roberto capellano manente in parochia Scī Bartholomei
quia intravit domum Claricie atte Grene in hamsok (iij s.)
. . . . De Henrico Gylur quia recepit Edmundum filium
suum fugientem (ij s.) . . . . De Johanne ffenning quia
fecit iniustam semitam ultra terras pertinentes ad ca-
pellam Scī Wynewaloy (xij d.) . . . . De Johanne Canum
quia emit duas summas frumenti ad unum molendinum
aquaticum per quod etc. (ij s., solvit xij d.) . . . . De
Roberto de Bergh carpentario manupasto Priorisse de
Carhowe quia emit bladum antequam etc. (xij d.) . . . .
De Thoma Jyce clerico pro transgressione facta Waltero
de Burtof (xij d.) . . . . De Edmundo Gylur quia fregit
domum Johannis de Berstrete capellani (cap :). De Johanne le Chaluner pro eodem (cap :). De Gocelina Kade
de Clakeston quia assueta est furari catalla (cap :). . . . .
De Willelmo Hervy serviente Galfridi de Bintre quia
furatus fuit unam Cumbam ordey (cap :). . . . . De Cle-
mente le Agulyer quia receptavit unam Camysiam furatam (ij s., solvit vj d.) . . . . De Waltero de Lenn quia
habet bussellum de stramine (ij s., solvit iiij d.) De
Rogero le Bakestere quia emit et vendit tanquam concivis.
De eodem Rogero quia emit cum quadam mensura de

John de Swerdeston pays on the Saturday before
the feast of St. Gregory from the Leet of Manecroft   21 s.
[Also on four following Saturdays 16 s., 4 s. 10 d.,
4 s., 18 d.; and afterwards 4 s. 10 d.]

Amercements of the Cooks . . . . Of Forestallers. . . . .
Paid by the hands of William Stanhard and
Walter Hibil on Saturday being the vigil of
the Annunciation of the Blessed Mary .   . 15 s.
Paid by the hand of the same on the Saturday
next following   .   .   .   .   .   . 11 s. 9 d.

LEET OF CONESFORD AND BERSTRETE.

Of Robert the chaplain, lodging in the parish of St. Bartholomew, because he entered the house of Claricia Attegrene in hamsoken (3 s.) . . . . Of Henry Gylur because he harboured his son Edmund when a fugitive (2 s.) . . . . Of John Fenning because he made a wrongful footpath beyond the lands pertaining to the chapel of St. Winwaloy (12 d.) . . . . Of John Canon because he bought two loads of wheat at a water mill, whereby etc. (2 s., paid 12 d.) . . . . Of Robert de Burgh, carpenter, mainpast of the Prioress of Carrow, because he bought corn before etc. (12 d.) . . . . Of Thomas Jyce, clerk, for making trespass on Walter de Burtoft (12 d.) . . . . Of Edmund Gylur because he broke open the house of John de Berstrete, chaplain (arrest). Of John the chaloner for the same (arrest). Of Goceline Kade of Claxton because she is wont to steal chattels (arrest). . . . . Of William Hervy, servant of Geoffrey de Bintry, because he stole a coomb of barley (arrest). . . . . Of Clement the needler because he received a stolen shirt (2 s., paid 6 d.) . . . . Of Walter de Lynn because he has a bushel of straw (2 s., paid 4 d.) Of Roger the baker because he buys and sells like a fellow-citizen. Of the said Roger because

AMERCIAMENTA AD LETAS NORWICI.

stramine (dī. mř., solvit xij d.) .... De Alexandro Pouel quia fecit vetitum namium[1] servientibus Ballivorum (ij s.) .... De Ricardo clerico ecclesie Scī Petri de Parmentergate quia non est in decenna (xij d.)

. . . .

Recepta Petri le Rus die Sabbati prox. post festum Scī Gregorii Pape. Soluta per manum eiusdem eodem die. . . . . viij s.
&c. . &c.

---

[1] This is always written *vetitum namium*, not *namii*. See Glossary.

he buys with a measure of straw (half a mark, paid
12 d.) . . . . Of Alexander Powel because he made vé
de naam against the serjeants of the bailiffs (2 s.) . . . .
Of Richard, the clerk of the church of St. Peter de Parmentergate,[1] because he is not in tithing (12 d.)

. . . .

Receipts of Peter le Rus on the Saturday next after
the feast of St. Gregory the Pope. Paid by the
hand of the same on the same day . . . . 8 s.

[1] See Introduction, X. 11.

V. [ROTULUS AMERCIAMENTORUM AD LETAS NORWICI A° R' REGIS EDWARDI XXI°.]

¹AMERCIAMENTA LETE DE CONESFORD ANNO REGNI REGIS EDWARDI FILII REGIS HENRICI XXI°.

. . . .

De Johanne de ffranshan capellano pro forstallo et vetito namio facto Ballivis (dī. mř.) . . . . De hominibus de Surlingham ² quia habent retia contra assissam cum quibus capiunt ffry et destruunt ripam Domini Regis (dī. mř.) De piscatoribus Prioris Norwyci pro eodem (dī. mř.) . . . . De Fratribus de Scō Augustino quia fecerunt purpresturam in vico de [Conesford] inferiori per quendam murum super Cokeye positum bene per viginti pedes in longitudinem et in latitudinem per tres pedes (—) . . . . De Martino le Belleyetere quia receptat quendam garcionem extra decennam (xij d.) . . . . De Thoma Molle quia fregit parvum pontem de Cokeye et asportavit bordas et meremium predicti pontis (xij d.) . . . . De Olyva le Orfevre quia vendit cervisiam cum chipho (dī. mř.) . . . .
De Sutoribus quia habent Gildam contra defensionem Domini Regis eo quod capiunt de apprenticiis suis duos

¹ A Roll of Amercements with the membranes fastened lengthwise.
² On the River Wensum, or Yare, about ten miles below Norwich. The jurisdiction of the Bailiffs and Coroner of Norwich extended as far as Breydon Water, near Yarmouth, the river all the way being then called the Wensum, not the Yare as it is now. (Customs Ch. 9; 'De submersis in aqua Norwici et communi Ripa usque ad aquam de Breything . . . fiat visus corone,' etc.)

V. [LEET ROLL OF 21 EDWARD I. 129⅔.]

AMERCEMENTS OF THE LEET OF CONESFORD IN THE 21st YEAR OF THE REIGN OF KING EDWARD, SON OF KING HENRY.

. . . .

Of John de Fransham, chaplain, for forestalment and vé de naam done against the bailiffs (half a mark). . . . . Of the men of Surlingham because they have nets contrary to the assize, with which they catch fry and destroy the lord king's river (half a mark). Of the fishermen of the Prior of Norwich for the same (half a mark) . . . . Of the Friars of St. Augustine because they have made a purpresture in the street of Nether Conesford by a wall set full on to the Cockey by twenty feet in length and three feet in breadth (—) . . . . Of Martin the bellfounder because he harbours a groom out of tithing (12 d.) . . . . Of Thomas Molle because he broke the small bridge of the Cockey and carried away the boards and timber of the said bridge (12 d.) . . . . Of Olyva the goldsmith [1] because she sells beer with a ciphe (half a mark).

Of the cobblers because they have a gild contrary to the prohibition [2] of the lord king, whereby they take of their

---

[1] This is the same as the 'wife of Henry Costinoble' amerced in the previous Roll in the Leet of Manecroft. She resided almost certainly in that Leet in Hosyergate, and in this Roll she is again amerced half a mark in the Leet of Manecroft for breaking the assize of ale. This offence may have been committed against a resident in the Leet of Conesford.

[2] See Introduction, Note B.

Solidos et de hiis [*sic*] qui exerceant officium sutoris per se dant decem solidos predicte Gilde (xx s.) De Sellariis quia habent similiter Gildam nocentem Domino Regi (j mr̄.) De Fullonibus pro eodem (dī. mr̄.) De Rogero de Coreston quia suffodit terram Willelmi de Kirkby et Willelmi le Pundreys infra metas et bundas inter eos positas (ij s.) .... De Johanne Petyt de Morlee quia fecit bladum Galfridi fratris sui ducere de dunston per carectam usque Norwycum et illud advocat tanquam suum proprium per quod Ballivi etc. (dī. mr̄.) De uxore Johannis le Ballif pro assissa cervisie fracta et non observata (vj d., solvit iij d., quieta est)..... De Avicia de Staunford pro eodem (xij d., cond: ad instantiam Henrici Clerici)..... De uxore Johannis le man pro eodem (xij d., cond: quia non braciat)..... De uxore Hugonis le carectere pro eodem (xij d., cond: quia non braciat).

. . . .

Soluta per manus Ranulphi Belle die sabbati
  prox. post festum Sc̄i Gregorii [1] . . . xv s. vj d.
Item soluta per manus Belle die sabbati prox. vj s.
Item soluta per manus eiusdem liberato G.
  clerico [2] . . . . ij s. vj d.
Item soluta per manus eiusdem . . . xviij d.

INCIPIUNT PRESENTATIONES LETE DE NEDHAM ET MANECROFT.

. . . .

De Stephano quondam serviente Willelmi de Totham quia habet quandam carectam euntem cum mercandizis suis tanquam concivis noster nec est de libertate (dī. mr̄.)

---

[1] 14 March, the fifth Saturday in Lent.
[2] One of the Bailiffs at this time was Galfridus Clericus or Kempe. The entry occurs in a similar manner in all the four Leets. The word *libato* in each case is clearly written. Perhaps some such words as 'In argento' may be understood.

apprentices 2 s., and those who carry on the business of
a cobbler on their own account give 10 s. to the said gild
(20 s.) Of the saddlers because they likewise have a gild
hurtful to the lord king (1 mark). Of the fullers for the
same (half a mark).
Of Roger de Causton because he digs the ground of William de Kirkby and William le Pundreys within the metes
and bounds between them set (2 s.) . . . . Of John Petyt
of Morley because he has had the corn of Geoffrey his
brother led from Dunston to Norwich by cart and avows
it for his own, whereby the bailiffs etc. (half a mark).
Of the wife of John the Bailiff for breaking the assize of
ale and not observing it (6 d., paid 3 d., quit.) . . . . Of
Avice de Stamford for the same (12 d., excused at the
request of Henry the clerk). Of the wife of John le Man
for the same (12 d., excused because she does not brew).
. . . . Of the wife of Hugh the carter for the same (12 d.,
(excused because she does not brew).

. . . .

Paid by the hands of Ranulph Belle on the Saturday next after the feast of St. Gregory . . 15 s. 6 d.
Item paid by the hands of Belle on the Saturday next . . . . 6 s.
Item paid by the hands of the same, delivered to Geoffrey the clerk . . . . . 2 s. 6 d.
Item paid by the hands of the same . . 18 d.

HERE BEGIN THE PRESENTMENTS OF THE LEET OF
NEDHAM AND MANECROFT.

. . . .

Of Stephen, formerly servant of William de Totham, because he has a cart which goes with goods as if he were
our fellow-citizen, and he is not of the freedom (half a

.... De Hugone Lekman¹ quia habet societatem cum quibusdam mercandizis cum quodam serviente suo et illa bona advocat tanquam sua propria per quod etc. (dī. mr̄.) De eodem Hugone quia receptat eundem servientem extra decennam (ij s.)

. . . .

INCIPIUNT PRESENTATIONES DE WYMER ET WESTWYK ANNO XXI°.

. . . .

De Nicholao Blakberd et Willelmo de Pangesford quia detinent duodecim denarios de langabulo Domini Regis de quadam insula sita in Ripa Domini Regis (dī. mr̄.) . . . . De Radulpho Gyn pro concelamento eo quod concelavit [quod] Johannes filius capellani asportavit meremium de domo que fuit quondam Galfridi Sewale (xij d., pauper). . . . . De Thoma Decano Norwyci quia fecit purpresturam super fossatum Domini Regis in Norwyco imponendo ibi arbores appropriando sibi terram. Et quia fecit ibi quandam pallaciam similiter (dī. mr̄.) . . . . De Martino de Tudenham pro falsa presentatione eo quod presentavit quod quedam mulier que vocatur Lecia occidit Olivam de Hemelington . que quidem presentatio non fuit advocata de decennariis suis nec de capitali plegio (ij s.) De Ricardo de Ho pro eodem (ij s.) De Radulpho Russell pro eodem (ij s.) . . . . De Johanne filio Johannis de Schotesham quia emit quendam pannum furatum pretii sex denariorum et noluit dicere warrantum suum de quo emit quia filum lane predicti panni furatum fuit ad domum Ade Ston (ij s.) . . . . De Johanne Brid de Gernemutha quia forbarravit Ripam Domini Regis cum quadam barrera ita quod caballi non possunt habere

---

¹ A 'Leekman' was a dealer in herbs. One of the market rows in the 13th century was called the 'Lekmarket,' the market for leeks or herbs. It adjoined the Apothecaria, the herbs being mostly used for medicinal purposes. In Roll XI., p. 71, it has become a surname, and the equivalent 'gardener' is added to it.

mark). . . . . . Of Hugh the gardener because he has
partnership[1] in certain goods with a servant of his and
avows those goods as his own, whereby the bailiffs etc.
(half a mark). Of the same Hugh because he harbours
the said servant out of tithing (2 s.)

. . . .

HERE BEGIN THE PRESENTMENTS OF WYMER AND
WESTWICK IN THE 21st YEAR.

. . . .

Of Nicholas Blackbird and William de Panxford because
they withhold twelve pence of the lord king's landgable
from a certain island situate in the lord king's river
(half a mark). . . . . Of Ralph Gyn for concealment, for
that he concealed that John, son of the chaplain, carried
off timber from the house which was formerly Geoffrey
Sewale's (12 d., poor). . . . Of Thomas, Dean of Norwich,
because he made a purpresture on the lord king's ditch
planting trees there and so appropriating land, and because
he has made a fence there likewise (half a mark). . . . .
Of Martin de Tudenham for false presentment, for that
he presented that a certain woman who is called Lecia
killed Oliva de Hemblington, which presentment was not
avowed by her [2] decennaries nor by the capital pledge (2 s.)
Of Richard de Howe and Ralph Russell for the same
(2 s. each). . . . . Of John, son of John de Shottisham,
because he bought a stolen cloth of the value of 6 d., and
declined to vouch his warrant from whom he bought it,
because the woollen yarn of the said cloth was stolen at
Adam Stone's house (2 s.) . . . . Of John Bird of Yarmouth because he has forbarred the lord king's river
with a bar, so that horses cannot have their easements

---

[1] The 39th chapter of Norwich
Customs forbids a citizen to receive
his 'serviens' into partnership in
making, buying, or selling until he
has solemnly made his entry and
become 'par civitatis.' The penalty
is fixed at 40 s. That chapter probably belongs to a generation later
than this Roll. The offence is that
two persons are reaping the profits
of trade, only one of whom bears the
burdens of citizenship.

[2] Or *his*. See some remarks on
this entry in Introduction, IV. 4.

aysiamenta sua sicut soliti fuerunt (xij d.) . . . . De Roberto de Wymundham leyner quia refutat mensuram Domini Regis rasam et non wult recipere eam nisi sit cumulatam [1] (ij s.) . . . . De Willelmo Pawe pro receptamento cuiusdam supertunice quam filia sua furata fuit de domo sua (—). . . . . De Rogero le Skeppere quia fecit vetitum namium [2] servientibus Ballivorum (xij d., solvit iij d., et quietus est). . . . . De Ida Bele pro assissa cervisie non observata (xij d., cond: quia tenet assissam).

. . . .

DE PRESENTATIONIBUS LETE ULTRA AQUAM.

. . . .

De Willelmo Bischop quia deforciat communem populum Civitatis Norwyci ita quod non possint defalcare quandam insulam pertinentem communitati et herbas ibidem coligere sicut soliti fuerunt (dī. mř.) . . . . De Johanne Bischop quia emit et vendit per talliam nec est de libertate (ij s., et fecit finem per xij d. et habet diem ad faciendum introitum a die Pasche in unum mensem). De quodam capellano serviente apud Normanspitellond quia verberavit servientes Ballivorum Norwyci et virgas suas fregerunt [1] (cond.) De Johanne Tutte . Johanne Knicht . Galfrido de Scā ffide . Willelmo Palefreyman pro eodem (condonantur). . . . . De Thoma Spik quia cepit mercedem de Ricardo Cluhoth qui furatus fuit unum correum vaccinum pretii quatuor solidorum de predicto Thoma et postea receptavit eundem Ricardum (—, debet). . . . . De Ricardo le Redde quia procuravit implacitari Willelmum le luminur in curia Christianitatis (ij s.) . . . . De Ricardo de Senges quia habet fimerum nocentem (xij d., fecit finem pro v s. pro omnibus etc). [3]

. . . .

---

[1] Sic in MS.
[2] MS. namiū.
[3] Just below his wife is amerced

2 s. for breaking the assize of ale. No other offences of his are presented in this Roll.

as they were wont (12 d.) .... Of Robert de Wymondham, woolman, because he refuses the lord king's measure when bare and will not take it unless it is heaped up (2 s.) ... Of William Pawe for receiving a stolen surcoat which his daughter stole from his house (—)..... Of Roger the basketmaker because he made vé de naam against the serjeants of the bailiffs (12 d., he paid 3 d. and is quit) .... Of Ida Bele (for not observing the assize of ale (12 d., excused because she keeps the assize).

. . . .

OF THE PRESENTMENTS OF THE LEET OVER-THE-WATER.

. . . .

Of William Bishop because he deforces the common people of the City of Norwich so that they cannot mow a certain island belonging to the commonalty and gather the grass there as they were wont (half a mark). .... Of John Bishop because he buys and sells by tally and is not of the freedom (2 s., and he made fine with 12 d., and he has a day to make his entry within one month from Easter). .... Of a certain chaplain serving at Normanspitel-land because he beat the serjeants of the Bailiffs of Norwich and broke their wands (excused). Of John Tutte, John Knight, Geoffrey de St. Faith, William Palfreyman, for the same (excused). .... Of Thomas Spik because he took reward of Richard Cluhoth who stole an ox-hide of the value of 4 s. from the said Thomas and afterwards harboured the said Richard (—, owing). .... Of Richard the Red because he procured that William the limner should be impleaded in the Court Christian (2 s.) .... Of Richard de Seething (because he has a noxious muck-heap (12 d., he made fine with 5 s. for all offences).[1]

. . . .

[1] The Roll closes with a long list of amercements of fishmongers, cooks, poulterers, for forestalling, and of tanners for having a gild etc., all as in Roll III.

VI. [ROTULUS AMERCIAMENTORUM AD LETAS NORWICI A° R' REGIS EDWARDI XXIIII°.]

[1] PRESENTATIONES LETE DE CONESFORD ET BERSTRETE ANNO XXIIIJ°.

. . . .

De Domino Petro Roscelin pro purprestura facta super Dominum Regem appropriando sibi quendam Rivulum qui vocatur Dallingflette per quendam murum ibidem positum (—) . . . . De Adam Benediscite quia appropriavit sibi terram Domini Regis in Conesford per stapellos et truncos ibidem positos (ij s.)

De Margareta de Brundale quia vendit cervisiam cum quadam olla de terra que non est de assissa Domini Regis (ij s.)

. . . .

Willelmus Stedefast reddit compotum primo
    die sabbati post medium quadragesime . xxxij s. viij d.
           et extra rotulum . . xviij d.
           etc. . etc.

PRESENTACIONES DE NEDHAM ET MANECROFT.

. . . .

De Johanne de Nelond pro defalta quia non venit (xij d.)
. . . . De Waltero Heghe quia habet truncum fullonis

---

[1] Roll VI. - A similar Roll to the last.

VI. [LEET ROLL OF 24 EDWARD I. 129⅝.]

PRESENTMENTS OF THE LEET OF CONESFORD AND BERSTRETE IN THE 24TH YEAR.

. . . .

Of Sir Peter Roscelin for making a purpresture on the lord king by appropriating to himself a streamlet called Dallingfleet by a wall there set (—). . . . . Of Adam Benedicite because he has appropriated to himself the ground of the lord king in Conesford by stakes and blocks there set (2 s.)

Of Margaret de Brundall because she sells beer with an earthen pot which is not according to the lord king's assize (2 s.)

. . . .

William Steadfast renders account on the first Saturday [1] after Midlent . . . . . 32 s. 8d.
        and outside of the roll . . . 18 d.
        etc., etc.

PRESENTMENTS OF NEDHAM AND MANECROFT.

. . . .

Of John de Nelond for default because he did not come (12 d.) [Thirteen other persons amerced ' for the same,' 12 d. each]. Of Walter Eye because he has a fuller's

[1] March 3.

faciendo falsitatem in opere (ij s.) . . . . De Thoma de
Aylesham pro purprestura facta super Dominum Regem
per quoddam calcetum positum prope pontis [*sic*] de
Cokeye (iij s.) De uxore Galfridi de Costeseye quia vendit
cervisiam contra communem proclamationem, videlicet
unam Lagenam cervisie pro duobus denariis et quod
vendit cervisiam cum duabus mensuris (ij s.) . . . . De
Ranulpho le Pessoner quia obviando ivit extra villam sub
Carehowe et ibi emebat unum batellum plenum piscium
contra communem proclamationem a cariorando forum
Norwyci (j mř.) De Roberto Suffold pro falsitate facta
etc. . vendendo oleum unius nature pro oleo alterius
nature (iiij s.) De Rogero Chaumpanye quia vendit
vitrum [1] mixtum cum vertegrez et arguel mixtum cum
fecibus vini (dī. mř.)

. . . .

Ricardus serviens reddit compotum suum die
   sabbati in festo Scī Wynnewaloy . . . j mř.
Item per manus eiusdem Ricardi secundo die . xlj s. ix d.
      et extra rotulum . . v s.
        etc.

PRESENTATIONES· DE WIMER ET WESTWYK.

. . . .

De Johanne de Weston quia suffodit terricidias de fossato
Norwyci exaltando calcetum tente sue (ij s.) . . . . De
Johanne de Scotia quia habet fenestras ad modum ap-
penticie nocentes equitantibus (dī. mř.) . . . . De Johanne Trukke de ffibrigge quia emebat unam vaccam
submersam in aqua et eam vendidit in foro Norwyci
per minimas particulas (iiij s.)
De Waltero de Berningham et tota decenna quia non venit
(xij d.) De Adam ffrend et tota decenna sua pro eodem
(iij s.) De decenna Nicholai filii Katerine pro eodem

[1] Materials used for dyeing or fulling.

block, so making fraud in his work (2 s.) . . . . Of Thomas de Aylsham for making a purpresture on the lord king by a causeway set by the Cockey bridge (3 s.) Of the wife of Geoffrey de Costessey because she sells beer contrary to the common proclamation—to wit, one gallon of beer for two pence and because she sells beer with two measures (2 s.) . . . . Of Ranulph the fishmonger because he went outside the town by Carrow to meet a boat full of fish and there he bought it contrary to the proclamation against heightening the market of Norwich (1 mark). Of Robert Suffield for making fraud etc., by selling oil of one kind for oil of another kind (4 s.) Of Roger Champanye because he sells woad mixed with verdigris and potter's clay mixed with lees of wine (half a mark).

. . . .

Richard the serjeant renders his account on
  Saturday being the feast of St. Winwaloy . 1 mark
Item by the hands of the said Richard on
  the second day [? Saturday] . . . 41 s. 9 d.
    And outside of the roll . . 5s.
      etc.

PRESENTMENTS OF WYMER AND WESTWICK.

. . . .

Of John de Weston because he digs turves out of the city ditch to raise the floor of his tenting-frame (2s.) . . . .
Of John de Scotia because he has windows in the fashion of a lean-to which are a nuisance to riders (half a mark).
. . . . Of John Trukke of Fibridge because he bought a drowned cow and sold it in Norwich market in little pieces (4 s.)
Of Walter de Barningham and his whole tithing[1] because he came not (12 d.) Of Adam Friend and his whole tithing for the same (8 s.) Of the tithing of Nicholas son of

---

[1] This is the only place in these Rolls where whole tithings are amerced.

(iij s.) De decenna Benedicti Berd quia non venit (iij s.) De Ricardo le Slopere et tota decenna sua quia non venit (ij s.) De Emma la Rede quia commiscuit allecia ostrea et alia mercimonia faciendo falsitatem vendendo predicta mercimonia extraneis hominibus (iij s., solvit vj d.) . . . . De Ricardo de Knapeton manente in Hospitali Sc͞i Egidii quia emit et vendit oleum et sotulares ad domum Ricardi de Grungelthorp nec est ad lottum et scottum [1] per quod etc. (iiij s.)

. . . .

DE PRESENTATIONIBUS ULTRA AQUAM.

. . . .

De Adam serviente Ricardi de Knapeton quia emit et vendit nec est de libertate (iiij s.) . . . . De persona de Eccles quia concelavit j denarium [? de] Jure Domini Regis (iiij s.) De Magistro Thoma de Depham pro eodem (iiij s.) . . . . De Johanne le Cartere quia emit et vendit cum catallis Johannis de Madelmarkette capellani ad dimidium lucri et ea advocat tanquam sua propria per quod etc. (iiij s.) . . . . De Willelmo de Attelburth quia emit et vendit tanquam concives [2] nec est de libertate (iiij s., condonatur quia cives [2] est). . . . . De Petro Pirmund pro purprestura facta super Dominum Regem per quandam liberam fletam in aqua inter ipsum et personam de Swanton (iiij s.) . . . . De Willelmo de Denham pro hamsok facta ad domum Alicie de Causton occidendo canem ipsius Alicie in domo sua (iiij s.) . . . . De Hugone clerico quia non est in decenna (ij s.) De Godefrido Tutte quia forbaravit forum ducendo mercatores secrete per singna ad domum suam emendo ab eisdem correa (iiij s.)

. . . .

---

[1] See Introduction, Note A. 4.   [2] Sic in MS.

Katherine for the same (3 s.)   Of the tithing of Benedict
Bird because he came not (3 s.)   Of Richard the slop-
seller and his whole tithing because he came not (2 s.)
Of Emma la Rede because she mixed herrings, oysters,
and other goods, so making fraud, and selling the said
goods to strangers (3 s., paid 6 d.) . . . . Of Richard de
Knapton, lodging in the Hospital of St. Giles, because he
buys and sells oil and shoes at the house of Richard de
Gringlethorp, and he is not at lot and scot, whereby
etc. (4 s.)

OF THE PRESENTMENTS OVER-THE-WATER.

Of Adam, servant of Richard de Knapton, because he buys
and sells and is not of the freedom (4 s.) . . . . Of the
parson of Eccles because he concealed one penny of the
right of the lord king (4 s.)   Of Master Thomas de
Deepham for the same (4 s.) . . . . Of John the Carter
because he buys and sells with the chattels of John de
Maddermarket, chaplain, going halves in the profit, and
avows them as his own, whereby etc. (4 s.) . . . . Of
William de Attleborough because he buys and sells as a fellow-citizen and is not of the freedom (4 s., excused because
he is a citizen). . . . . Of Peter Pirmund for making a purpresture on the lord king by a free fleet in the water
between himself and the parson of Swanton (4 s.) . . . .
Of William de Denham for making hamsoken at the
house of Alice de Causton and killing the said Alice's dog
in her house (4 s.) . . . . Of Hugh the clerk because he
is not in tithing (2 s.)   Of Godfrey Tutte because he forbarred the market, privily leading merchants by signs to
his house, and buying hides of them (4 s.)

De Ranulpho le Pessoner pro forstallo et forbarramento piscium in foro Norwyci et super Cayum de ffibrigge etc. (j marc̄).

. . . .

De Pulletariis . . . . De Regratariis Caseorum . . . . De Cocis . . . . De Braciatoribus . . . .

. . . .

De Mulieribus que faciunt Braseum.
De Margareta de Eston quia emit bladum antequam venit ad forum per quod etc. . . . . et quia emunt et vendunt nec sunt de libertate [1] (ij s.)

. . . .

De Tannatoribus . . . . quia habent Gildam nocentem Domino Regi.

. . . .

De hiis qui emunt filum lane in foro Norwyci et faciunt forstallum etc. . . . .

---

[1] Women were admitted to citizenship. A few cases occur in the earliest existing Assembly Roll, of 1365-1369.

[Here follow amercements of Ranulph and the other fishmongers, poulterers, regraters of cheese, and cooks, all as before, mostly the same persons: 61 fishmongers are amerced; 10 marked 'mortuus est'.]

[Then the brewers throughout the city.]

. . . .

Of women who make malt.

Of Margaret de Easton because she buys corn before it comes to the market, whereby etc. . . . . and because they buy and sell and are not of the freedom (2 s.)

[8 other women are amerced 2 s. each.]

. . . .

[Then the tanners for fraud and having a gild, as before.]

. . . .

Of those who buy woollen yarn in Norwich market and make forestalment.

[7 women, 2s. each.]

VII. [ROTULUS AMERCIAMENTORUM AD LETAS NORWICI A° R' REGIS EDWARDI XXVIII°.]

Afferatores {Matheus Thusceyns.
Rogerus de Batesford.
[1] Tempore Regis Edwardi filii Regis Henrici XXVIII°.

[2] PRESENTACIONES LETE DE CUNESFORD ANNO XXVIII°
TEMPORIBUS JOHANNIS CLERICI . ROGERI DE
TUDENHAM . SOCIORUMQUE EORUM.

De Willelmo filio Bartholomei de Redham quia stetit in Civitate Norwyci per annum et diem et non est in decenna (xij d.) De Galfrido de Matishale pro eodem (xij d., clericus). De Roberto de Daleby quia non habet pancllum [3] suum sicut debuit (xij d.). .... De omnibus pistoribus et Braciatoribus pro assissa fracta et quia pistores vendunt unum panem pro sterlingg et alium pro poll' [4] et sic faciunt duas assissas contra voluntatem Regis. De Braciatoribus quia vendunt unam lagenam servisie pro sterling et aliam pro poll'. De Tannatoribus quia faciunt falsitatem in opere videlicet dubbant corria bovina in fraudem totius populi Domini Regis. .... De Paulino Stanhard pro hamsok noctanter facta super Margaretam le Clerk (iiij s.) De Andrea de Virly (xij d.), Andrea de Colneye pro eodem (xij d.) .... De Margareta uxore Ri-

---

[1] Added by a later hand.
[2] Roll VII.—A long Roll of Amercements. On the Affeerers see Introd. IV. 6.
[3] Perhaps the list of Capital Pledges for his district.
[4] The use of these coins had been strictly prohibited by the 'Statutum

VII. [LEET ROLL OF 28 EDWARD I. $\frac{1299}{1300}$.]

Affeerers, Matthew Tusceyns, Roger de Batisford.
In the time of King Edward, son of King Henry, 28th [year].

PRESENTMENTS OF THE LEET OF CONESFORD IN THE 28TH YEAR, IN THE TIMES OF JOHN THE CLERK, ROGER DE TUDENHAM, AND THEIR FELLOWS.

Of William, son of Bartholomew de Reedham, because he has been in the city for a year and a day and is not in tithing (12 d.) Of Geoffrey de Mattishall for the same (12 d., clerk). Of Robert de Dalby because he has not his panel as he ought to have had (12 d.) . . . . Of all the bakers and brewers for breaking the assize and because the bakers sell one loaf for sterling and another for pollards and so make two assizes, contrary to the will of the king. Of the brewers because they sell one gallon of beer for sterling and another for pollards. Of the tanners because they make fraud in their work—to wit, dub oxhides to the defrauding of all the lord king's people. . . . . Of Pauline Stanhard for making hamsoken by night on Margaret le Clerk (4 s.) Of Andrew de Virly and Andrew de Colney for the same (12 d. each). . .
Of Margaret, wife of Richard the clerk, because she drew

de falsa moneta' in May of the year preceding this Leet. The city authorities, however, show no disposition either here or in the later Rolls to adopt so summary a reform

cardi clerici quia traxit sanguinem de Beatricia de Irstede (xij d., J. Clericus). . . . . De Ricardo le Combere quia recepit unam libram lane pretii vj den. furatam per unam feminam ingnotam (—). . . . . De Emma Pruding de Trous attornata uxoris Johannis Rodlond quia emit bladum ad opus dicte uxoris Johannis Rodlond antequam etc., per quod etc. (ij s.) De Willelmo Molendinario pro eodem (ij s.) De Johanne le Blekestere quia implacitavit Johannem le Newebrid in Curia Cristianitatis per quod Ballivi amittunt placita sua (dī. mī.) De Ranulpho Saluz quia procuravit predictum placitum (ij s.) De Johanne Canum quia extraxit bundas positas inter ipsum et Rogerum de Melton et obstuppavit viam predicti Rogeri[1] ita quod ipse non habet ingressum ad terram suam etc. (ij s.) . . . . De Thoma de Melton curlevage quia non est in decenna et quia facit se concivem (xij d.) De Braciatoribus de Conesford.

De uxore Alexandri del Sartrin pro assissa servisie non observata et quia vendit unam lagenam cervisie pro j sterling et aliam pro poll' et crok' et quia emit bladum antequam venit ad forum per quod Dominus Rex amittit custumam suam et quia recusat mensuram rasatam et quia advocat bona extraneorum tanquam propria per quod Dominus Rex etc. (ij s., solvit, quieta est). . . . . De uxore Willelmi de Keteringham pro eodem (ij s., condonatur quia serviens). . . . . De uxore Galfridi sutoris pro eodem (ij s., non braciat). . . . . De uxore Johannis de Weston pro eodem (ij s., Tudenham . Poringlond). . . . . De Clara de Toftes pro eodem (ij s., non braciat).

. . . .

Lucas solvit die Sabbati prox. ante clausum
pascha . . . . xij s.
Item die Sabbati prox. in festo Scī Georgii . . xxviij s.
Item idem eodem die de Incremento . . . vj s.
    Carcatur lx s. vj d.

[1] This, like many other offences presented, would surely in later times have been treated as a matter for redress by writ, not by presentment.

LEET ROLL OF 1299/1300. 51

blood of Beatrice de Irstede (12 d., John the clerk). . . . .
Of Richard the Comber because he received a pound of
wool, of the value of 6 pence, stolen by a woman unknown (—). . . . . Of Emma Pruding of Trowse, attorney
of the wife of John Rodland, because she buys corn to
the use of John Rodland's wife before etc., whereby
etc. (2 s.) Of William the miller for the same (2 s.) Of
John the Bleacher because he impleaded John le New-
bird in the Court Christian, whereby the Bailiffs lose their
pleas (half a mark). Of Ranulph Saluz because he procured the said plea (2 s.) Of John Canon because he has
removed the bounds set between himself and Roger de
Melton and has blocked Roger's way so that he has no
entry to his own land (2 s.) . . . . Of Thomas de Melton
curlevage because he is not in tithing and makes himself
a fellow-citizen (12 d.)
Of the brewers of Conesford.
Of the wife of Alexander del Sartrin for not observing the
assize of ale and because she sells one gallon of beer for
one penny sterling and another for pollards and crockards,
and because she buys corn before it comes to the market,
whereby the lord king loses his custom, and because she
refuses bare measure and because she avows the goods of
strangers as her own, whereby the lord king etc. (2 s.,
she paid it and is quit). . . . . Of the wife of William de
Keteringham for the same (2 s., excused because he is a
serjeant). . . . . Of the wife of Geoffrey the Cobbler for
the same (2 s., she does not brew). . . . . Of the wife of
John de Weston for the same (2 s., Tudenham, Poringland). . . . . Of Clara Toftes (2 s., she does not brew).

. . . . . .

Luke pays on the Saturday [1] next before the close
   of Easter .   .   .   . 12 s.
Item on Saturday being the feast of St. George . 28 s.
Item on the same day for increment .   .   . 6 s.
   He is charged with 60 s. 6 d.

[1] April 16th, 1300.

INCIPIT LETA DE NEDHAM ET MANECROFT.

. . . .

De Ricardo de Berton quia rapuit uxorem Willelmi Stedefast cum bonis mariti sui (—). De Willelmo Tolle quia vendit unum vitulum qui vocatur Gogge (iiij s.) . . . . De omnibus candelariis pro quadam convencione inter eos facta videlicet quod nullus eorum venderet libram candele minus quam alter. . . . . De Paulo Bendiste quia vendidit totum cepum suum hoc anno sine visitatione trone Domini Regis et quia vendidit corria sua secrete in domo (dī. mr̄.) . . . . De Johanne le palmer uno de capitalibus plegiis pro defalta (xij d.) De Roberto de Hikelingg pro eodem (xij d.) De Wyoto Quinton pro eodem (xij d.) De Johanne Bunthequel capitali plegio pro eodem (xij d.) . . . . De Galfrido de Brandon manupasto Ricardi de Snoringg quia non est in decenna (xij d.) De eodem Ricardo pro receptamento eiusdem (xij d.) . . . . De Nicholao de Banham pro thesauro invento videlicet unum[1] misericordem pretii xviij d. et non liberavit ballivis Regis (xij d.) . . . . De Johanne de Tacolston quia fugit contra letam (xij d.) . . . . De Johanne le pantermakere de Cantebrigg quia non est in decenna (xij d.) De Johanne serviente Galfridi le taverner et manupasto pro eodem (xij d.) De Galfrido le taverner pro receptamento eiusdem Johannis (xij d.) De Roberto le Barbur quia receptat quendam servientem suum extra decennam (xij d.) . . . . De Roberto de Wymundham quia habet unam falsam lagenam (iij s.) De Galfrido de Blafeld pro eodem de dimidia lagena (ij s.) . . . . De Johanne Taliur pro cloaca facta (iiij s.) . . . . De Rogero de Suthfeld quia imposuit servienti suo quod furatus fuit xviij den. sterlingg et postea ipsum retinuit quousque finem fecit cum eo de duobus solidis et retornavit predictum argentum (iij s.)

---

[1] MS. *unā misericord'*.

HERE BEGINS THE LEET OF NEDHAM AND
MANECROFT.

. . . .

Of Richard de Berton because he carried off the wife of William Steadfast with her husband's goods (—). Of William Tolle because he sold a calf called a gogge (4 s.) . . . . Of all the chandlers for making an agreement amongst themselves—to wit, that none of them should sell a pound of candle at less than another. [8 persons amerced.] Of Paul Benedicite because he has been selling all his tallow this year without using the lord king's beam, and because he has sold his hides privily in his house (half a mark). [14 others amerced.]
Of John the Palmer, one of the Capital Pledges, for default (12 d.) Of Robert de Hickling [and] Wyot Quinton for the same (12 d. each). Of John Bunthequel, a Capital Pledge, for the same (12 d.) . . . . Of Geoffrey de Brandon, mainpast of Richard de Snoring, because he is not in tithing (12 d.) Of the said Richard for harbouring him (12 d.) . . . . Of Nicholas de Banham for treasure trove—to wit, a dagger, of the value of 18 d., which he delivered not to the king's bailiffs (12 d.) . . . . Of John de Tacolneston because he fled to escape the leet (12 d.) . . . . . Of John de Cambridge the bird-snare-maker because he is not in tithing (12 d.) Of John, the servant of Geoffrey the taverner and his mainpast, for the same (12 d.) Of Geoffrey the taverner for harbouring him (12 d.) Of Robert the barber because he harbours a servant of his out of tithing (12 d.) . . . . Of Robert de Wymondham because he has a false flagon ((3 s.) Of Geoffrey de Blofield for the same with a half-flagon (2 s.) . . . . Of John the tailor for making a privy (4 s.) . . . . Of Roger de Suffield because he charged his servant with stealing 18 d. sterling and afterwards kept him till he made fine with him with two shillings and returned the said money (3 s.)

LETA DE WYMER ET WESTWYK.

De Adam de Stirston clerico quia receptavit meremium trebuchetti[1] (iiij s.) . . . . De Radulpho de Birston pro falsa fullonia cum fece vini (xij d., ad Pentecostem). . . . . De Sarra le hattere quia refutat poll' et crok' pro servisia (dī. mř.) . . . . De Galfrido filio Beatricie de Smalberth quia fullat pannos cum fecibus vini. (ij s.) . . . . De Willelmo le lacebreydere manente in redditu Willelmi de Bliclingg quia non est in decenna et stetit per annum et diem etc. (ij s.) . . . . De Radulpho de Sprouston quia traxit filium suum in Curia Cristianitatis (xij d.) . . . . De Caterina de Schelfanger quia habet duos filios suos extra decennam (xij d.) . . . . De Roberto de Stowe quia vendit cepe [sic] occulte et candelas (xij d.)

Walterus de Aswardeby solvit die Sabbati prox. ante
Pascha clausum . . . . xx s.
Item solvit die Sabbati in festo Sēi Georgii . . xl s.
Carkatur de lvj s. ix d.

LETA ULTRA AQUAM. ANNO XXVIIJ°. DE PRESENTACIONIBUS.

De Bartholomeo Provyns quia assuetus est levare utesium super uxorem eius iniuste et super alios extraneos homines xij d. . . . . . De Johanne filio Milicentie quia receptavit bladum noctanter de quodam fratre de la hospitall' Sēi Egidii in Norwico de quibus amittitur Tolnetum (dī. mř.) . . . . De Ricardo de Kyrkeby quia emit correa ad domum suam secrete contra defensionem Domini Regis (iij s.) . . . . De Alano de Hindringham quia emit correa

---

[1] The tumbrell or tre-buckct. The word must here mean the frame from which the cucking-stool was let down into the water.

LEET OF WYMER AND WESTWICK.

. . . .

Of Adam de Sturston clerk because he has received timber of the tumbrell (4 s.) . . . . Of Ralph de Burston for fraudulent fulling with lees of wine (12 d., at Whitsuntide). . . . . Of Sarah the hatter because she refused pollards and crockards [1] for beer (half a mark). . . . . Of Geoffrey, son of Beatrice de Smalburgh, because he fulls cloths with lees of wine (2 s.) . . . . Of William the lace-braider, lodging in William de Blickling's rent, because he is not in tithing and has been [in the city] for a year and a day etc. (2 s.) . . . . Of Ralph de Sprowston because he drew his son into the Court Christian (12 d.) . . . . Of Catherine de Shelfhanger because she has her two sons out of tithing (12 d.) . . . Of Robert de Stowe because he sells tallow and candles secretly (12 d.)

Walter de Aswardeby paid on the Saturday next
before the close of Easter . . . . . 20 s.
Item he paid on Saturday being the feast of St.
George . . . . 40 s.
He is charged with 56s. 9d.

LEET OVER-THE-WATER—28TH YEAR—OF PRESENTMENTS.

. . . .

Of Bartholomew Provyns because he is wont to raise the hue wrongfully on his wife and others who are strangers (12 d.) . . . . Of John, son of Melicent, because he has received corn by night from a brother of the Hospital of St. Giles in Norwich, whereby toll is lost (half a mark). . . . . Of Richard de Kirkby because he buys hides at his house privily contrary to the prohibition of the lord king (3 s.) . . . Of Alan de Hindringham because he buys hides with pollards and crockards and has delivered them

[1] See p. 50, note 4, above.

cum pollard' et crok' et ea tradidit tannatoribus ad tannandum contra communem proclamationem Domini Regis (ij s.)

Johannes de Sweynsthorpe solvit . . . xxx s.
Item . . . . xxiiij s. Item de Incremento . ix s.
 Carcatur de li s.
De Piscatoribus, Pulletariis etc.
Johannes Gerard . . . . carcatur de compoto . iij li xv s.

VIII. [ROTULUS PRESENTATIONUM AD LETAM DE CONESFORD IN CIVITATE NORWICI TEMPORE INCERTO.]

[1] ADHUC CONESFORD . BERSTRETE.

Parochie Sōi Sepulcri—Sōi Bartholomei de Berstrete—Sōi Michaelis de Berstrete—Sōi Johannis de Berstrete—Sōi Martini—Omnium Sanctorum del Swynemarket-hill—Sōi Wynwaloy de Parva Newegate.

Capitales Plegii, Johannes le heye (jur), Johannes Calf (jur), Johannes Lothale (jur) etc., etc.

Capitales Plegii presentant quod Simo Skriveyn de Helgeton traxit sanguinem de Isabella Baxtere per quod levavit utesium.
 etc., etc. .   . . .

---

[1] Roll VIII.—This Roll is only a fragment, containing, on a single membrane, presentments for the district of Berstrete in the Leet of Conesford. It has no date. In form and appearance it closely resembles the other fragment of the Conesford Leet for 12$\frac{89}{90}$. But it is of a later date, as appears from the names, which do not occur in the earlier Rolls, but some are found in the Roll of 1313. I have dated it approximately at c. 1307. It specifies the names of the parishes forming the subject of Berstrete, which are not found elsewhere.

to the tanners to tan contrary to the common proclamation of the lord king (2 s.)

[John de Swainsthorp makes two payments of 30 s. and 24 s., and 9 s. of increment. He is charged at 51 s.]

[Then follow amercements of fishmongers, poulterers, cooks, and regraters as before.

At the end John Gerard is charged on his account £3 15 s.]

VIII. [LEET ROLL WITHOUT DATE. c. 1307 ?]

CONTINUATION OF CONESFORD—BERSTRETE.

Parishes of St. Sepulchre—St. Bartholomew de Berstrete—St. Michael de Berstrete—St. John de Berstrete—St. Martin—All Saints of Swinemarket-hill—St. Winwaloy of Little Newgate.[1]

Capital Pledges. John le heye [and 11 others all marked 'sworn.']

The Capital Pledges present that Simon Scriven of Helhoughton drew blood of Isabella Baker, whereof she raised the hue.

(No entries of interest.)

---

[1] The Prioress of Carrow claimed the view of frankpledge in Little Newgate until 1290, when by a composition she released it to the City. The Church of St. Winwaloy was afterwards known as that of St. Catherine.

IX. [ROTULUS AMERCIAMENTORUM AD LETAS NORWICI A° R' REGIS EDWARDI FILII REGIS EDWARDI VI°.]

¹ CONESFORD.

De Rogero Taliur quia traxit sanguinem de Everardo de Troux et vulneravit ipsum noctanter per quod Alicia uxor dicti Everardi levavit hutesium super ipsum Rogerum iuste, per plegium Willelmi Hamund et Willelmi de Olyf (xij d.) . . . . . De omnibus phelipariis quia dubbant et divertunt pannos faciendo falsitatem in opere (—). De Martino Ern manente apud Trox quia albisitat corea equorum porcorum et ovium furata et ea sic albisitat ut non agnoscantur (xij d.) . . . . De Thoma le Norice quia emit smeltes apud Trox et alios pisces aque rescentis venientes versus forum Norwyci faciendo forstallum cariorando victualia per quod etc. (ij s.) . . . . De Rosia filia Willelmi Gerberge de Chategrave quia emit bladum et vendit braseum tanquam consivis nec est de libertate (xij d.) De Margeria sorore predicte Rose pro eodem (xij d.) De Milisio quondam apprentisio Ade Stalun quia emit et vendit per talliam nec est de libertate (ij s.) De Priorissa de Carhowe quia concelavit Jus Domini Regis videlicet quatuor denarios annui redditus quos Ballivi Domini Regis solebant participere de quodam betemayo ² (dī. mr̄.) . . . . De Roberto le Quern-

---

¹ Roll IX.—An unusually long, broad, and full Roll of Amercements. It consists of 9 membranes extending to a total length of seventeen feet. It has no heading. The only date is towards the end, as noticed below (p. 61).
² See Glossary.

IX. [LEET ROLL OF 6 EDWARD II.—131⅔].

CONESFORD.

Of Roger Tailor because he drew blood of Everard de Trowse and wounded him by night, whereof Alice, wife of Everard, raised the hue on Roger rightfully, by the pledge of William Hammond and William de Olyf (12 d.)
. . . . Of all the fripperers because they dub and turn cloths, so making fraud in their work (—). Of Martin Ern, lodging at Trowse, because he whitens stolen hides of horses, pigs and sheep, and whitens them in such wise that they may not be recognised (12 d.) . . . . Of Thomas le Norice because he buys smelts at Trowse and other freshwater fish coming to Norwich market, so making forestalment and heightening victuals, whereby etc. (2 s.)
. . . . Of Rose, daughter of William Gerberge of Chedgrave, because she buys corn and sells malt like a fellow-citizen and is not of the freedom (12 d.) Of Margery, sister of the said Rose, for the same (12 d.) Of Miles formerly apprentice of Adam Stalun, because he buys and sells by tally and is not of the freedom (2 s.) . . . . Of the Prioress of Carrow because she has concealed the lord king's due, to wit, four pence of annual rent which the Bailiffs of the lord king have been wont to receive from a certain bitmay (half a mark). . . . . Of Robert

hacker pro hamsoken facto super Rogerum le Daubere et fratrem eius verberando ipsos in domo ipsius Rogeri (vj d.) De eodem Roberto quia fecit hamsoken super uxorem Rogeri le Daubere in domo sua per quod ipsa levavit utesium super ipsum iuste (vj d.) . . . . De Christiana Avenant quia deobstupavit quandam gutteram ad domum quondam Willelmi de Valeyns per quam diversa sordia corruptibilia exeunt ad nocumentum vicinorum [1] (xl d.)

Berstrette.

De Rogero Gente quia abstulit capucium de Margareta Helwyse per quod dicta Margareta levavit utesium (vj d.) . . . . De Ricardo de Porynglond draper quia nocte proxima post festum conceptionis beate Marie ultimo preterito [sic] abstulerit de Willelmo de Castre unam zonam et unam bursam de serico cum duobus denariis infra contentis et unum sigillum de nomine suo et j claveum [2] ap forcerium suum et unum misericordem per quod dictus Willelmus levavit hutesium super ipsum Ricardum (xij d.) De Adam de Lincoln pellipario pro eodem per quod dictus Willelmus levavit hutesium pro eodem [sic] (vj d.) . . . . De Thoma de Cuttyng quia non venit ad letam per suum capitalem plegium (vj d.) . . . . De Piscenariis qui emunt ante horam primam contra communem proclamationem et defensionem ballivorum Domini Regis.

LETA DE NEDHAM ET MANECROFT.

De Alicia matre Johannis de Appyngg quia abstulit de Alicia Canon unum capitium cum quadam festuca argenti pretii duorum denariorum per quod predicta Alicia

[1] This house lay between the street of Nether Conesford and the river, so that the nuisance could hardly have affected any one but the occupiers of the adjoining land.

[2] I can only suppose this word to be meant for *clavem*. A 'forcer' was a small box. The other word is *ap* (? apud), not *ad*. 'Clave ad forcerum' occurs in *Records of Nottingham*, i. 234.

the Quernhacker for making hamsoken on Roger the
Dauber and his brother, beating them in Roger's house
(6 d.) Of the same Robert because he made hamsoken
on the wife of Roger the Dauber in her house, whereof
she raised the hue on him rightfully (6 d.) . . . . Of
Christiana Avenant because she has blocked up a gutter
at the house formerly of William de Valeyns, whereby
much putrid filth runs out to the nuisance of the
neighbours (40 d.)

Berstrete.

Of Roger Gent because he took away a cape from Margaret
Helwys, whereof Margaret raised the hue (6 d.) . . . . Of
Richard de Poringland, draper, because on the night next
after the feast of the Conception of the Blessed Mary last
past he took away from William de Caister a girdle and a
silk purse with two pence in it and a seal with his name
and a key for his box and a dagger, whereof the said
William raised the hue on Richard (12 d.) Of Adam de
Lincoln, skinner, for the same, whereof the said William
raised the hue (6 d.) . . . . Of Thomas de Cuttying because he came not to the leet by his Capital Pledge[1] (6 d.)
. . . . Of the Fishmongers who buy before the hour of
prime contrary to the common proclamation and prohibition of the Bailiffs of the lord king.[2]

. . . .

LEET OF NEDHAM AND MANECROFT.

Of Alice, mother of John de Happing, because he took from
Alice Canon a cape with a silver clasp [?] of the value of
two pence, whereof the said Alice Canon raised the hue

---

[1] Some special circumstance not explained must be the ground for this presentment.
[2] Evidently here the Bailiffs of the City. In the Customs (ch. 33) they are distinguished from others so called by the title 'principales Ballivi.'

Canon levavit hutesium (vj d.) . . . . De Johanne Keyc quia noctanter fregit domum Johannis Koc per quod idem Johannes levavit hutesium (cap.) De Thoma Lewyne pro eodem (cap.) . . . . De Johanne le Clerc de Rugham barber et Johanne manipasto suo quia verberaverunt et proiecerunt Johannem le Barburg de Castelhacr' in luto¹ per quod ipse levavit hutesium (xij d.) . . . . De Johanne Samer quia traxit sanguinem de Willelmo Wrangel (cap.) . . . . De Alicia que fuit uxor Ricardi de ffornessete [quia ipsa] et servientes sui emebant unum quarterium frumenti extra villam obviando versus forum regium et illud frumentum abduceret [sic] ad molendinum et ibidem redigere faceret in farinam per quod Ballivi amittunt tolnetum (xij d.) . . . . De Hugone Tyvillie quia fecit rescussum Johanni Birks [²] subballivis Domini Regis auferendo ab eis unum bukettum et unam cordam (xij d.) . . . . De Thoma del Percie³ quia assuetus est emere bladum in foro et incontinentim illud dividit in dimidios bussellos in fraudem Domini Regis ut non deberet tolneari per quod Ballivi etc. (xij d.) . . . . De Thoma de Denton Armigero quia fecit hamsoken super Warinum de Tudenham per [quod] idem Warinus levavit hutesium super predictum Thomam (ij s.) . . . . De Johanne Tolle quia scienter emebat quendam porcum furiosum de Waltero le Grey curreur et illum interfecit et vendidit per talliam que quidem caro fuit corumpcionelibus hominis⁴ [sic] et hoc fecit contra communem proclamationem Domini Regis (ij s.) . . . . ⁵ De Roberto Kep de Marsham capitali plegio pro concelamento . in mīā . eo quod concelavit quod Johannes de Birkelce de Scothowe emebat et vendidit per talliam tanquam concivis et non est de libertate.

. . . .

¹ *in luto* added above the line. This expression, common afterwards, is not found in the earlier Rolls.
² Blank in MS.
³ This name can hardly be correctly written. It may be meant for

'del Mercerie' or 'del Speceric,' two of the Market Rows.
⁴ Are these two words a mangled relic of '*corrupta et non sana corporibus hominum*'?
⁵ The Capital Pledges of St. Peter Mancroft. See Introduction VIII. 3.

(6 d.) . . . . Of John Key because by night he broke the house of John Koc, whereof John raised the hue (arrest). Of Thomas Lewyn for the same (arrest). . . . . Of John le Clerk of Rougham, barber, and John his mainpast because they beat and cast in the mud John de Castle- acre the barber, whereof he raised the hue (12 d.) . . . . Of John Samer because he drew blood of William Wran- gel (arrest)[1]. . . . . Of Alice who was wife of Richard de Forncet [because she] and her servants bought one quarter of wheat outside the town, meeting it on the way to the king's market, and carried the corn to the mill and there got it ground to flour, whereby the Bailiffs lose toll (12 d.) . . . . Of Hugh Tyvill because he made rescue on John Birks and . . . . sub-bailiffs of the lord king, carrying off from them a bucket and a cord (12 d.) . . . . Of Thomas del Percie because he is wont to buy corn in the market and forthwith divides it into half-bushels to the defrauding of the lord king so that it might not be taxed, whereby the Bailiffs etc. (12 d.) . . . . Of Thomas de Denton, Esquire, because he made hamsoken on Warin de Tudenham, whereof Warin raised the hue on Thomas (2 s.) . . . . Of John Toll because he wit- tingly bought a mad pig from Walter the Gray, currier, and killed it and sold it by tally, which flesh was corrupt [and unfit for the bodies of] men, and this he did contrary to the common proclamation of the lord king (2 s.) . . . Of Robert Kep of Marsham, Capital Pledge, for conceal- ment—in mercy—for that he concealed that John de Berkeley of Scottow bought and sold etc. (12 d.) (22 other Capital Pledges similarly amerced.)

. . . .

---

[1] A curious feature in this Roll is the treatment of the offence of 'blood-drawing.' In the Leet of Conesford twenty-six offenders are amerced either 12 d. or 6 d. In the other three Leets there are over 100 such offenders presented, not one of whom is amerced, all (with very few exceptions) being marked 'cap.' Observe especially, on p. 58, the different penalties meted out to three acts of rescue, and to a fourth which was accompanied by blood-drawing, and similarly the first two entries in the Leet ultra Aquam, on p. 59.

WYMER ET WESTWYK.

De Willelmo le Wayte quia abstulit a Beatrice de Cringelthorp leprosa duas Bestas[1] per Walterum le lindraper nomine districtionis captas per [quod] ipsa Beatricia levavit hutesium (vj d.) .... De Johanne de Schotesman[1] fullone quia fecit forstallum Roberto de Pikenham et Andree de Morle subballivis quando fecerunt districtionem pro Nicholao de Poswyk (vj d.) De eodem Johanne quia fecit forstallum Roberto de Pikenham et Andree venientibus cum Johanne de Castre colectore ad distringendum pro tallagio communitatis (vj d.) De Margareta de Brundale manente in Holdtor pro rescussu facto Roberto de Pikenham subballivo (xij d.) De Hugone Tyvillie quia fecit rescussum Willelmo le Nothne [sic] et traxit sanguinem ab eo (cap.) .... De Roberto de Colvyston et uxore eius quia vexaverunt Ricardum Sussan in curia Christianitatis a festo Pasche ultimo preterito usque ad festum Sc̄i Michaelis ultimum preteritum super hiis que non tangunt testamentum neque matrimonium (xij d.) De Thoma de Brok quia vexavit Johannem de Schotesham fullonem coram Decano Norwyci super hiis etc. (xij d.) .... De Ricardo Fhis quia assuetus est [se] subtrahere[2] contra letam (vj d.) .... De Willelmo ffleghe quia verberavit Robertum de Rothering in domo sua per quod idem Robertus languebat per quindenam faciendo hamsok super ipsum Robertum (xij d.) .... De Roberto Mentel quia receptavit unam aucam venientem de Strahie[3] nec liberavit illam Ballivis (vj d.) .... De Willelmo de ffornessete curlevacher manente juxta ecclesiam Sc̄i Stephani [quia] emit bladum antequam venit ad forum per quod Ballivi amittunt tolnetum (xij d.) .... De Willelmo de Happesburgh quia insultavit Rogerum

---

[1] Sic in MS.
[2] Cf. Stat. Wallie: 'De hiis qui contra adventum et iter Justiciariorum se subtraxerunt et post iter Justiciariorum redierunt.'
[3] 'de Straio.'

WYMER AND WESTWICK.

Of William the Watchman because he took away from Beatrice de Cringlethorp, a leper, two beasts seized by Walter the linendraper in the name of distraint, whereof Beatrice raised the hue (6 d.) . . . . Of John de Shottisham, fuller, because he made forestalment against Robert de Pickenham and Andrew de Morley, sub-bailiffs, when they made distraint for Nicholas de Postwick (6 d.) Of the same John, because he made forestalment against Robert de Pickenham and Andrew, coming with John de Caister, the collector, to distrain for the tallage of the commonalty (6 d.) Of Margaret de Brundall, lodging in Holdthor, for making rescue on Robert de Pickenham, sub-bailiff (12 d.) Of Hugh Tyvill because he made rescue on William le Nothne and drew blood from him (arrest) . . . . Of Robert de Colveston and his wife because they vexed Richard Sussan in the Court Christian from the feast of Easter last past to the feast of St. Michael last past, concerning things which touch not wills nor marriage (12 d.) Of Thomas de Brooke because he vexed John de Shottisham, fuller, before the Dean of Norwich, concerning things which etc. (12 d.) . . . . Of Richard Fish because he is wont to withdraw himself to escape the leet (6 d.) . . . . Of William Fleg because he beat Robert de Rothering in his house, whereof the said Robert was sick for a fortnight, so making hamsoken on Robert (12 d.) . . . . Of Robert Mentel because he received a goose coming astray and did not deliver it to the Bailiffs (6 d.) Of William de Forncett, curlevacher, lodging near the church of St. Stephen, because he buys corn before it comes to the market, whereby the Bailiffs lose toll (12 d.) . . . . Of William de Happisburgh because he assaulted

de Lopham, Willelmum Gerard et Johannem del Stonhus ballivos¹ Domini Regis ducentes quasdam communes meretrices extra civitatem Norwyci et predictos ballivos de predictis meretricibus rescutere voluit et illas rescuere vincebatur in contemptum ballivorum Domini Regis etc. (cap.) De Johanne Dereday et Johanne fratre eius pro eodem (cap.) . . . . De Adam de Merston quia fecit hampsok super Johannem de Bernham apportando unum pannum extra domum suam contra voluntatem suam (xij d.)

ULTRA AQUAM.

De Hugone le Stotere quia fecit hampsok super Thomam le Glaswryth et vulneravit ipsum in domo sua (ij s.) . . . . De eodem Hugone quia traxit sanguinem de predicto Thoma (cap.) De Johanne le Rus filio Claricie Atteyates quia fregit hostia domus Johannis de Riston dum iacuit in feretro et ibidem noctanter verberavit executores dicti Johannis videlicet Stephanum Keye et alios per quod ipsi levaverunt hutesium (cap.) . . . . De Petro Pirmund quia exaltavit viam regiam ex opposito messuagii quondam Thome Godesman cum gravella et sabilone ita quod per illam exaltationem obstupavit cursum aque de Muspol ² [et] non potest transire iuxta portas fratrum predicatorum versus pontem de ffibrigge sicut currere solebat per quam obstupacionem dicta aqua de Muspol inundat et submergit domos vicinorum valde noscenter (xl d.) . . . . De Ricardo de Catton qui desponsavit filiam Rogeri de Honeworth quia mercandizat cum viginti cumbis ordei et aliis bonis cuidam leproso manenti extra portas Sc̄i Augustini et illa bona advocat sua propria per quod

¹ The City Bailiffs for this year were Robert de Lopham, William Bateman, William But, and Robert de Holveston. The 'Bailiffs of the lord king' mentioned in this entry must be the persons elsewhere described as 'sub-bailiffs.' They were probably more than mere serjeants, for one of them bears the same surname as one of the City Bailiffs, and the surname of another, 'del Stonhus,' is usually restricted to the owners of stone houses, which were rare.

² This was a pool or spring from which, it seems, a considerable flow

LEET ROLL OF 1312/3.   59

Roger de Lopham, William Gerard, and John of the Stonehouse, Bailiffs of the lord king, as they were leading some common harlots out of the city of Norwich and tried to drive off the Bailiffs from them, and he was prevented from rescuing them, in contempt of the lord king's Bailiffs (arrest). . . . . Of John Dereday and John his brother for the same (arrest). . . . . Of Adam de Merston because he made hamsoken on John de Burnham, carrying off a cloth out of his house against his will (12 d.)

OVER-THE-WATER.

Of Hugh the Stutterer because he made hamsoken on Thomas the glass-wright and wounded him in his house (2 s.) Of the said Hugh because he drew blood of the said Thomas (arrest). . . . . Of John le Rus, son of Claricia Attegates, because he broke the doors of John de Riston's house while he lay on his bier, and there by night beat the executors of the said John—to wit, Stephen Key and others —whereof they raised the hue (arrest). . . . Of Peter Pirmund because he has raised the king's highway opposite to the messuage late of Thomas Godesman with gravel and sand, so that by that raising he has blocked the course of the water of Muspol [and] it cannot pass near the gates of the Friars Preachers towards the bridge of Fibrigge as it was wont to run, by which obstruction the said water of Muspol overflows and floods the houses of the neighbours to their great nuisance (40 d.) . . . . Of Richard de Catton who married the daughter of Roger de Hunworth, because he trades with a certain leper,[1] lodging outside St. Augustine's gates, with 20 coombs of barley

of water issued at this date. It gave its name to the adjoining church of St. George de Muspol or de Colgate. The Friars Preachers originally settled in this district (Introduction, IV. 4). Afterwards they moved to the opposite side of the river, where their church still exists under the name of St. Andrew's Hall.

[1] On the isolation of lepers, see below, Roll XI. (p. 71). Trading with a leper is not here treated as an offence.

Ballivi tolnetum et custumam suam amittunt (ij s.)
. . . . De Roberto serviente Annacorie [1] de Newbrigge quia suffodit viam regalem extra portas Sēi Augustini (ij s.) . . . . De Margareta Dukke et filia eius manipasta sua quia traxerunt sanguinem de Johanne filio Rogeri le Cobeler (cap.)

[2] *De Regratariis Avene.*—De uxore Roberti le Prestesson quia emit avenam antequam venit ad forum et quia similiter vendit per pekkes que non sunt mensure Domini Regis (xij d.)

De Regratariis Caseorum.—De Estrilda de Elmham quia emit caseum buttyrium et ova venientia versus forum et alia victualia antequam veniunt ad forum faciendo forstallum (ij s.)

De Phelippariis.—De Ricardo Baldewyne quia habet truncum fullonem [sic] et dubbat pannos faciendo falsitatem in opere (ij s.)

De Pulteariis.—De Ricardo Daumesson quia assuetus est emere aucas gallinas et alia volatilia venientia versus forum ante horam primam contra communem proclamacionem etc. (xl d.)

De Candelariis.—De Ricardo de Schipedham pro falsitate facta opere operando scilicet sul.[3] hono. cepo in candelis suis (xl d.)

De Carnificibus.—De Rogero Nel quia vendit cepum per weygh sine visitatione trone Domini Regis (ij s.)

De Cocis.—De Ricardo de Totyngton quia recalefacit carnes pisces et pastillos post biduum seu triduum contra defensionem Ballivorum Domini Regis (xl d.)

[1] There were several of these recluses in the city. They were regarded with great respect and had many testamentary gifts made to them. More than once their servants are mentioned in these Rolls. They chiefly lived at the corners of churchyards.

[2] The definitions of trade offences in this Roll are specially full and precise.

[3] This and the next word are clearly written, but cannot be correct.

and other goods and avows them as his own, whereby the Bailiffs lose their toll and custom (2 s.) . . . . Of Robert, servant of the Anchoress of Newbrigge, because he digs up the king's highway outside St. Augustine's gates (2 s.) . . . . Of Margaret Dukke and her daughter, her mainpast, because they drew blood of John, son of Roger the cobbler (arrest).

Of the Regraters of Oats.—Of the wife of Robert, the Priest's son, because she buys oats before they come to the market, and likewise sells them by pecks which are not the lord king's measures (12 d.) [10 others amerced, 8 of them women.]

Of the Regraters of Cheese.—Of Estrilda de Elmham because she buys cheese, butter, and eggs coming to the market etc. (2 s.) [12 others amerced, all women.]

Of the Fripperers.—Of Richard Baldwin because he has a fuller's block and dubs cloths, so making fraud in his work (2 s.) [10 others amerced.]

Of the Poulterers.—Of Richard Damson because he is wont to buy geese, hens, and other fowls coming to the market before the hour of prime contrary to the common proclamation (40 d.) [6 others amerced.]

Of the Chandlers.—Of Richard de Shipdham for making fraud in doing his work, to wit [?] with tallow in his candles (40 d.) [9 others amerced.]

Of the Butchers.—Of Roger Nel because he sells suet by weight without using the lord king's beam (2 s.) [13 others amerced.]

Of the Cooks.—Of Richard de Tottyngton because he warms up meat, fish and pasties after the second or third day contrary to the prohibition of the lord king's Bailiffs (40 d.) [18 amercements].

De Braciatoribus de Nedham et Manecroft Anno Sexto.—De uxore Willelmi Bele pro assissa cervisie fracta et non observata secundum proclamacionem Domini Regis et quia vendit per cyphos que [*sic*] non sunt mensure Domini Regis [1] (xij d.)

De Tannatoribus.—De Rogero de Helmham quia tannat cum alia cortice quam cum cortice quercinea [2] faciendo falsitatem in opere. Et quia emit corea in domibus secrete contra communem proclamacionem Domini Regis (ij s.) . . . .

---

[1] The amercements for this offence are: Conesford 49, Manecroft 93, Wymer 56, Ultra Aquam 52 = 250.
[2] MS. has *fraxina* in error.

Of the Brewers of Nedham and Manecroft in the 6th year.[1]—
Of the wife of William Bele for breaking the assize of
ale and not observing it according to the lord king's
proclamation, and because she sells by ciphes which are
not measures of the lord king (12 d.)

Of the Tanners.—Of Roger de Elmham because he tans
with other bark than oak bark, so making fraud in his
work, and because he buys hides in houses secretly,
contrary to the common proclamation of the lord king
(2 s.) [18 amercements.]

---

[1] This is undoubtedly the sixth year of Edward II. The contemporary Conveyance Rolls furnish the requisite evidence on this point. I am glad to fortify this conclusion by the authority of Kirkpatrick, who frequently quotes the Roll as of that date in the *Streets and Lanes of Norwich*. In the Guildhall 'Repertory' it is assigned to 'c. 1374.'

X. [ROTULUS DE VEREDICTIS LETARUM NORWICI A° R' REGIS EDWARDI TERTII XLIX°.]

[1] ROTULUS DE VEREDICTIS LETARUM CORAM HENRICO SKIE, HUGONE DE HOLAND, JOHANNE LATIMER, ET WILLELMO GERARD BALLIVIS CIVITATIS NORWICI ANNO REGNI REGIS EDWARDI TERCII A CONQUESTU QUADRAGESIMO NONO.

[Conesford] Capitales plegii presentant subscripta videlicet quod Willelmus Coyt Botman fecit hamsok' super Johannam Warwyk et verberavit eam cum cultello extracto contra pacem (viij d.) Quedam serviens Johannis Paternoster levavit hutesium super eundem iuste (vj d.) Cecilia de Taverham levavit hutesium super monachum ecclesie Sce̅ Trinitatis iniuste (xij d.) .... Galfridus de Bixton et Willelmus le Blacomoor emebant blada per forstallum diversi generis ad summam cccc quarteriorum et eadem blada advocaverunt tanquam sua ad portas civitatis et alibi tamen sua non fuere quousque mensurata fuere absque tolneto (x ti.) .... Rogerus de Bergham similiter emebat per forstallum tam per vicos venellas portas et pontes obviando diversa blada videlicet ccc quarteria frumenti lx quarteria siliginis et cc quarteria ordei et avene in magnam caristiam mercati unde Ballivi amise-

---

[1] Roll X.—For the features by which this and the next Roll are distinguished from the earlier ones which have been already dealt with see Introd. XI. 1. An interval of 63 years separates this from the last. These two Rolls are both in the form of presentments with the amercements added. The four Great Leets are not mentioned in either. The subleets are themselves treated as Leets. They are ten in number with

X. [LEET ROLL OF 49 EDWARD III. 137⅘].

ROLL OF VERDICTS OF THE LEETS BEFORE HENRY SKIE, HUGH DE HOLAND, JOHN LATIMER, AND WILLIAM GERARD, BAILIFFS OF THE CITY OF NORWICH IN THE 49TH YEAR OF THE REIGN OF KING EDWARD THE 3RD AFTER THE CONQUEST.

[Conesford] ¹ The Capital Pledges present the underwritten [offences]—to wit, that William Coyt, boatman, made hamsoken on Johanna Warwick, and beat her with a drawn knife contrary to the peace (8 d.) A maidservant of John Paternoster raised the hue upon him rightfully (6 d.) Cecilia de Taverham raised the hue on a monk of the church of the Holy Trinity wrongfully (12 d.) . . . . Geoffrey de Bixton and William the Blackamoor bought corn by forestalment of different sorts to the amount of 400 quarters and avowed it as their own at the city gates and elsewhere (notwithstanding it was not their own), until it was measured without toll (£ 10)². . . . . Roger de Bergham likewise bought by forestalment divers kinds of corn, going to meet it in streets and lanes, at gates and bridges—to wit, 300 quarters of wheat, 60 quarters of rye, and 200 quarters of barley and oats, to the great heighening of the market, whereby the Bailiffs have lost

the addition of a new Leet, of the Castle Fee.
¹ In this Roll six of the Leets are not introduced by any name or heading. They all begin 'Capitales plegii presentant etc.'

² These persons fraudulently at various times obtained the introduction and measurement of 400 quarters of corn without paying toll on any of it.

runt tolnetum (x. mr.) Nicholas de Bietlee similiter emebat per forstallum ccc quarteria et dimidium ordei et avene et lx cumbas pisarum albarum in magnam caristiam (xl. s., cond.) . . . . Rogerus Calf emebat per forstallum quatuor batellos plenos oystr' diversis vicibus unde pretium unius c acrescebat ad unum denarium et ob.[1] per unum diem et est communis forstallator (xx. s., cond.)

non parus[2] Petrus Nethyrde emit et vendit et non est civis (xij d.) . . . . Ricardus de Framyngham recepit thefbote[3] quod Andreas Gurnay habuit ex quodam latrunculo iniuste (vj d.) . . . . Robertus Papungeay et tres servientes eius non venerunt ad letam[4] (ij s.) . . . .

[Horstrete] Johannes de Gaywode taverner forstallavit tanta ova in mercato ut implevit [sic] xxviij barellos diversis vicibus et illa mandavit extra Regnum ad partes externas et similiter forstallavit butirum et caseum ad magnam summam unde magna caristia crevit in civitate victualium et hoc per iiij. annos (xx. s.) Johannes de Wynterton similiter forstallavit diversa blada in magnam caristiam et ea abduxit extra Regnum etc. (lx s.) . . . . Petrus persona ecclesie Scē Katerine emit multum ordeum et inde fecit fieri braseum in domo Hugonis de Lakenham et non est civis (xx s.) Simon persona ecclesie Scē Margarete in Westwyk est communis emptor bladorum, lane, fili lane, oof et warp et communis est mercator per totum annum et non est civis (xx s.) Katerina Skynner similiter est communis hukster et non est civis (vj d., cond.) Henricus Curreyour emit et vendit et habet duos apprenticios et non est civis (x d.) . . . . Johannes de Burghwode non est in decenna neque venit ad letam (iiij d.) . . . .

---

[1] The ordinary price of 100 oysters was 1½d. See below, p. 65.
[2] This expression is only used here in the Leet Rolls. In this Roll the equivalent expression *non cives* is used in other sublects. For some remarks on the word see Introd. Note A. 2.
[3] Something taken in amends for theft without licence of the king's court.
[4] This offence, which is very rarely mentioned in the thirteenth century Rolls, is one of the chief subjects of presentment in these two Rolls. It does not appear whether the de-

toll (10 marks). Nicholas de Beetley likewise bought by forestalment 300 quarters and a half of barley and oats, and 60 coombs of white peas to the great heighening etc. (40 s., excused) .... Roger Calf bought by forestalment 4 boats full of oysters at divers times whereby the price of 100 rose 1½ d. for one day, and he is a common forestaller (20 s., excused).

not peers Peter Neatherd buys and sells and is not a citizen (12 d.) .... Richard de Framingham received thefbote which Andrew Gurnay had wrongfully from a certain young thief (6 d.) Robert Papungay and three servants of his came not to the leet (2 s.) [13 others amerced.]

[Derstrete] John de Gaywood, taverner, forestalled so many eggs in the market that he filled 28 barrels at divers times and sent them out of the kingdom to foreign parts, and likewise forestalled butter and cheese to a large amount, whereby there accrued great dearness of victuals in the city, and that for four years (20 s.) John de Winterton likewise forestalled divers kinds of corn to great heighening, and exported them out of the kingdom (60 s.) .... Peter, parson of the church of St. Katherine, bought a great deal of barley and had it made into malt in Hugh de Lakenham's house, and he is not a citizen (20 s.) Simon, parson of the church of St. Margaret in Westwick, is a common purchaser of corn, wool, woollen yarn, woof and warp, and has been a common merchant for a whole year, and is not a citizen (20 s.) Katherine Skinner likewise is a common huckster, and is not a citizen (6 d., excused). Henry the Currier buys and sells and has two apprentices, and is not a citizen (10 d.) .... John de Burwood is not in tithing, nor did he come to the leet (4 d.)

faulters had been specially summoned to answer for some offence, or whether they were simply presented for non-attendance. The frequent presentment of servants with a master rather favours the latter supposition.

[Sćī Stephani]   Johannes Colde communis felliparius est torkeynando[1] veteres pannos in deceptionem (xviij d.) . . . . Rogerus de Bergham in tantum forstallavit diversa genera bladorum per se et servientes in mercato vicis venellis et portis civitatis quod precium unius cumbe frumenti acrescebat de xl & ij d. usque ad v s. in magnam caristiam et contra sacramentum suum unde Ballivi perdiderunt tolnetum plurimum (x mr̃.) . . . . Thomas Kebbe est communis braciator et vendit cervisiam per ciphos[2] et discos et non continue per mensuras sigillatas contra proclamationem et fregit assissam (xij d.) . . . .

[Sćī Petri de Manecroft] Johannes de Northiks cordwaner una nocte fecit hamsok' vi et armis super duos duchemen in domo Johannis Disse minans eis ad verberandum et interficiendum per quod dicti duchemen fugerunt civitatem et dictus Johannes depredatus fuit dictis duobus hominibus extra Nedhamgates vij d. ob. et est communis noctivagus et male fame (cap.) Filius Ranulphi Moreman apprenticius nuper Ricardi Armourer furatus fuit de dicto Ricardo brasas[3] brestplates et similia ad valenciam xx s. et illa vendidit Johanni Coo sporier et dictus Johannes Coo sciens [sic] dicta catalla fuisse furata (cap.) . . . . Johannes de Norton fecit districcionem super Nicholaum Fyppes draper absque licencia Ballivorum et fecit deliberacionem eiusdem contra consuetudinem (xl d.) . . . . Johannes Prentys Blake Herry Robertus Boteler fullere et Nicholaus fullere cantor vi et armis ceperunt de Johanne Sandresson alieno xl d. per extorsionem et confederacionem inter eos prehabitam et similiter ceperunt eodem modo de Johanne Hant fullere dimidiam marcam et predicti Herry Robertus et Nicholaus sunt communes noctivagi et male fame (cap.) . . . . Herveus de Eggemere est communis forstallator frumenti et aliorum bladorum et illa vendit extra regnum (alibi). . . . .

Sći Egidii   Ela serviens Johannis Rollesby traxit sanguinem de Margareta Kempe et fecit hamsok' super eam et levavit

[1] ? *torquinando*, twisting about. [3] Armour for the arms. 'Cath.
[2] See Glossary.   Angl.' s.v. *Bracc*.

[St.Stephen] John Colde is a common fripperer, turning old clothes to the defrauding etc. (18 d.) . . . . Roger de Bergham to such an extent forestalled divers kinds of corn by himself and his servants in the market and in the streets, lanes, and gates of the city, that the price of one coomb of wheat rose from 42 pence to 5 shillings, to great heightening, and contrary to his oath, whereby the Bailiffs have lost much toll (10 marks). . . . . Thomas Kebbe is a common brewer and sells beer by ciphes and discs, and not constantly by sealed measures, contrary to the proclamation, and has broken the assize (12 d.)

[St. Peter de Mancroft] John de Northwick, cordwainer, one night made hamsoken by force and arms on two Dutchmen in the house of John Diss, threatening to beat and kill them, whereby the said Dutchmen fled from the city, and the said John robbed them of 7½ d. outside Nedham Gates, and he is a common night-rover and of ill fame (arrest). Ranulph Moreman's son, who was sometime apprentice to Richard the armourer, stole from Richard braces, breastplates and like goods to the value of 20 s., and sold them to John Coo, spurrier, and John Coo knew well that the said goods were stolen (arrest). . . . . John de Norton made distraint on Nicholas Fypps, draper, without licence of the Bailiffs, and made release of the same contrary to the custom (40 d.) . . . . John Prentice, Henry Blake, Robert Butler, fuller, and Nicholas Fuller, singer, by force and arms took from John Sanderson, an alien, 40 d. by extortion and conspiracy between them premeditated, and likewise they took in the same way from John Hant, fuller, half a mark, and the said Henry, Robert, and Nicholas are common night-rovers and of ill fame (arrest). . . . . Hervey de Edgmere is a common forestaller of wheat and other corn, and sells it out of the kingdom (elsewhere). [64 persons are here amerced for forestalling, 12 'ad traducendum,' *i.e.* for exportation.]

St. Giles Ela, servant of John Rollesby, drew blood of Margaret Kemp and made hamsoken upon her, and raised the hue

hutesium super dictam Margaretam iniuste et dicta Margareta levavit hutesium super dictam Elam iuste (cap.) Johannes de Walsingham et Matilda uxor eius receperunt de Johanna Kempster xiij slabbes scientes quod dicta Johanna ea depredavit (xij d.) Eadem Johanna Kempster depredavit unum par Kardes [1] de Johanna uxore Johannis Andes et predicta Johanna uxor Johannis Andes recepit dictos Kardes retro sine Ballivis (xij d.) Eadem Johanna depredavit de Petro de Scothowe vj ulnas de warp de brown et est communis fur (cap.) . . . . Johannes de Gyssyngg iniuste occupavit le Bytemay cum c carectatis plenis fimi et cepit de diversis hominibus pecuniam ad ponendum ibidem fimum illorum ad nocumentum ripe (ij s.) . . . . Andreas Miller fecit molare xxx cumbas frumenti et illa [sic] mandavit apud Jernemutham tempore piscium (xij d.) . . . . Petrus de Stodeye est communis felliparius torkeynando veteres pannos in novam formam in decepcionem populi (xij d.)
. . . .

Gregorii Quidam serviens Andree Millere furatus est de iiij^{or} cumbis bladi xviij libras farine ad magnum dampnum (ij s.) . . . . Willelmus Fesant persona ecclesie de Pakefeld emebat per forstallum diversis diebus mercatoriis in Norwico ita quod infra vij dies pretium unius cumbe frumenti accrevit ad xx d. (c s.) . . . . Rogerus Calf assuetus est emere per forstallum oystres in diversis batellis ita quod quando j batellus sit apud le Stathe ad vendendum, j alius batellus vel duo batelli erunt apud Thorp [2] quousque ille primus batellus evacuetur et vendatur et tunc ceteri batelli veniunt ad vendendum et ubi communitas habere [solebat] c oystres pro j denario et j obolo ille Rogerus vendit pro ij d. vel iij d. (alibi). . . . . Jacobus Jakes non venit ad letam neque est in decenna Domini Regis [3] (xij d.) Willelmus de Eton et duo servientes eius non venerunt ad letam (xij d.) . . . . Cle-

---

[1] For carding wool.
[2] About 1½ mile below Norwich.
[3] This expression, unused in the earlier Rolls, seems to mark the silent progress of the social revolution by which the 'decennarius'

LEET ROLL OF 137⅘.   65

on Margaret wrongfully, and Margaret raised the hue on Ela rightfully (arrest). John de Walsingham and Matilda his wife received from Johanna Kempster 13 slabs, knowing that the said Johanna stole them (12 d.) The same Johanna Kempster robbed Johanna, wife of John Andes, of a pair of cards, and Johanna, John Andes' wife, took the cards back without licence of the Bailiffs (12 d.) The same Johanna robbed Peter de Scottow of 6 ells of brown warp, and she is a common thief (arrest). . . . . John de Gissing has wrongfully occupied the bitmay with 100 cartloads of muck, and has taken money from divers persons to lay their muck there, to the nuisance of the river (2 s.) . . . . Andrew the miller had 30 coombs of wheat ground, and he exported them at Yarmouth in the fishing season (12 d.) . . . . Peter de Stody is a common fripperer, turning old clothes into new shapes, to the defrauding of the people (12 d.) . . . .

St. Gregory A servant of Andrew the miller stole 18 pounds of flour from 4 coombs of corn, to the great damage etc. (2 s.) . . . . William Pheasant, parson of the church of Pakefield, bought by forestalment on divers market days in Norwich, so that within seven days the price of one coomb of wheat went up 20 d. (100 s.) . . . . Roger Calf is wont to buy oysters by forestalment in divers boats, so that when one boat is at the Staith for the sale of [oysters] another boat or two shall be at Thorpe until the first boat is emptied and sold, and then the rest of the boats come up for sale ; and whereas the common people [were wont] to have 100 oysters for 1½ d., Roger sells them for 2 d. or 3 d. (elsewhere). . . . . James Jakes came not to the leet, and is not in the lord king's tithing (12 d.) William de Eton and his two servants came not to the leet

ceased to be a unit of mutual responsibility, and became either a 'suitor of a court' or merely a 'sworn liege'—one who had sworn allegiance at the view of frankpledge. See the quotation from Kitchin, below, Roll XVII., p. 94, n. 4.

mens Spycer et duo filii eius fecerunt similiter (xij d.) Quidam serviens Thome Berd et manupastus eius fecit similiter (vj d.) Johannes de Becclys et quinque servientes eius non venerunt ad letam (xviij d.) . . . .

Sči Andree Trumpyngton serviens Henrici Coteler traxit sanguinem de quodam mendicante et dictus pauper levavit hutesium super eum iuste (xviij d.) . . . . Adam de Horsted goldsmyth Robertus Flesshewer et Thomas Toftes simul pugnaverunt in domo Barestaf et sunt communes lusores ad talos (cap.) . . . . Alicia filia Roberti Shedere furata fuit de Roberto de Massyngham magistro suo unum cloce duplicem unum cote [de] furro unum par lintheamentorum et alia jocalia ad valenciam xx d. (cap.) . . . . Gilbertus de Sechgeford fecit districcionem super Johannem Smyth tenentem Ricardi Smyth videlicet j belewe sine licencia etc. (xij d.) . . . . Ranulphus Moreman posuit unum magnum lapidem in Regia via contra hostium suum ad magnum nocumentum et vicini rogant ut amoveatur (vj d.) . . . . Johannes Silkman emit et vendit et habet apprenticium et non est civis (ij s.) Alicia Wigemaker similiter emit et vendit et non est civis (ij s.) Agnes Bookbynder similiter non est civis (xij d.) Andreas Lanternemaker fecit similiter (xl d.) Ricardus Clerk cardemaker fecit similiter (vj d.) Edmundus de Metton webster fecit similiter (xviij d.)

[Sči Georgii] Willelmus Stugs recepit j blanket pretii xij d. quam Katerina famula sua furata fuit de eo nomine Thefbote (vj d.) . . . . Johannes Neloth emebat j coverlytum pretii xx s. quod Alicia Kutere furata fuit de Thoma Dencok magistro suo (xx s.) Herveus de Eggemere vi et armis cum cultello extracto die dominica prox. post festum Epiphanie Domini Anno xlviij°[1] fecit hamsok super Oliverum Rounkyn in Conesford et eadem hora ibidem in Margaretam Diggard et Thomam filium eius cum dicto cultello extracto insultum fecit et eam verbe-

[1] Edward's 40th year began on 25 Jan. preceding the holding of this court; the Epiphany in his 48th year would therefore be in the January just passed.

LEET ROLL OF 137¼.

(12 d.) Clement the spicer and his two sons did likewise (12 d.) A servant of Thomas Bird, and his mainpast, did likewise (6 d.) John de Beccles and his five servants came not to the leet (18 d.)

St. Andrew Trumpington, a servant of Henry the cutler, drew blood of a certain mendicant, and the said poor man raised the hue on him rightfully (18 d.) .... Adam de Horstead, goldsmith, Robert Fleshhewer and Thomas Toftes fought together in the house [called the] Bearstaff, and are common dice-players (arrest). .... Alice, daughter of Robert Sheder, stole from Robert de Massingham, her master, a double cloak, a fur coat, a pair of sheets, and other valuables worth 20 d. (arrest). .... Gilbert de Sedgeford made distraint on John Smith, tenant of Richard Smith—to wit, one bellows without licence (12 d.) .... Ranulph Moreman has set a great stone in the king's highway opposite his door, to the great nuisance of his neighbours, and they pray that it may be removed (6 d.) .... John the silkman buys and sells, and has an apprentice, and is not a citizen (2 s.) Alice the wig-maker likewise buys and sells, and is not a citizen (2 s.) Agnes the bookbinder likewise is not a citizen (12 d.) Andrew the lantern-maker has done likewise (40 d.) Richard Clerk, card-maker, has done likewise (6 d.) Edmund de Metton, webster, has done likewise (18 d.)

St. George William Stugs took back in the name of thefbote a blanket, price 12 d., which Katherine his maidservant stole from him (6 d.) . .... John Neloth bought a coverlet, price 20 s., which Alice Kuter stole from Thomas Dencock, her master (20 s.) Hervey de Edgmere by force and arms with a drawn knife, on Sunday next after the feast of the Epiphany of the Lord, in the 48th year, made ham-soken on Oliver Rounkyn in Conesford, and at the same hour and place made assault with the said drawn knife on Margaret Diggard and Thomas her son, and beat her

ravit pannos delaceravit et eam in lutum deiecit et unam markam in pecunia numerata in una bursa ad pectus pendente cepit et asportavit et eis minatus fuit ad interficiendum (xij d.) . . . . Galfridus Bagwell submersit batellum suum in regia ripa sub ponte Episcopi in purpresturam magnam et ad detrimentum eiusdem ripe (xij d.)

[Michaelis[1]] Walterus Baldewyne Tayllour et Johannes de Palegrave Tayllour invenerunt unum bidew in Regia via et illum custodiverunt et concelaverunt a Ballivis (xl d.) . . . . Walterus Quell capellanus furatus fuit de Johanne Longspy lanam pretii vij s. circa festum Nativitatis[2] beate Marie et asportavit et insuper cepit vi et armis lectum suum in domo dicti Johannis arestatum et asportavit. Idemque Walterus elongavit de Roberto de Costeseye uxorem dicti Roberti per tres vices [sic, ? dies] cum bonis et catallis suis et noctanter fregit clausum dicti Roberti et dictum Robertum postea inde eiecit de domo sua vi et armis per tres noctes continuas et dicunt quod est noctivagus communis et male fame et quod est communis Webber°[3] (cap.) . . . .

[Clementis] Isabella Walswymman fecit hamsok super Johannam Warner et sustulit pannos lineos et proiecit in lutum et illam conculcavit ad grave dampnum (cap.) Johanna Warner fecit hamsok super eandem Isabellam iniuste et verberavit eandem Isabellam contra pacem Domini Regis (cap.) . . . . Uxor Roberti de Staumford cepit unum agnellum de straio vagantem qui fuit Constancie Bullok et illum vendidit pro xij d. in contemptum Ballivorum (vj d.) Henricus Taillour fecit rescussum Johanni de Eggefeld Taxatori communis taxationis de uno pelvi et una lavatoria in contemptum etc. (vj d.) Johannes de Banham fecit similiter taxatoribus et fregit sigillum eorum quod posuerunt nomine arrestacionis in contemptum Domini Regis et Ballivorum (xij d.) . . . .

---

[1] St. Michael ultra Aquam. [2] September 8.
[3] Sic. Meaning doubtful. Weaver (?)

and tore her clothes and cast her in the mud, and took and carried away one mark in coined [1] money in a purse that hung at her breast, and he threatened to kill them (12 d.) . . . . Geoffrey Bagwell has sunk his boat in the king's river under Bishop's Bridge in great purpresture and detriment of the said river (12 d.)

St. Michael Walter Baldwin, tailor, and John de Palgrave, tailor, found a dagger on the king's highway, and kept it and concealed it from the Bailiffs (40 d.) . . . . Walter Quell, chaplain, stole from John Longspy wool worth 7 s. about the feast of the Nativity of the Blessed Mary, and carried it off; and moreover he seized by force and arms in the house of the said John his bed which had been taken in distraint, and carried it off. And the said Walter carried away from Robert de Costessey Robert's wife three times with his goods and chattels, and by night he broke into the close of the said Robert, and afterwards ejected him from his house by force and arms for three whole nights, and they say he is a common night-rover and of ill fame, and is a common webber (arrest).

St. Clement Isabella Walswoman made hamsoken on Johanna Warner, and took away her linen clothes and cast her in the mud and trampled on her to her grave damage (arrest) Johanna Warner made hamsoken on the said Isabella wrongfully and beat her, contrary to the king's peace (arrest). . . . . Robert de Stamford's wife took a lamb which belonged to Constance Bullock, as it wandered astray, and sold it for 12 d., in contempt of the Bailiffs (6 d.) Henry the tailor made rescue from John de Edgfield, taxer of the common tax, of one basin and one ewer, in contempt etc. (6 d.) John de Banham did likewise to the taxers, and broke their seal which they set [on the goods] in the name of seizure, in contempt of the lord king and the Bailiffs (12 d.)

[1] Or *counted*.

[Castri Feodi]

Veredictum Lete novi feodi Castri[1] **coram Henrico Skye et sociis suis prenominatis anno xlix°.**

Johannes de Northik cordwaner, Thomas of the Mersh, Johannes Prentys commorans cum Willelmo Skeynkill [et] Ricardus serviens Walteri Bond cum aliis iiij^{or} ignotis servientibus sunt communes malefactores et perturbatores pacis et confederati sunt invicem ad diversa mala perpetranda in dicta civitate etc. et sunt communes noctivagi et male fame incedentes tam per diem quam per noctem armati ad modum guerre etc. (cap.) . . . . Adam de Hyndryngham barbour assuetus est continue ponere fimum suum in regia via per totum annum et similiter carectas suas tam per diem quam per noctem ad magnum nocumentum vicinorum et omnium ibidem confluentium unde dicta via semper est profunda et turpis in incumbracionem (xij d.) . . . . Thomas Tytel webstere est leprosus, ideo exeat. Ricardus Jobbe manens in quadam domo apud Normanspitel est leprosus.

[1] Introduction, Note F.

[Castle Fee] **Verdict of the Leet of the new Fee of the Castle before Henry Skye and his fellows aforesaid in the 49th year.**

John de Northwick, cordwainer, Thomas of the Marsh, John Prentice, lodging with William Skeynkill, [and] Richard, the servant of Walter Bond, with four other servants unknown, are common evildoers and disturbers of the peace, and have conspired together to do divers evil deeds in the said city, and are common night-rovers and of ill repute, going about as well by day as by night armed as in time of war etc. (arrest). . . . . Adam de Hindringham, barber, is wont constantly to lay his muck in the king's highway through the whole year, and likewise his carts as well by day as by night, to the great nuisance of the neighbours and of all that gather together there, whereby the said way is always deeply and foully encumbered (12 d.) . . . . Thomas Tytel, webster, is a leper; therefore he must go out [of the city]. Richard Jobbe, lodging in a house at Normanspital, is a leper.

XI. [ROTULUS DE VEREDICTIS LETARUM NORWICI A° R' REGIS RICARDI SECUNDI XIIIJ°.]

¹ ROTULUS DE VEREDICTIS LETARUM CIVITATIS NOR-
WICI CORAM WILLELMO EVERARD, HUGONE DE
HOLAND, THOMA HERT ET WILLELMO DE CRAKE-
FORD BALLIVIS DICTE CIVITATIS ANNO REGNI
REGIS RICARDI SECUNDI XIIIJ°.

[Conesford] Veredicta Lete de Conesford capta die Martis in secunda septimana XL⁎. anno predicto.

Capitales Plegii presentant quod Rogerus Sperlyngg noctanter vi et armis insultum fecit super Johannem Merygo capellanum in Regia via in affraiam et eum verberavit et ad terram proiecit contra pacem et dictus Johannes levavit utesium super eum iuste (xl d.) . . . . Johannes Turry vi et armis insultum fecit super Johannem Mas3on noctanter in Regia via et eum percussit verberavit et in terram proiecit contra pacem et dictus Johannes Turry cum quodam baculo et dagger intravit domum Roberti Bedyngham noctanter in hamsok et magnam affraiam (xl d.) . . . . Asselina atte Grene intravit clausum Stephani Collys in hamsok et ibidem unum naperon et unum kerchef depredavit et asportavit et dicta Asselina traxit sanguinem de uxore dicti Stephani contra pacem (cap.)

¹ Roll XI.—The Roll consists of two long closely written membranes fastened at the top. It is especially valuable for its precise indication of the different districts as organised at this period and of the names which they bore. It also stands alone in specifying in the case of each district on what day the presentments were made. See Introd. III. 3.

XI. [LEET ROLL OF 14 RICHARD II. 139⁹⁰/₁.]

ROLL OF THE VERDICTS OF THE LEETS OF THE CITY OF NORWICH BEFORE WILLIAM EVERARD, HUGH DE HOLAND, THOMAS HERT, AND WILLIAM DE CRACKFORD, BAILIFFS OF THE SAID CITY IN THE 14TH YEAR OF THE REIGN OF KING RICHARD 2ND.

[Conesford] **Verdicts of the Leet of Conesford**[1] **taken on Tuesday in the second week of Lent in the year aforesaid.**

The Capital Pledges present that Roger Sperlyng by night with force and arms[2] made assault upon John Merygo, chaplain, in the king's highway in affray, and beat him and cast him to the earth, contrary to the peace, and the said John raised the hue upon him rightfully (xl d.) . . . . John Turry by night with force and arms made assault upon John the mason in the king's highway, and struck him, beat him, and cast him to the earth ; and the said John Turry with a stick and dagger entered the house of Robert Bedyngham by night in hamsoken and great affray (40 d.) . . . . Asselina Attegreen, entered the close of Stephen Collis in hamsoken and there stole and carried away one napkin and one kerchief and drew blood from Stephen's wife, contrary to the peace (arrest)

---

[1] This is not the Great Leet of Conesford as in the thirteenth century Rolls, but the two combined subleets so called. The day is 21 February.

[2] The various component elements of a legal assault here described were apparently unknown to the jurors of 100 years before.

.... Johannes Merygo, capellanus assuetus est ascultare noctanter sub parietibus vicinorum et est communis noctivagus (xl d., cap.) .... Johannes Atteker de Wightelyngham et Thomas filius suus depredaverunt de Willelmo Attemeer anguillas ad valentiam xxx s. et dictus Johannes Atteker et Thomas depredaverunt pisces rescentes videlicet perches roches et pikerelles ad valentiam x s. (cap.) .... Philippus Lumbard intravit clausum Johannis Souter in hamsok et cum scala quadam ascendit ad fenestram domus sue et ibidem intravit et pisces vocatos baukynnes et alia bona ibidem inventa ad valentiam xiij s. iiij d. cepit et asportavit (cap.) ....
——[1] Barbour assuetus est iactare sanguinem [2] corruptum in Regia via in abhominacionem (xij d.) .... Johannes Wake lyster assuetus est iactare cineres paste et alia multa de arte sua provenientia in Regia Ripa ad obsturpacionem [sic] dicte Ripe (xx s.) .... ——[1] vexavit Johannem Lenn Wright coram decano iniuste et est communis procurator decani (xij d.) .... Simon Asshfeld fregit assissam panis contra proclamacionem (dī. mr̄.) .... Hugo Baxster fecit similiter (x s.) .... Simon Bawburgh non venit ad letam nec est in decenna (xij d.) .... Johannes Godyng assuetus est vendere cervisiam per ciphos et discos et fregit assissam contra proclamacionem (xviij d.)

[Berstrete] **Veredicta Lete de Berstrete die Jovis in secunda septimana XLme Anno predicto.**

Capitales Plegii presentant quod .... Rogerus Smyth depredavit c latthis de Herveo Skott et maremium et stagyngg murorum Civitatis et est communis latro (—). ..... ——[3] serviens Nicholai ffastolf clerici parochialis [4] Sc̄i Stephani intravit gardinum Willelmi Ides bis noctanter et ibidem depredavit poma et pira sua etc., et asportavit contra pacem et dictus Nicholaus receptavit

[1] The name is too defaced to be legible.
[2] Illegible.
[3] The barbers were the chief practisers of medicinal bleeding.
[4] MS. *poch*. See Glossary.

. . . . John Merygo, chaplain, is wont to listen by night under his neighbour's eaves, and is a common night-rover (40 d., arrest). . . . . John Atteker, of Whitlingham, and Thomas his son robbed William Attemere of eels to the value of 30 s., and the said John and Thomas stole fresh fish—to wit, perches, roach, and pike—to the value of 10 s. (arrest). . . . . Philip Lumbard entered the close of John Souter in hamsoken, and with a ladder climbed up to the window of his house and there entered and seized and carried off fish called haukyns and other goods there found, to the value of 13 s. 4 d. (arrest). . . . . ——, barber, is wont to throw putrid blood into the king's highway in abominable offence (12 d.) . . . . John Wake, dyer, is wont to throw cinders, paste, and many other things issuing out of his craft into the king's river, to the blocking of the river (20 s.) . . . . —— has vexed John Lynn, wright, before the Dean wrongfully, and is a common touter of the Dean (12 d.) . . . . Simon Ashfield has broken the assize of bread, contrary to the proclamation (half a mark). Hugh the baker has done likewise (10 s.) [7 others.] . . . . Simon Bawburgh came not to the leet and is not in tithing (12 d.) [10 others.] . . . . John Godyng is wont to sell beer by ciphes and discs, and has broken the assize, contrary to the proclamation (18 d.) [23 others.]

[Berstrete] **Verdicts of the Leet of Berstrete on Thursday in the second week of Lent in the year aforesaid.**

The Capital Pledges present that . . . . Roger Smith stole 100 laths from Hervey Scott, and timber and staging of the City walls, and he is a common thief (—). . . . . A maidservant of Nicholas Fastolf, parochial clerk of St. Stephen, entered the garden of William Ides twice by night, and there stole his apples and pears etc. and carried them off, contrary to the peace, and the said

VEREDICTA LETARUM NORWICI.

dictam servientem suam cum pomis et piris sic depredatis sciens eam depredasse ea (—). . . . . Johannes Lekman Gardyner obstupavit quoddam commune Cokey distans a Wastelgate[1] usque Newgatesend ad nocumentum (vj d.) . . . . Johannes ffrank talyor subtraxit bundas inter ipsum et tenementum nuper Henrici Cole positas absque assensu vicinorum (xij d.) . . . . Thomas Sylet non est civis (vj d.). Et similiter dictus Thomas vendit corea equina et vitulina pro coreo bovium in deceptionem populi (vj d.) . . . . Christiana uxor Willelmi Matteshall est communis procuratrix decani (xij d., cap.) Matildis de Parys est communis procuratrix officialis correctoris[2] et decani et fecit quamplures homines et mulieres perdere argentum suum iniuste (xviij d.; cap.) Margeria Wonder est communis procuratrix correctoris et decani (cap.) . . . . Johannes Hengham candeler nocte diei Jovis[3] prox. post festum Exaltationis Sc̄e Crucis Anno regni regis Ricardi secundi xij° imprisonavit Willelmum Glasen bocher in Norwyco in ffibriggate in domo sua et ibidem eum detinuit et non abhinc voluit eum abire quousque finem cum ipso fecisset de ij marcis et alia enormia ei intulit contra pacem (xx s., cap.) . . . . Ricardus Wilby utitur pondere contra proclamacionem (vj d.) . . . . Robertus Cook est communis recalefactor omnium victualium et vendidit fratri Thome Walsham unam aucam recalefactam in periculum etc. (xl d.) Robertus Lardner assuetus est vendere carkeys ovium et boum et similiter corea boum et pelles lanutas in domo et non in mercato contra consuetudinem civitatis et est communis forstallator ovium boum vitulorum et agnorum unde magnus clamor est (x s.) . . . . Thomas ffuystor est leprosus. Isabella nuper uxor Luce de Iklyngham est leprosa.[4]

[1] The street now called Red Lion Street (S. and L. 15, 17).
[2] An official with this title is still appointed by the Bishop in each Archdeaconry of the diocese of Norwich.
[3] September 14.
[4] It appears from the notices of this person that, although a known leper, she was not isolated. Under the name of 'Isabella Lucas' she is fined below for having a foul gutter

Nicholas received his said maidservant with the apples and pears so stolen, knowing she had stolen them (—) .... John Leekman, gardener, has obstructed a common Cockey, extending from Wastlegate to Newgates-end, to the nuisance etc. (6 d.) .... John Frank, tailor, has withdrawn the bounds set between himself and the tenement late of Henry Cole, without the assent of the neighbours (12 d.) .... Thomas Sylet is not a citizen (6 d.), and likewise the said Thomas sells hides of horses and calves for ox-hides to the defrauding of the people (6 d.) .... Christiana, wife of William Mattishall, is a common touter of the Dean (12 d., arrest). Matilda de Paris is a common touter of the Official Corrector and the Dean, and has caused many men and women to lose their money wrongfully (18 d., arrest). Margery Wonder is a common touter of the Corrector and the Dean (arrest). .... John Hingham, chandler, on the night of Thursday next after the feast of the Exaltation of the Holy Cross in the 12th year of the reign of King Richard 2nd, imprisoned William Glasen, butcher, in Norwich, in Fibriggate, in his house, and there detained him, and would not let him go thence till he had made fine with him for 2 marcs, and other enormities he committed against him contrary to the peace (20s., arrest). .... Richard Wilby uses a weight contrary to the proclamation (6 d.) [23 others.] .... Robert the cook is a common cooker-up of all victuals, and he sold to Friar Thomas Walsham a cooked-up goose to the peril etc. (40 d.) Robert Lardner is wont to sell carcases of sheep and oxen and likewise ox-hides and woolfels in his house and not in the market, contrary to the custom of the city, and is a common forestaller of sheep, oxen, calves, and lambs, whereof is great outcry (10 s.) .... Thomas Fuystor is a leper. Isabella, formerly wife of Luke de Icklingham, is a leper. ....

and also for breaking the assize of ale. The same persons are presented for leprosy in several leets, as is the case with other offences in this and the preceding Roll. 'Isabella Lucas' is a curious example of the growth of surnames. 'Lucas' was her husband's Christian name.

[Sĉi Stephani] **Veredicta lete Sc̄i Stephani die lune in secunda septimana XLme Anno predicto.**

Willelmus fframingham in regia via insultum fecit super Willelmum Stoke sherman cum cultello extracto in affraiam pacis (xx d.) .... Simon de Bayfeld assuetus est emere per majorem bussellum et vendere per minorem bussellum in deceptionem populi (xl d.) .... Johannes ffoly utitur arte sua et emit et vendit et non est civis (vj d.) .... Uxor Henrici Lant assueta est emere pullos gallinas caupones et alia in mercato diebus sabbati et ea diebus dominicis vendere ad portas Trinitatis[1] in magnam caristiam et forstallum et est communis forstallator unde magnus clamor existit (xij d.) .... Rogerus Metton utitur pondere contra statutum (vj d.) .... Isabella Lucas habet et manutenet unam vilem gutteram currentem de messuagio suo in Regiam viam ad nocumentum (vj d.) .... Isabella Lucas est leprosa. Thomas ffuystor est leprosus.

[Sĉi Petri de Manecroft] **Veredicta lete Sc̄i Petri de Manecroft die Jovis in tertia septimana XLme anno predicto.**

Walterus Gressenhall percussit quendam duchman et de eo etc. (ij s.) .... Johannes Breton fecit districcionem in Regia via super Andream Ketyll capellanum iniuste contra consuetudinem civitatis (vj d.) .... Willelmus Roper attachiavit Robertum Baxster de ffornesete debitorem suum et eum deliberavit sine licencia Ballivorum (xx d.) .... Johannes Raymond assuetus est vendere vinum per mensuras non sigillatas contra proclamacionem (xl d.)

non cives Walterus Goldesmith utitur arte sua et non est civis (dī. mr̄.) .... Omnes pistores fregerunt assissam panis.

Braciatores. .... Walterus Gressenhall assuetus est vendere cer-

---

[1] The Cathedral.

LEET ROLL OF 139¾. 72

[St.Stephen] **Verdicts of the Leet of St. Stephen on Monday in the second week of Lent in the year aforesaid.**

William Framingham on the king's highway made assault on William Stoke, shearman, with a drawn knife, in breach of the peace (20 d.) . . . . Simon de Bayfield is wont to buy by a greater bushel, and sell by a less bushel, to the defrauding of the people (40 d.) . . . . John Foly exercises his craft and buys and sells, and is not a citizen (6 d.) [31 others.] . . . . The wife of Henry Lant is wont to buy fowls, hens, capons and other things in the market on Saturdays and sell them on Sundays at the gates [of the church] of the Holy Trinity, to great heighening and forestalling, and is a common forestaller, whereof great outcry has arisen (12 d.) . . . . Roger Metton uses a weight contrary to the statute (6 d.) . . . . Isabella Lucas has and maintains a foul gutter running from her messuage into the king's highway, to the nuisance etc. (6 d.) . . . . Isabella Lucas is a leper ; Thomas Fuystor is a leper. . . . .

[St. Peter de Manecroft] **Verdicts of the Leet of St. Peter de Manecroft on Thursday in the third week of Lent in the year aforesaid.**

Walter Gressenhall struck a certain Dutchman and drew blood etc. (2 s.) . . . . John Breton made distraint in the king's highway on Andrew Ketyl, chaplain, wrongfully, contrary to the custom of the city (6 d.) . . . . William Roper attached Robert Baker of Forncett, his debtor, and delivered him without licence of the Bailiffs (20 d.) . . . . John Raymond is wont to sell wine with unsealed measures, contrary to the proclamation (40 d.)

not citizens Walter Goldsmith exercises his craft and is not a citizen (half a mark). [31 others.] . . . . All the bakers have
Brewers broken the assize of bread. . . . . Walter Gressenhall is

VOL. V. L

visiam etc. (ij s.) .... ¹Floritius Talyor pro Beer (ij s.) Johannes Trewlove . tip' cervisie (xij d.) ¹Walterus Goldsmith alienus . tip' (xij d.)

[Sēi Gregorii] **Veredicta lete Sēi Gregorii die Veneris in secunda septimana XLme Anno predicto.**

Johannes Shuldham habet et manutenet plurima ligna et stulpes posita et fixa in Regia Ripa de messuagio suo nuper Reginaldi Cobbe in obstupacionem et artacionem dicte Ripe (xx s.) Johannes Longg lyster assuetus est iactare et ponere fimum cineres et alia vilia iuxta les stulpes et stakes unde multum decidit in Regiam Ripam in obstupacionem Ripe (dī. mr̄.) Idem Johannes de Shuldham per quendam Rieder servientem suum iactavit fimum multum et alia vilia de reparacione domorum suarum in Regiam Ripam in obstupacionem et coartacionem dicte Ripe ita quod nullus batellus possit ibidem transire sicut solebat (dī. mr̄.) .... Johannes Storell assuetus est capere yongfry in Regia Ripa et vendere hominibus de Crowmeer² et aliis hominibus de villis adiacentibus pro bayte et est communis forstallator in caristiam totius communitatis (x s.) .... Thomas Pennyng assuctus est accipere equos cum peddys diversorum extraneorum et ducere in domum suam unde Ballivi amittunt custumam suam et est communis forstallator piscium eundo extra portas civitatis contra proclamacionem (dī. mr̄.) .... Radulphus Rieder est communis forstallator arundinum et tegularum in magnam caristiam totius communitatis (x s.) ....

[Sēi Egidii] **Veredicta lete Sēi Egidii die Veneris in quarta septimana XLme anno predicto.**

Johannes ffraunceys depredavit unum equum apud Keswykhall et vendidit eum apud feriam de Horning (j mr̄.)

---

¹ Added at the side in MS.
² The well-known pleasure resort on the north coast of Norfolk. It was at this time a fairly prosperous fishing port. An outlying portion called Shipden had, however, already been swallowed up by the sea, and just at the date of this Roll steps

wont to sell beer etc. (2 s.) .... Floritius Taylor, for beer (2 s.) John Truelove is a tippler of beer (12 d.) Walter Goldsmith, an alien, is a tippler (12 d.)

[St. Gregory] **Verdicts of the Leet of St. Gregory on Friday in the second week of Lent in the year aforesaid.**

John Shouldham has and maintains a great many logs and stulps set and fixed in the king's river from his messuage, lately Reginald Cobbe's, to the obstructing and straitening of the said river (20 s.) John Long, dyer, is wont to throw and lay muck, cinders, and other refuse by the stulps and stakes, whereof much falls into the king's river, to the obstructing of the river (half a mark). The same John de Shouldham, by a certain reeder, his servant, has thrown much muck and other refuse from the repairing of his houses into the king's river, to the obstruction and straitening of the river, so that no boat can pass by as they were wont to do (half a mark)..... John Storell is wont to catch young fry in the king's river, and sell them to the men of Cromer and other men of the adjacent towns for bait, and is a common forestaller, to the heighening of the whole commonalty (10 s.) .... Thomas Pennyng is wont to receive divers strangers' horses with peds, and take the peds into his own house, whereby the Bailiffs lose their custom, and he is a common forestaller of fish, going outside the gates of the city contrary to the proclamation (half a mark). Ralph the reeder is a common forestaller of reeds and tiles, to the great heighening of the whole commonalty (10 s.) ....

[St. Giles] **Verdicts of the Leet of St. Giles on Friday in the fourth week of Lent in the year aforesaid.**

John Francis stole a horse at Keswick Hall and sold it at Horning fair (1 mark[1]). The same John Francis stole a

were taken to build a pier to form a new harbour (Rye, *Cromer Past and Present*, p. 47).
[1] A contrast to the penalty for stealing a horse in later times. Keswick is 3 miles south of Norwich. Horning is on the river Bure 11 miles to the north east.

Idem Johannes ffraunceys depredavit unum equum de Galfrido Carter et penes eum detinuit per unum quarterium et est communis latro (xij d.)

non cives Johannes Dey utitur arte sua et habet ij apprenticios et non est civis (viij s.) . . . . Johannes de Well quam pluries vexat Henricum Smyth de Berstrete coram correctore et decano et fecit ipsum perdere xl d. iniuste (cap.) . . . . Ricardus Walpole est communis forstallator frumenti emendo xxx cumbas et custodiendo in forstallum (ij mr̄.)

[Sc̄i Andree] **Veredicta lete Sc̄i Andree die lune in quarta septimana XLme anno predicto.**

Johannes Turnor alienus fecit hamsoken super Walterum Gressenhall et abstulit unum harneys celle dicti Walteri (cap.) Walterus Gressenhall traxit sanguinem de Johanne Turnor alieno contra pacem (vj d.)

non cives Johannes Wymer utitur arte sua et non est civis et habet j apprenticium (xij d.)

Johannes Walsham mercer advocat bona et catalla Ricardi fratris sui contra sacramentum suum (xij d.) . . . . Simon Asshfeld, Hugo Hedenham, Johannes Erlham, Thomas Bloker, et Willelmus atte Water, confederaverunt et conspiraverunt custodire[1] mercatum in forstallum frumenti et aliorum bladorum in caristiam totius communitatis unde magnus clamor oritur et existit (c s.) Johannes Burgate ffuller emebat frumentum in mercato, videlicet unam cumbam pro v s. ubi alii emebant pro iiij s. iiij d. in forstallum (xij d.) . . . . Johannes Miller de Trous et socius suus ceperunt de Johanne Alberd xij libras de iij bussellis frumenti et de Henrico Acrys v libras de uno bussello frumenti et sic assueti sunt facere quam pluribus de civitate (j mr̄.) Stephanus Miller de Calkemylles cepit de Johanne Debenham Smyth xiiij libras de uno bussello cum dimidio (j mr̄.) . . . . Henricus Wylde pro Beer (tip', xij d.). Johannes vanlere alienus pro bere (tip', xij d.)

[1] To control the price.

horse from Geoffrey Carter and detained it in his possession for a quarter, and is a common thief (12 d.)

not citizens John Day exercises his craft and has two apprentices, and is not a citizen (8 s.) [34 others.] .... John de Well very many times vexes Henry Smith of Berstrete before the Corrector and the Dean, and has caused him to lose 40 d. wrongfully (arrest)..... Richard Walpole is a common forestaller of corn, buying 30 coombs and keeping them in forestalment (2 marks).

[St. Andrew] **Verdicts of the Leet of St. Andrew on Monday in the fourth week of Lent in the year aforesaid.**

John Turnor, an alien, made hamsoken on Walter Gressenhall, and took away Walter's saddle harness (arrest). Walter Gressenhall drew blood of John Turnor, alien, contrary to the peace (6 d.)

not citizens John Wymer exercises his craft and is not a citizen and has one apprentice (12 d.) [51 others.]

John Walsham, mercer, avows the goods and chattels of Richard his brother, contrary to his oath (12 d.) .... Simon Ashfield, Hugh Hedenham, John Erlham, Thomas Bloker, and William Attewater have confederated and conspired to keep the market in forestalment of wheat and other corn to the heighening of the whole commonalty, whereof great outcry exists (100 s.) John Burgate, fuller, bought wheat in the market in forestalment, to wit, one coomb for 5s., whereas other people were buying for 4 s. 4 d. (12 d.) .... John the Miller of Trowse and his partner took of John Alberd 12 lbs. out of 3 bushels of wheat and of Henry Acres 5 lbs. out of 1 bushel of wheat and so are they wont to do to very many of the city (1 mark). Stephen the Miller at the Calk Mills took from John Debenham, smith, 14 lbs. out of one bushel and a half (1 mark)..... Henry Wylde for beer (tippler, 12 d.); John van lere, alien, for beer (tippler, 12 d.)

[Sĉi Georgii] **Veredicta lete Sc̄i Georgii die Martis in quinta septimana XL^mo anno predicto.**

Robertus Tytell invenit x hespys de Irlondyern pretii iiij d. (iiij d.) .... Ricardus Pattesle assuetus est commiscere flotiscum cum bono cepo in deceptionem populi (xij d.) .... Johannes Lymmes Lyster assuetus est ponere multum fimum et paste continue iacentem in Regia via sub muro cemeterii Sc̄i Martini ad nocumentum (ij s.)

[Sc̄i Michaelis] **Veredicta Lete Sc̄i Michaelis die Jovis in quarta septimana XL^mo anno predicto.**

Johannes Hert de Heylesdon assuetus est adducere bestias suas in communitatem[1] Norwici et ibidem pascere eas in destruccionem communitatis (vj d.) .... Willelmus Gerard habuit unum equum per longum tempus iacentem in Regia via iuxta ecclesiam Sc̄i Michaelis de Colgate in magnam abhominacionem et corrupcionem (xij d.)

[Sc̄i Clementis] **Veredictum[2] Lete Sc̄i Clementis die luno in quinta septimana XL^mo Anno predicto.**

Johannes Worthsted parchemyner assuetus est procurare custumarios Willelmi Drawer aliis firmariis portarum Civitatis[3] ad grave dampnum (xij d.) .... Filii Walteri Blower ex procuracione et abbetto dicti Walteri assueti sunt depredare garbas in autumpno de Adam Swan et aliis et dictus Walterus receptavit dictas garbas depredatas (xl d.) .... Robertus Hegham est utlagatus et mīātur[4] capitalis plegius dī. mr̄.

---

[1] Sic in MS.: but ? should be *communam*. See below, Roll XVI. (p. 92, n. 1).
[2] Sic, singular in MS.
[3] The City Gates with the tolls were farmed out, and it appears that some of the farmers had outlying touters to intercept country people going towards other gates and bring them in by theirs. 'Custumarii' would be 'toll-payers.'
[4] MS. *mīāt*.

[St. George] **Verdicts of the Leet of St. George on Tuesday in the fifth week of Lent in the year aforesaid.**

Robert Tytell found 10 hesps[1] of Irish yarn, price 4 d. (4 d.) .... Richard Pattesley is wont to mix grease with good tallow, to the defrauding of the people (12 d.) .... John Lymmes, dyer, is wont to lay much muck and paste continually lying in the king's highway under the wall of St. Martin's churchyard, to the nuisance etc. (2 s.)

[St. Michael] **Verdicts of the Leet of St. Michael on Thursday in the fourth week of Lent in the year aforesaid.**

John Hert of Hellesdon is wont to bring his beasts into the common land of Norwich and pasture them there, to the injury of the commonalty (6 d.) .... William Gerard has had a horse lying for a long time in the king's highway near the church of St. Michael de Colegate to abominable offence and poisoning [of the air] (12 d.)

[St. Clement] **Verdict of the Leet of St. Clement on Monday in the fifth week of Lent in the year aforesaid.**

John Worstead, skinner, is wont to procure the customers of William Drawer for the other farmers of the City gates, to [his] great damage (12 d.) .... The sons of Walter Blower, by the procurement and abetting of the said Walter, are wont to steal sheaves in autumn from Adam Swan and others and Walter has received the said stolen sheaves (40 d.) .... Robert Heigham is outlawed, and the Capital Pledge is amerced half a mark.

---

[1] A fourth part of a spindle of yarn. *Prompt. Parv.*

[Feodi Castri]

Veredicta lete novi feodi Castri die lune[1] proxima post festum Sc̄e̅ Petronille virginis Anno xiiij°.

Thomas Alderman persona ecclesie Sc̄i Botulphi in Norwico die lune proxima post festum Sc̄i Georgii[2] Martiris Anno regni regis Ricardi secundi xiiij° vi et armis intravit domum Ricardi Oxburgh talyor contra pacem et bona et catalla ipsius Ricardi videlicet pannos lectum vasa lignea tabulas et alia bona et catalla ibidem inventa ad valentiam xiij s. iiij d. cepit et penes se detinet contra pacem (ij s.) Egidius Alberd fecit unum Sawyngpit in Regia via et ibidem factum est unum fimerum ad nocumentum et similiter incumbravit Regiam viam ibidem cum una carecta per longum tempus ad nocumentum omnium vicinorum (vj d.)

[1] June 5. [2] April 23.

[Castle Fee] **Verdict of the Leet of the new Fee of the Castle on Monday next after the Feast of St. Petronilla the Virgin in the 14th year.**

Thomas Alderman, parson of the church of St. Botulph in Norwich, on the Monday next after the Feast of St. George the Martyr in the 14th year of the reign of King Richard 2nd by force and arms entered the house of Richard Oxburgh, tailor, contrary to the peace and seized the said Richard's goods and chattels—to wit, clothes, bed, wooden vessels, tables and other goods and chattels therein found—to the value of 13 s. 4 d. and detains them in his possession, contrary to the peace (2 s.) Giles Alberd has made a sawing pit in the king's highway and a muck heap has been made there in nuisance, and likewise he has encumbered the king's highway there with a cart for a long time to the nuisance of all the neighbours (6 d.)

XII.[1] [COMPOTUS AMERCIAMENTORUM AD LETAS NORWICI A° R' REGIS EDWARDI TERTII XXXVII°.]

Shimpling[2] reddit de iiij s. vj d. de amerciamentis curie[3] in primo rotulo. Et de ix s. in secundo rotulo.

[Conesford] De amerciamentis letarum de Conesford iiij li vj s. x d. Et de xxxvj s. iiij d. de Berstret. Summa vj li iij s. ij d. Inde soluta per Indenturam[4] iiij li xiiij s. In vadiis liberatis ballivis xix s. Item de diversis cruce[5] signatis xij s. x d. Summa xij s. x d. Unde solvit super compotum ij s. Et debet preter vadia x s. x d.
Summa totalis solutionis cum vadiis cxvij s. iiij d. Item iij s. Summa totalis vj li iiij d.

De Willelmo Gadthorp districto per j cote
  et j sellam . . . . . pro ij s.
Robertus de Bonewell 1 ollam eneam . pro ij s.
Petrus Nethird j ollam . . . pro iij s.

[1] Roll XII. Account Roll.—This Roll is a single membrane, of value because no similar one appears to have survived. It is very badly written and difficult to decipher. It has no heading.
[2] MS. *Shimpl'*. Shimpling is a village in Norfolk and occurs as a surname. The person here named was either a temporarily appointed Collector, as in the earlier Rolls, or more probably each of the four Great Leets had at this time a more permanent official appointed for this purpose.
[3] This must refer to some other court than the Leets. See below, in Wymer.
[4] The Roll. By Statute 1 E. III. c. 17 all indictments were ordered to be made by Roll indented, one part to remain with the indictors, the other with the Sheriff or Bailiff of Franchise who held the Inquest.
[5] By ch. 45 of Norwich Customs citizens failing to attend on public business when summoned were to be marked with a cross (+) with a view to amercement (Introd. VI. 6). If we could be sure that the mark was

XII. [ACCOUNT ROLL OF 37 EDWARD III. 1364.]

Shimpling renders account of 4 s. 6 d. of amercements of the court in the first roll. And of 9 s. in the second roll.

[Conesford] Of the amercements of the leets of Conesford £4 6 s. 10 d. And of 36 s. 4 d. of Berstrete. Sum £6 3 s. 2 d. Thereof paid by Indenture £4 14 s. In gages delivered to the Bailiffs 19 s. Also of divers persons marked with a cross 12 s. 10 d. Sum 12 s. 10 d. Whereof he has paid on his account 2 s. And he owes besides gages 10 s. 10 d. Sum total of the payment with gages 117 s. 4 d. Also 3 s.   Sum total £6 4 d.[1]

Of William Gadthorp distrained by 1 coat and 1
   saddle [or, 1 seat] . . . . . for 2 s.
   Robert de Bunwell 1 brass pot . . . for 2 s.
   Peter Neatherd 1 pot . . . . . for 3 s.

---

used in this sense here it would furnish important evidence of the presence of leading citizens in the Leet Courts as assessors. But in each of the four Great Leets here three items of accounts are specified: (1) payments by Indenture (*i.e.* cash received, as in Roll II.); (2) Gages; (3) an item entered in the other Leets as 'De respectuatis:' 'de' (as a rule) is used of persons, 'in' of money or gages; so that this would be '*of* persons respited,' and the item ought to correspond with the 'debet' or arrears of Roll II. But, except in the case of St. Giles below, the amounts seem too small for that. Still I see no other meaning for 'de respectuatis.' If 'de diversis cruce signatis' means the same, the use of the expression is contrary to that adopted elsewhere, viz. absence without excuse.

[1] Shimpling's accounts are not so intelligible as those of his colleagues.

Johannes Dun j cote pro muliere . . pro ij s.
Alicia uxor Johannis Sterr j pelvim
 j lavatoriam . . . . . pro xviij d.
Milicentia Bone ij patellas . . . pro xviij d.
Johannes filius Johannis Yve j capetium pro vj d.
Ricardus de Oxewyk 1 ollam . . pro xl d.

[Wymer] Ladd reddit de Leta Sc̄i Gregorii xxiiij s. viij d. Et de xlv s. de leta Sc̄i Andree. Et de lxxviij s. x d. de leta Sc̄i Georgii. Summa vij ℔ viij s. vj d. Inde soluta per indenturam v ℔ xij s. In vadiis xxviij s. ij d. De respectuatis iiij s. iiij d.
Summa vij ℔ iiij s. vj d. Et debet iiij s.
Idem de curia a festo Michaelis usque ad festum translationis Sc̄i Thome Martiris [1] xj s. j d.
Inde soluta per indenturam ix s. et debet ij s. j d.
Reddit vadia Ladd. De Henrico de Carleton j cloth j cortepi pro muliere furr' pro ij s. Thoma Skip j [rustum][2] pro xij d. De Johanne de Marlyngford xij d. Johanne de Linn Souter j cloth pro vj d. Bartholomeo j pelvim j lavatoriam pro xviij d. Johanne Solby j pelvim j lavatoriam pro xviij d. Thoma Surlingham viij paria cerotecarum pro ij s. Ada Bad j cloth pro xl d. De Ricero de Hoo j [vannum] pro xvj d. De Johanne Taverner j [peciam] pro xl d. Ricardo Harpel j par [Trand] cum uno firmaculo xlj d. De Ricardo ffish j ollam de peutero pro xl d.

[Mancroft] De leta Sc̄i Stephani xxj s. vj d. Inde soluta per Indenturam xij s. iij d. In vadiis vj s. ix d. De respectuatis ij s. vj d.
De leta Sc̄i Petri viij ℔ xvj s. ij d. Inde soluta per Indenturam iiij ℔ iij s. x d. In vadiis iiij ℔. xvij s. vj d. De respectuatis xiiij s. x d.

---

[1] From September 29 to July 7.
[2] The letters in this Roll are so very indistinctly formed that it is mere guess work to say what some of the words are meant for. Those in a bracket are doubtful or unintelligible.

John Dun 1 woman's coat . . . . for 2 s.
Alice wife of John Ster 1 basin 1 ewer . . for 18 d.
Milicent Bone 2 plates . . . . . for 18 d.
John, son of John Yve, 1 cape . . . for 6 d.
Richard de Oxwick 1 pot . . . . for 40 d.

[Wymer] Ladd renders account from the Leet of St. Gregory 24 s. 8 d. And of 45 s. from the Leet of St. Andrew. And of 78 s. 10 d. from the Leet of St. George. Sum £7 8 s. 6 d. Thereof paid by Indenture £5 12 s. In gages 28s. 2 d. Of persons respited 4 s. 4 d.
    Sum £7 4 s. 6 d. And he owes 4 s.
Also of the court from the feast of Michael to the feast of the translation of St. Thomas the Martyr, 11 s. 1 d. Thereof paid by Indenture 9 s. and he owes 2 s. 1 d.
Ladd renders account of the gages. Of Henry Carleton 1 cloth 1 short furred coat for a woman for 2 s. Thomas Skip 1 russet cloth [?] for 12 d. Of John de Marlingford 12 d. John de Linn, shoemaker, 1 cloth for 6d. Bartholomew 1 basin 1 ewer for 18 d. John Solby 1 basin 1 ewer for 18 d. Thomas Surlingham 8 pairs of gloves for 2 s. Adam Bad 1 cloth for 40 d. Of Richer de Howe 1 fan for 16 d. Of John Taverner 1 piece[1] for 40 d. Of Richard Harpel 1 [?] with 1 buckle 41 d. Of Richard Fish 1 pewter pot for 40 d.

[Mancroft] Of the Leet of St. Stephen 21 s. 6 d. Thereof paid by Indenture 12 s. 3 d. In gages 6 s. 9 d. Of respites 2 s. 6 d. Of the Leet of St. Peter £8 16 s. 2 d. Thereof paid by Indenture £4 3 s. 10 d. In gages £3 17 s. 6 d. Of respites 14 s. 10 d.

[1] Perhaps *pece*, a drinking cup. Morris and Skeat, *Specimens of Early English*, Part II. 435.

79 COMPOTUS AMERCIAMENTORUM AD LETAS NORWICI.

De leta Sc̄i Egidii vj ƚi xix s. vij d. Inde soluta xlvij s. x d. In vadiis lix s. viij d. De respectuatis xxxij s. j d.
Ladde. Summa totalis vj ƚi ij s. iiij d. Summa in vadiis xxiiij s. ij d. Summa totalis vij ƚi vj s. viij d.
Inde solvit per Indenturam cxiiij s. Et debet viij s. preter vadia.

[Ultra Aquam] Nusun. Idem reddit. De leta Sc̄i Michaelis ultra aquam xlix s. vj d. De quibus solvit per Indenturam xxxviij s. xj d. In vadiis vij s. vij d. De respectuatis iij s.
Item de leta Sc̄i Clementis xlvij s. ij d. De quibus solvit per Indenturam xxv s. xj d. In vadiis cum [namiis] xvj s. De respectuatis v s. iij d.
Mem: quod omnibus computis [1] die sabbati proxima post festum Sc̄i Petri ad vincula anno regni domini Edwardi Regis tertii xxxvij Willelmus Nusun reddit de amerciamentis lete Sc̄i Michaelis ultra aquam de Denariis receptis xlv s. ix d. Item in vadiis de amerciamentis eiusdem lete ix s. vj d. Idem reddit de amerciamentis lete Sc̄i Clementis de denariis receptis xlj s. v d. Item in vadiis iij s. ix d. Item de denariis Novi feodi xiiij s. iij d.
Summa in denariis v ƚi xvij d.
Summa vadiorum [2]
Item reddit de xiiij s. iij d. de amerciamentis lete Novi feodi.
Et de ij s. in vadiis. Summa totalis xvj s. iij d.
De quibus solvit ballivis per Indenturam [2]

XIII. [NOMINA EORUM QUI IN DECENNIS IRROTULANTUR IN] LETA DE NEDHAM ET MANECROFT ET DE MAGNA NEWEGATE.

. . . . .

[1] MS. *comput͡*. The Feast of St. Peter ad Vincula was on Aug. 1.
[2] Left unfinished.

Of the leet of St. Giles £6 19 s. 7 d.   Thereof paid [1] 47 s. 10 d. In gages 59 s. 8 d.   Of respites 32 s. 1 d.
Ladde.   Sum total £6 2 s. 4 d.   Sum in gages 24 s. 2 d. Sum total £7 6 s. 8 d.
Thereof he has paid by Indenture 114 s.   And he owes 8s. besides gages.

[Over-the-Water]   Nusun.   He also renders account.   Of the leet of St. Michael over the Water 49 s. 6 d.   Whereof he has paid by Indenture 38 s. 11d.   In gages 7 s. 7 d.   Of respites 3s.

Also of the leet of St. Clement 47 s. 2 d.   Whereof he has paid by Indenture 25 s. 11 d.   In gages with distraints 16 s. Of respites 5 s. 3 d.

Memorandum—that at all the reckonings on Saturday next after the feast of St. Peter in Chains in the 37th year of the reign of our lord King Edward the Third William Nusun renders account of the amercements of the leet of St. Michael over the Water of moneys received 45 s. 9 d. Also in gages of the amercements of the said leet 9 s. 6 d. Also he renders account of the amercements of the leet of St. Clement of moneys received 41 s. 5 d.   Also in gages 3 s.. 9 d.   Also of moneys of the New Fee 14 s. 3 d.

Sum in moneys £5 17 d.
Sum of gages

He also renders account of 14 s. 3 d. of the amercements of the leet of the New Fee.   And of 2 s. in gages.   Sum total 16 s. 3 d.   Whereof he has paid to the Bailiffs by Indenture

XIII. THE TITHING ROLL OF MANECROFT.

[For a description of this Roll see Introduct. VIII. IX. X.]

---

[1] Supply 'per indenturam' omitted.   The subleet of St. Giles is here reckoned in the Greet Leet of Manecroft, not in Wymer as before.

XIV. [PLACITA CORAM BALLIVIS NORWICI A° R' REGIS EDWARDI TERTII XXIII° ET XXIIII°.]

PLACITA CORAM GALFRIDO BOTILER ET SOCIIS EIUS' BALLIVIS CIVITATIS NORWICI DIE LUNE PROXIMA POST FESTUM EPIPHANIE DOMINI ANNO REGNI REGIS EDWARDI TERTII A CONQUESTU XXIIJ°.

Compertum est per inquisitionem captam die et anno supradictis per Ricardum de Attelburgh . . . quod Willelmus Brok carnifex vendidit carnes boum et multonum succematas coruptas et pro vetustate putridas per quod consideratum est per curiam quod predicte carnes comburentur et dictus Willelmus Brok pro falsitate committatur prisone et judicio pillorelle.

. . . , ...

Memorandum quod presentatum fuit coram Ballivis civitatis Norwici per xij Juratores die Mercurii in vigilia Nativitatis Sēi Johannis Baptiste anno r' r' Edwardi tertii a conquestu xxiiij quod David Fishmonger piscenarius aque dulce emebat pisces aque dulce de diversis hominibus venientibus ad dictam civitatem causa pisces vendendi ante pulsationem misse beate Marie ad ecclesiam Sēē Trinitatis in prejudicium populi civitatis et patrie.

---

[1] Roll XIV.—This Roll, consisting of a single membrane with a small slip attached, is catalogued among the Leet Rolls. Though not actually connected with the Leets it refers to matters which were dealt with at those courts. As it is the only surviving Roll of its kind, no conclusion can be formed from it. There is nothing to show that the offences inquired into had previously been presented at the Leets. More probably they were

XIV. [ROLL OF PLEAS, 1350.]

PLEAS BEFORE GEOFFREY BUTLER AND HIS FELLOWS BAILIFFS OF THE CITY OF NORWICH ON MONDAY NEXT AFTER THE FEAST OF THE EPIPHANY OF THE LORD IN THE 23RD YEAR OF THE REIGN OF KING EDWARD THE THIRD FROM THE CONQUEST.

It was found by an inquisition taken on the day and year aforesaid by Richard de Attleburgh [and eleven others], that William Brok, butcher, sold meat of oxen and sheep measly, bad, and putrid through age; wherefore it was decided by the court that the said meat should be burned and that the said William Brok for his fraud be committed to prison and the judgment of the pillory.[1]

. . . . . .

Be it remembered that it was presented before the Bailiffs of the City of Norwich by twelve Jurors on Wednesday being the Vigil of the Nativity of St. John Baptist in the 24th year of the reign of Edward the Third from the Conquest that David Fishmonger, dealer in fresh water fish, bought fresh water fish from divers men coming to the said city to sell fish before the tolling of the Mass of the Blessed Mary at the church of the Holy Trinity, to the prejudice of the people of the city and the country. And the said

inquests taken quite independently and may serve as an early example of the absorption of the business of the Leets by the Municipal Assembly. The date of the Roll is the year after the Black Death, which may partly account for the small number of entries.

[1] Another butcher had been previously dealt with in the same way.

Et dictus David presens in curia Civitatis predicte hoc non potest dedicere set ponit se in gratiam Ballivorum. Ideo in mīā. Et dictus David juravit quod amplius huiusmodi emptiones non committeret. Et mīā per Ballivos condonatur. Et dictum est predicto David per Ballivos et Communitatem quod amplius huiusmodi non committeret sub pena.

. . . .

Memorandum quod Nicholaus Stotere et Johannes Mounfort et Thomas Stannard et Thomas Skip et Thomas Grange allocuti coram Ballivis Civitatis Norwici in Congregatione Civitatis tenta die Veneris proxima post festum Nativitatis Sc̄i Johannis Baptiste anno regni regis Edwardi tertii post conquestum Anglie xxiiij^{to} quod predicti Nicholaus et omnes alii assueti sunt emere omnia victualia piscis que ducuntur ad Civitatem ad vendendum de omnibus dictum piscem portantibus vel cariantibus ante pulsationem ad missam beate Marie ad ecclesiam Sc̄e Trinitatis per quod omnes ementes victualia piscis carius emunt contra consuetudinem Civitatis. Et quesiti qualiter se velint inde acquictare. Et predicti Nicholaus Johannes Thomas et Thomas et Thomas presentes non possunt hoc dedicere. Ideo in mīā. Set dicta mīā per ballivos et communitatem perdonatur. Et tamen dicti Nicholaus Johannes Thomas Thomas et Thomas invenerunt securitatem dictis ballivis et communitati videlicet unusquisque manucepit alterum quod amplius hoc non committerent atque corporale prestiterunt juramentum tactis sacrosanctis Evangeliis et sub pena.

[7 Entries between Thursday before Epiphany, 31 Dec. 1349, and Saturday after the Nativity of the Virgin Mary, 10 Sept. 1350.
Only the first two offenders adjudged to the pillory.]

David being present in the court of the said City cannot deny this but places himself on the grace of the Bailiffs. Therefore in mercy. And the said David swore that he would no more make such purchases. And the amercement is pardoned by the Bailiffs. And it is declared to the said David by the Bailiffs and Commonalty that he should no more do the like deeds under a penalty.

. . . .

Be it remembered that Nicholas Stutterer and John Mumfort and Thomas Stannard and Thomas Skip and Thomas Grange were charged before the Bailiffs of the City of Norwich at an Assembly of the City held on Friday next after the Nativity of St. John Baptist in the 24th year of the reign of King Edward the Third from the Conquest [for] that the said Nicholas and all the others are wont to buy all kinds of fish victuals which are being brought to the City for sale, from all who bring or carry the said fish, before the tolling of the Mass of the Blessed Mary at the church of the Holy Trinity, whereby all who buy fish victuals buy more dearly, contrary to the custom of the City. And they were asked how they would acquit themselves. And the said Nicholas, John, Thomas, Thomas and Thomas being present cannot deny this. Therefore in mercy. But the said amercement is pardoned by the Bailiffs and Commonalty. And nevertheless the said Nicholas, John, Thomas, Thomas and Thomas found surety to the said Bailiffs and Commonalty—that is to say, every one was mainpernor for another that they would no more do this thing and they took a corporal oath by touching the Holy Gospels and under a penalty.

. . . .

PRESENTMENTS AND AMERCEMENTS AT THE TOURNS AND LEETS HELD BEFORE THE SHERIFFS OF THE CITY OF NORWICH.

1551 TO 1698.

XV. [ROLL OF LEETS AND TOURNS. 5 EDWARD VI. 1551.]

¹ **Leta Sci Gregorii infra Wardam de Wymer.**

Civitas Norwici

² Inquisitio in predicta leta domini Regis capta et tenta apud Norwicum predictum in Guyhald Civitatis predicte ibidem coram Thoma Morley & Johanne Walters vicecomitibus eiusdem Civitatis xxvj die Februarii Anno quinto regni Edwardi Sexti Dei gratia Anglie ffrancie & Hibernie Regis ffidei defensoris et in terra ecclesie Anglie & Hibernie supremi Capitis per sacramentum Thome Wynter . . . [14 names] . . .

ts Cappleg'

Qui dicunt super eorum sacramentum quod Johannes Eldrytche occupat artem suam infra Civitatem Norwici tanquam civis eiusdem Civitatis & non est civis juratus. Ideo ipse in mīa . . vj d.
Willelmus Nutteth pro consimili . . . . vj d.

fforcyns

. . . [22 others] . . .

. . . .

---

¹ Roll XV. 1551.—These Rolls are not complete. They relate partly to the Leets held in February and March 155⁰/₁, and partly to the second Tourn held in April. The returns for both are incomplete and those for the first Tourn held in the previous October are altogether missing. For the divisions of the City at this time, see Introduction, II. 13.

² The returns for each Leet or Ward in this and the succeeding Rolls are made on a separate membrane. They are mostly in English. Sometimes the headings are in Latin. The presentments for the Leet of St. Gregory are entirely in Latin. 'St. Gregory' was one of the old subleets; 'Wymer' here is the Great Ward of Wymer, formerly the Leet of that name.

86 LEET IN NORWICH, 155¾.

Cuiv' Et quod Johannes Webster ffyshmonger habet gutturam nocument' [sic] per quam permittit aquam corruptam exire et eodem [sic] in regia via ad nocumentum etc. . . . . iij d.
. . . [4 others] . . .

Typplers Et quod Thomas Pate exposuit et vendidit servisiam in domo sua per mensuras illicitas et insigillatas contra formam statuti inde editi & provisi . iij d.
. . . [4 others] . . .

Noysaunce of the king's hijghe wey Et quod Thomas Nicolls nocet Regiam viam cum fimo lignis et truncis ac aliis nocumentis. Ideo in mīa . . . . vj d.
. . . [6 others] . . .

Noysaunce le ryver Et quod Johannes Lowe Dyer nocet Regiam Ripam cum fimo et aliis sordidis in magnum detrimentum eiusdem Ripe et nocumentum populi Domini Regis. Ideo in mīa . . . . vj d.

corrupt vittell Et quod Rogerus Stannowe vendidit in foro dicte Civitatis victualia corrupta et insana pro corporibus populi sive leges¹ Domini Regis viz. le myssell bakon. Ideo in mīa . . . . iiij d.

Ille rule Et quod Robertus Clerk manutenet diversos suspectos in domo sua ludendo ad jòca² illicita et lege prohibita temporibus illicitis et prohibitis. Ideo in mīa . . . . xij d.
Clement pro consimili . . vj d.
Et quod Camerarii predicti nocent Regiam viam apud le cokkeye infra presinctum huius lete ad graunde nocumentum populi et leges¹ Domini Regis viz. apud lez Cockeyz in parochiis Sc̄ōrum Gregorii, Laurentii et Seynte Croyse. Ideo in mīa iiij s.
Et quod nullus Capitalis Plegius huius lete discooperabit consilium nostrum in aliquibus causis sub pena forisfacture³ . . . . . x s.

---

¹ *lieges.* ² *games.* tion is made at the end of each set
³ This or an equivalent declara- of presentments in all these Rolls.

Berstret.

The Citie of Norwich

The Lete of our Soveraigne Lord the king holden in the Guyldhall of the said Citie before Thomas Morley and John Walters Shrevis of the Citie aforesaid the ij daye of Marche in the Vth yere of the Raigne of our Soveraigne Lorde Edward the Syxt by the grace of God King of Englond ffraunce & Irelond defendor of the ffaith and in earthe of the Churche of Englond and also of Irelond Supreme hede— for the Warde of Berstret within the said Citie by the Othis of
[13 persons]—sworn
Which sayeth by vertue of thir said Othis that thes persons here next after namyd Do Inhabite the said warde and occupie thir occupacions within the said Citie as Citizens and ben non—wherfor they ben amercied as folowyth
fforynors—[9]

Typplers.

These persons next after namyd ben amercyed for typplyng of ale and bere with unlawfull metts & measures & ben amercied as folowith.
. . . [2 persons] . iij d.

Bordall howsez.

Robert Heywarde for that he kipeth a bordall howse and suffer[1] suspect persons to resorte to the same wherefor he is amercied . . . . . ij s.
[2 persons for resorting thither . . . iij s.]

Brawlyng.

John Pirkyn by cawse he is a Common Brawler with his neybors . . . . . iij d.
The Churchwardens of Saynt Martyns at the Bale for noyeing the King's heye waye with mucke & compasst . . . . iij d.
Howe browne for suffering his gutter to be corrupt into the anoyans of the Kyngs Lege people . iij d.

[1] This form of the 3rd person singular is still in use.

John Marsham for encroching the Kyng's hie waye
in Saynt Myhells Lane is amercyed . . iij s. iiij d.
The Chamberlaynes of this Citie for not lokyng to
the Corrupt Lane callyd Saynt Bartylmewes Lane v s.
Also yf any of our company shall bewraye the
King's counsell his fellows or his owne he shall
lose & forfet . . . . x s.

[SHERIFFS' SECOND TOURN. 1551.]

Norwich

The turn for our Soveraygn lorde Kyng Edward the Sext holden in the Gylde hall there the xx^{tl} day off apryll the fyfth yere of hys majesties Reign before Thomas Morley and John Walters then beyng Shreffs off the Citye of Norwiche.

The Ward of berstrete Conford and trowse.[1]
[15 Jurors.]
fforeyns.
And they say by the othe that they have takyn that
Wylliam Stewyns occupieth as a freman and ys
non therefore he ys mercyd . . . . ij d.
[26 others, 2 previously presented at Berstrete Leet.]
[Then follow other presentments, as in the Leets.]

Norwyche.
Wymer and Mydyll Wymer & also Est Wymer Warde.[2]
The turne with ye resydue [3] of ye Lete holden in ye guyld hall in ye xxj^{tl} daye of Apryll in ye reigne of Edwarde ye Syxte by ye grace of God Kyng . . . . ye vth yere in ye yere of Thomas Morley Alderman & John Walterrs Schrevys of ye seyd cyte of Norwyche.
The namys of the enquest.
[12 Jurors—none on the three Juries of these three Leets.]

[1] The Great Ward (formerly Leet) of Conesford. Trowse was a suburb which had not belonged to the sub-leet of South Conesford. It was within the bounds of the County of the City under the Charter of Henry IV. in 1403.
[2] The Great Ward of Wymer was divided into the three Small Wards of West, Middle and East Wymer.
[3] See Introduction, XII. 4.

Whiche seythe upon yer othe that thes hereafter insuyng being fforeyners do occupye yer crafts & occupacions within ye lybertyes of ye seyd cyte whiche is a great detriment & hyndraunce of ye cytezens And yerfor yei bo amercicd as it apearyth.

William Whylwryght vj d. and he to be cytezen on yc feast of ye natyvyte of Seynt John baptyst next insuyng upon the penaltye of iij s. & iiij d.

[5 others—5 out of 6 were presented at the Leets.]

Also whereas ye baxter bake breade undyr thassyse therfor he is amercyd as it appeare . Jaffrey Mychell iij s. & iiij d.

Also of dyverse and sondrye for noyeing of ye King's leche people with layeing of tymbre & mucke yerfor yei be amercyd which be thes . Thomas Nycoll . iij s. & iiij d. Wylliam Sandryngham & Edmond Downing churchwardens of ye parysche churche of Seynt Gregorye . vi d. Mr. Hubberd viij d. The Chamberleyns x s. George herryson iij d.

Also of those y^t noyethe the Kyng's ryver yei be amercyd as it apeare which is . John Betts, vi s. & viij d.

[None of these last offences were presented at the Leets.]

XVI. ¹[SHERIFFS' TOURNS. 1 AND 2 PHILIP AND MARY. 1554 AND 1555.]

[THE FIRST TOURN. OCTOBER 1554.].

Civitas Norwici

The Shrives Turne holden in the Guyldhall of the Cite of Norwiche before Mr. Thomas Malby and William Myngey Shrives of the same Cite the — ² daye of October in the firste & seconde yeres of the reyne of our Soverayne Lorde and Lady Phylyp and Mary by the grace of God King & Quene of Ingland ffraunce Napylls Jerusalem and Irelande Defenders of the feyth prynce of Spayne and Cicyll Archduke of Austryche Duke of Myllane Burgundye and Brabaunt Counteys of Haspurge fflanders and Tyroll for the warde of Connesforde Bestrete [sic] and Trows within the seid Cite by the othes of . . . [14 Jurors.]

Whiche do say upon their said othes that all theis persons here next under named do inhabyte the seyde Warde and do occupy their occupacions and be no Citezens Wherefore they be amercied as folowith.

	Thomas Debney . .	vj d.	
ult. turn	John Cowell . . .	vj d.	[88 presentments.
ult. turn	John Pallyng . .	xij d.	7 marked 'ult. turn.'
let.	Robert Hemmyng .	iij d.	14 marked 'let.']
let.	Robert Roper . .	ij d.	

. . . .
. . . .

¹ Roll XVI. 1554 and 1555.— These Rolls also are incomplete. They contain returns from the first Tourn, in October 1554, and the second Tourn, in May 1555, with references to the Leets held in the interval and also to those of the preceding year.
² Each membrane in these later

TOURN IN NORWICH, 1554.

The Verdicte of the enqueste of the firste turne for y⁰ warde of Mancrofte holden .... [before the same Sheriffs in the same year] .... y⁰ xxiij daye of October. ....

[Presentments of persons who trade and 'be no fremen.' 37 presentments, 2 marked 'ult. turn,' 1 'prim. turn,' 23 marked 'let.']

John Sturgen for maynteinyng and suffering mens sarvants to spend ther money in his house to y⁰ great hynderaunce of ther maysters and to the evell example of others is amarcyed . . . . . . iij s. iiij d.

Mestres Conye beyng authorized to kepe a victualling house doth not only denye to sell ale to y⁰ king and quenes subjects having sufficient store in her house but also do sell her said ale be an unreasonable gayne yᵗ is to say after v d. or vj d. y⁰ galon contrary to the statutes of this cyte therupon provided, deceyvyng y⁰ king & quenes subjectes Wherefor she is amercyd . . . iij s. iiij d.

Thomas Glene for delyvering his stuffe to poore folke to be wrought by a waight a great deale above y⁰ standard¹ deceyvyng y⁰ poore subjectes etc. . . . . . xij d.

The Shrevis Turne holden .... [before the same Sheriffs in the same year] the — daye of October .... for the Warde Beyonde the Water.

Rolls has a full heading. In a large number of them the date of the day and frequently the month are left blank or filled in with different writing. Yet the presentments and amercements are written by the same hand as the heading.

¹ He paid his workpeople for making so much material by weight, whereas he really got a greater weight of material made for the money paid.

TOURN IN NORWICH, 1555.

[27 presentments for unauthorised trading, 2 marked 'ult. turn,' 17 marked 'let.']

. . . .

Symond Crabbe for forstalling of worsted
  yarne & other victualls . . . . x s.
And except the said Symond doth ceasse from
  hensforth from forstallyng any of the pre-
  misses we payne hym . . . . xl s.

[2ND TOURN. MAY AND JUNE 1555.]

The turne thear holden . . . . [before the same Sheriffs in the same year] . . . . the — daye of the monythe of Maye . . . . for the warde over the water by the othe of

The knyghts of ye turne . . . . [12 Jurors.]

. . . .

[37 presentments of 'foreyners,' 3 marked 'primo turn,' 19 marked 'let.']

. . . .

John Catbye for overleying y⁰ comon¹ with his
  horssez and neate therefor he is amercyd . iij s. iiij d.
William Marche for selling of woll oyle which
  is mekyt with traye oyle . . . . xij d.
[only 7 presentments in all.]

The Shreves Turne . . . . the vjth daye of June . . . . for the warde of Wymer.

Milites Turni [14 Jurors.]

. . . .

[30 foreigners, 1 marked 'ult. turn,' 4 'let.'
Annoyance of Stokks & blokks.
ffalse weights and mesures amercyed.
Anoyance of the kyng's heywayes with gutturs, cokeys muck and other ffilth . . . .]

---

¹ This probably refers to some land outside St. Stephen's Gates, a very ancient possession of the Commonalty. It is now called the Town Close and the rents have for many generations been divided amongst the Freemen. Recently an unsuccessful attempt was made to claim it by the Mayor and Corporation on behalf of the Citizens. The estate has been formed into a Charitable Trust to be administered on behalf of the Freemen.

XVII. [SHERIFFS' TOURNS AND LEETS. 1681 AND 1682.]

[FIRST TOURN. OCTOBER 1681.]

Civitas
Norwici

[2] Extracta Indentata finium et amerciamentorum forisfactorum taxatorum ad Curiam visus ffranciplegii Domini Regis tentam apud Guihald Civitatis Norwici Coram Johanne Westhorpe et Willelmo Salter vicecomitibus Civitatis predicte in Turno suo ibidem die lune vizt. vicesimo die Octobris Anno Domini 1681 pro Warda de Conesford Becrestrecte et Trowse.

. . . .

[14 Jurors.]

The several persons whose names are subscribed are severally amercied for their several offences following—
[16 Amercements.
11 for not paving or cleansing streets.
3 for drawing beer without licence.
2 for unsealed measures in selling beer.]

. . . .

Wee whose names are subscribed being Justices of the peace within the Citty of Norwich doe affeare the severall

---

[1] Roll XVII. 1681 and 1682.— Fragmentary Returns of the two Tourns with notices of the intermediate Leets.

[2] Estreats indented. The Statute of 1 E. III. was confirmed by 1 E. IV. c. 2, by which indictments and presentments at Tourns and Leets were required to be delivered to Justices of the Peace to be sanctioned by them. The estreats were then to be enrolled and by indenture delivered to the Sheriff. It appears that the whole process from presentment to amercement sometimes occupied two years.

94   LEETS IN NORWICH, 168½.

Amerciaments above expressed according to the forme of the statute etc.[1]

[Mayor 1681 and 1682]   Hugh Bokenham   O
                         Jn° Mingay   O
                         Rob*t*. Bendish. O

[Presentments were made on the same day and in the same form for the Ward of Mancroft, the Ward of Wymer, and the Ward ultra Aquam.]

[LEETS, MARCH 168½.]

Civitas Norwici

[2] Extracta Indentata omnium et singulorum finium et Amerciamentorum Assessatorum Taxatorum et forisfactorum in seperalibus Curiis Visus ffranciplegii Domini Regis tentis apud Norwicum in Guihald Civitatis predicte coram venerabilibus Johanne Westhorpe et Willelmo Salter vicecomitibus Civitatis predicte in separalibus letis suis ibidem separalibus diebus postea mencionatis.

Leta de Conisford

Leta de Conisford tenta ibidem sexto die Martii[3] Anno Dñi 1681.

De Jacobo Sherwood x s.
[12 others amerced x s. each.]

. . . .

Quilibet jur'[4] predicti qui defectum fecerunt in non comperiendo ad letam predictam in miā ut supra.

[1] See previous note.
[2] This and the two similar returns for 1693 and 1698 are on separate membranes and there is no note of time to show at what court the amercements were made. It must no doubt have been at the second Tourn or Residue of the Leet which next followed the holding of the Leet Courts. (Introd. XII. 5.)
[3] The first Monday in Lent.
[4] This word is never written out. For an attempt to solve the meaning of these amercements see Introduction, XII. 9. The language used is very similar to some given by Kitchin, *Le Court Leete*, p. 51.

'Item presentant super eorum sacramentum quod Johannes Rigge (4 d.) etc. . . . sunt resiantes infra precinctum visus franciplegii predicti. Et ad hunc diem fecerunt defaltam. Ideo quilibet eorum in misericordia, ut patet super eorum capita. (In margin : Decenn. qui foc' defalt'.) Item presentant quod Ricardus Wrench (2 d.) etc. . . . inhabitaverunt infra precinctum hujus visus franciplegii per spatium unius anni & diei & amplius et non jurantur dominæ Reginæ pro logiantia. Ideo quilibet eorum in miā, etc. (In margin : Non jur' in decennar'.) '

Leta de Beerstreet

Leta de Beerstreet ibidem tenta septimo die Martii Anno Dñi 1681.
[16 persons amerced x s. each.]

. . . .

Quilibet Jur' etc. etc. [Repeated after each Leet.]

Leta Sc̄i Stephani . octavo   die Martii . 12 amercements.
„   „ Petri   . nono   „   . 15   „
„   „ Benedicti . decimo   „   . 15   „
„   „ Gregorii . undecimo   „   . 17   „
„   „ Andree   . tertio decimo „   . 13   „
„   „ Georgii   . quarto decimo „   . 12   „
„   de Coslany   . quinto decimo „   . 11   „
„   de ffibridge . sexto decimo „   . 15   „

. . . . . .

Wee whose names are subscribed being Justices etc. etc.
Sessions 14 January 1683.[1]
William Helwys, Mayor.   Robt. Davy.   John Lowe.
○   ○   ○

[SECOND TOURN. APRIL TO JUNE 1682.]

Civitas Norwici

Extracta Indentata finium . . . . ad Curiam Visus ffranci plegii Dñi Regis tentam . . . . coram venerabilibus Johanne Westhorpe & Willelmo Salter . . . . in Turno suo ibidem vicesimo sexto die Aprilis Anno Dñi 1682 pro Warda de Mancroft.
[12 persons amerced x s. each.
only 1 in Leet of St. Peter before and 1 in St. Stephen.]
Quilibet Jur' predicti qui defectum fecerunt in Comperiendo ad Letam ultimam predictam in mīā ut supra.
De Richardo Baker qui comperuit ad hanc Curiam
et sine licensia inde decessit & abiit in contemptu
Curie.   Ideo finatus ad   .   .   .   .   . xl s.
Sessions 14 January 1683.[1]
Wee whose names &c. &c.
William Helwys, Mayor.   Robt. Davy.   John Lowe.

[1] A later insertion, two years after the holding of the Leets.

Civitas Norwici

Extracta Indentata finium etc. . . . [before the same Sheriffs] . . . . in Turno suo ibidem die Mercurii vizt. tertio die Maii Anno Dñi 1682 pro Warda de Conisford Beerstreet & Trowse.

[12 Jurors.]
43 amercements for nuisance, offences in beer selling and baking etc. None for unauthorised trading.]

. . . .

Extracta etc. . [same day] .
pro Warda de Wymer.
[13 Jurors.
36 similar amercements.]

. . . .

[Same day] . . . pro Warda Ultra Aquam.
[13 Jurors.
62 amercements for similar offences.]

. . . .

[At foot of each membrane—]
Sessions 14 January 1683.
Wee whose names etc. etc.
William Helwys, Mayor.   Robt. Davy.   John Lowe.
     O   O   O

[1] Extracta Indentata etc. . . . ad Curiam visus ffranci plegii Dñi Regis super exteriorem montem adversus pontem Castri Norwici pro leta predicta tempore venerabilium Johannis Westhorpe et Willelmi Salter vicecomitum Civitatis Norwici die Martis vizt. vicesimo septimo die Junii Anno Dñi 1682.

[14 Jurors.   28 amercements.]

. . . .

We whose names etc . . Sessions 14 January 1683.
William Helwys, Mayor.   Robt. Davy.   John Lowe.
     O   O   O

[1] The Leet for the Castle Fee. The Shirehall had now been removed to the Castle Hill by the north side of the Keep. This Leet must have been held on the old spot in the open air.

XVIII. [TOURNS AND LEETS. 1692 AND 1693.]

[FIRST TOURN. OCTOBER 1692. NO RETURNS.]

[LEETS. MARCH 169⅔.]

Civitas Norwici

[1]Extracta Indentata omnium et singulorum finium et amerciamentorum Assessatorum taxatorum et forisfactorum in separalibus Curiis visus ffranciplegii Domine Regine tentis apud Norwicum in Guihald Civitatis predicte coram venerabilibus Gamaliel Sugden et Petro Thacker vicecomitibus Civitatis Norwici in separalibus Letis suis ibidem separalibus diebus postea mentionatis.

Leta de Conisford

Leta de Conisford tenta ibidem sexto die Martii [2] Anno Dñi 1692.
De Johanne Tompson, xiij s. iiij d.
[18 others amerced xiij s. iiij d. each.]
Quilibet jur' qui defectum fecerunt in non comperiendo in Leta predicta in mīā ut supra.

Leta de Beerstreete . septimo die Martii   19 amercements.
„ Sc̄i Stephani . . [no date]. . . . 14 „
„ Sc̄i Petri . . . nono die Martii . 14 „
„ Sc̄i Benedicti . decimo   „   . 13 „
„ Sc̄i Gregorii . undecimo.,,   . [torn]

---

[1] Roll XVIII. 169⅔.—The returns for the October Tourn are all lost. The membrane containing the amercement of defaulters at the Leets is mutilated, so that three Leets are missing.

[2] The first Monday in Lent.

¹[Leta Sc̄i Andree . quarto decimo die Martii
  „   Sc̄i Georgii . quinto decimo   „
  „   de Coslany . sexto decimo   „   ]
  „   de ffibridge . decimo septimo „   17 amercements.
                                              xiij s. iiij d.

[On separate membrane.]

Civitas Norwici
Leta de Coslany

²Extracta Indentata etc. ad Curiam visus ffranciplegii Dn̄i Regis et Dn̄e Regine [before the same Sheriffs] pro Leta predicta decimo sexto die Martii Anno Dn̄i 1692.
[12 jurors.]

The severall persons hereunder written are severally amercied for their severall offences following—

Mr. Timothy Knights for not repairing his streete in S^t. Georges of Colgate John Alexander Grocer tenant	00 06 08
Mr. John Chapman Chamberlaine for not repairing the Towne Walls	20 00 00
Thomas Cowhell at the Stagg in S^t. Martines in the Oake for a fflaggon not sealed . .	00 02 06
John Wearing in S^t. Martines in the Oake for drawing Beere or Ale with [sic] a License .	01 00 00
Adam Pye in S^t. Michaells of Coslany for a fflaggon not sealed	00 02 06
John Rumble in S^t. Michaells of Coslany for a short yardswann³	00 02 06
Thomas Ellis in S^t. Michaells of Coslany for a fflaggon not sealed	00 02 06

Wee whose names [are] hereunder written being their Majesties Justices of the Peace have perused these Estreates and doe affeare the same.
[Not signed.]

¹ These three Leets have been restored conjecturally.
² A solitary return from one of the old Leet Courts, the last of its kind. It is given in full.
³ *Yard wand*, or *measure*.

[SECOND TOURN. APRIL & MAY 1693.]

Civitas Norwici

[1] Extracta Indentata etc. in Turno suo ibidem die Jovis vicesimo septimo die Aprilis 1693 pro Warda de Conisford Beerestreete and [sic] Trowse.

[13 Jurors. 15 Amercements.]

* * * * *

Same day, pro Warda de Mancroft.
[12 Jurors. 29 Amercements.]

* * * * *

Same day, pro Warda de Wymer.
[13 Jurors. 30 Amercements.]

Mr. John Chapman Chamberlaine for the Walls not mending betweene S^t. Gyles Gates & S^t. Bennetts 50 00 00

* * * * *

William Salter Esq. Scavenger for not Cleansing the Cockey at haigham gate . . . 50 00 00

* * * * *

William Salter Esq. Scavenger for not repairing the Cockey in S^t. Sweetings . . . 10 00 00

* * * * *

Same day, pro Warda ultra Aquam.
[14 Jurors. 37 Amercements.]

* * * * *

St. Augustines

Mr. John Chapman Chamberlaine[2] for the Walls betweene S^t. Martines and S^t. Augustines Gates want building up . . . 40 00 00

[No other presentment similar to those in the Leet of Coslany.]

[At foot of each Membrane—]
Wee whose names etc. . . . . have perused these Estreates and doe affeare the same.
[Not signed.]

* * * *

Castle Fee. 12 May.

---

[1] The second Tourn, in April.
[2] This would be the same portion of the City walls as that of which presentment was made at the Leet of Coslany. The City Chamberlain is always presented by every Jury for the neglect of some public work and they always put the cost at a high figure.

XIX. [LEETS. MARCH 169⅞.]

Civitas Norwici

[1]Extracta Indentata omnium et singulorum finium etc.
. . . in separalibus Curiis . . . . coram venerabilibus
Johanne Cocke et Augustino Metcalfe vicecomitibus Civitatis predicte in separalibus Letis suis ibidem separalibus
diebus postea mentionatis.

Leta de Conisford [missing].   [ments.
„ de Beerestreete tenta xvj° die Maii, 1698, 19 Amerce-
„ Sc̄i Stephani   „ [2]xiij° „ Martii, 1697, 17 „
„ Sc̄i Petri   „ xvij° „   „   „   17 „
„ Sc̄i Benedicti   „ xvij° „   „   „   15 „
„ Sc̄i Gregorii   „ xix°   „   „   „   20 „
„ Sc̄i Andree   „ xxj°   „   „   „   19 „
„ Sc̄i Georgii   „ xxij° „   „   „   18 „
„ de Coslany   „ xxiij° „   „   „   18 „
„ de ffibridge   „ xxiiij°„   „   „   18 „
„ Castri feodi   „   ij°   „ Junii, 1698, 16 „
                [Each Amercement is xiij s. iiij d.]

[After each Leet—]
Quilibet Jur' qui defectum fecerunt in non comperiendo in
Leta predicta in mīa ut supra.

[At foot of membrane—]
Wee whose names [are] hereunder subscribed being her
Majesty's Justices of the Peace have perused these
Estreates and doe affeare the same.

        Samuel Warkhouse, Mayor ○
        Robt. Davy ○
        Nicholas Helwys ○

---

[1] Roll XIX. 169⅞.—We have here the last surviving notice of the Leets in their old form. The 13th March in this year was Sunday. The 14th was the first Monday in Lent.

[2] This date must be given in error.

XX. [QUEST OF WARDS. 1629.]

¹ 'The presentment of the Quest of Wards for the Great Ward of Mancroft as followith holden att the Sessions in the Guyldhall Norwich being the 14th day of December 1629.'

. . . . .

Presentment for 'not paving streets,' for 'unlicensed tiplers,' etc.
In margin, 'S^t. Stephen,' 'Mancroft,' 'S^t. Giles.'

. . . . .

Another for the Great Ward of Wymer, on 15th day of December, 1629.
In margin, 'East Wymer,' 'Middle Wymer,' 'West Wymer.'

. . . . .

In Dec. 1636, in the Ward of Mancroft, presentments are made for 'not attending Church.'

XXI. PRINTED FORM, 1802 ETC.

'We the Inquest sworn to inquire for our Sovereign Lord the King and the great Ward of [Conisford] in the said City and County Do present the several persons hereafter named for the several Nuisances, defective Pavements, and other matters and things set forth and expressed in this our presentment against their respective names.'

No defective weights and measures are presented.

---

¹ XX. and XXI.—These two extracts are given as specimens of the way in which the ground formerly occupied by the Leets was in later times encroached upon by several agencies. The Justices of the Peace to whom these presentments were made were the Aldermen of the Wards. The date of holding the 'Quests' shows that they were not connected with the Sheriffs' Tourns. Numerous returns made by parish constables are mixed up with these Rolls. Perhaps the presentments were based upon them.

GLOSSARY.

Baco, s.m., a pig : s.f., pork. The genders are clearly distinguished in several places.

Bitmay. A portion of the river bank sometimes, or always, surrounded by water.

Cariorare. See **Heighen**.

Ciphi, Disci. Kitchin (*Le Courte Leete*, p. 11 b) gives the English equivalent of these words: 'auxi si Tiplers vendent par cuppes ou dishes est inquirable.' A 'ciphe' is described as an unauthorized measure, p. 61. A 'dish' was a sort of bowl.

Clericus ecclesie (p. 41), **parochialis** (p. 70). An attendant with the title 'clericus parochialis' or 'aquæ bajulus,' holy-water porter, was generally recognised in early times. Such an attendant may be meant on p. 41. But the reference on p. 70 seems to be rather to the parochial 'chaplain,' for an 'aquæ bajulus' would hardly have a servant.

Cockey. A local word of uncertain derivation, now used for a gutter or drain. In the thirteenth century the word occurs constantly in the Norwich Conveyance Rolls to describe certain watercourses which ran through the city and furnished convenient abuttals to pieces of land. The largest flowed to the east of the market. About that time they began to be covered over, and were finally utilised as public drains. They are enumerated in *Streets and Lanes of Norwich*, p. 99.

Curlevasche, curlevage, curlevacher. Meaning unknown. See Introduction, Note G. p. xciii.

Dealbare. To whiten hides. See Introduction, Note G. p. xciv.

Disci. See **Ciphi**.

Dubbare. To clean and thicken cloth. See Introduction, Note G. p. xciv.

Flotiscum (p. 75). 'Flotis' is the grease or scum floating on the surface of the boiling fat (Halliwell). The termination 'cum' may be an erroneous repetition of the word which follows.

Forbarramentum. Forbarring. The distinction in these Rolls between this and the kindred offence of forestalling may be thus described. Forbarring was stopping goods from entering, or from being exposed in, the market, with a view to selling them outside the city, thus diminishing the supply (*forum deteriorare*). Forestalling was intercepting goods outside the city, in order to sell them at a higher price in the market, thus raising

the market price (*forum cariorare*). Regrating was buying in the market to re-sell in smaller quantities. This was permitted under certain conditions.

Forstallum. This word is used in two distinct senses in the Rolls. 1. Forestalling goods.—2. 'facere forstallum Ballivis,' or, 'servientibus Ballivorum.' To assault, make violent rescue of distraints. See Statutum Wallie, 'De forstall', id est, de rescussu averiorum.'

Gogge. A calf (p. 52).

Heighen. To raise the price. A local word in common use for raising rent, wages etc. It is spelt in various ways, and pronounced 'hain.'

Lagena (p. 52). Here used in its proper sense, a flagon. Elsewhere it is used as equivalent to *galona*, a gallon.

Namium. See Vetitum namium.

Ped. A basket or panier which was slung over a horse's back and in which goods were afterwards exposed for sale in the market. A similar basket was called a 'lep,' and a 'spatium unius lepstede' in the market was sometimes the subject of a grant by deed.

Redditus. A habitable tenement (p. 2). A 'redditus' is said to have 'fenestras' (p. 30).

Scondere, Scowthere. Leather-dresser. The same as 'qwyttower,' *i.e.* white-tawer, dresser of white leather. See Introduction, Note G. p. xcv.

Selda. A shed. Sometimes spelt 'solda.'

Stulp. A low post.

Superseminatus (Fr. *surseme*). Spotted with measles.

Tallia. A tally, or notched stick, was good evidence in a plea of a citizen against a citizen, but a 'foreigner' was required to prove his debt by witnesses. Hence to buy and sell 'by tally' was to claim the privilege of a citizen. Kirkpatrick in the *Streets and Lanes of Norwich* translates the expression 'ad talliam' on p. 8 'by retail.' Gross (*Gild Merchant*) also gives 'Tallia, retail.' The translation certainly suggests itself in some places, but I cannot find any proof of its authority.

Thefbote. Compensation for stolen goods accepted by the aggrieved party without leave of the lawful court.

Trepha. Meat rejected by the Jewish inspector. See Introduction, Note G. p. xcv.

Truncus. The creating a nuisance 'cum truncis et stapellis' appears to be the same as 'noyeing the highway with stokks and blokks' (p. 92). The offence probably consisted in laying blocks (*truncos*) or logs of wood in the miry streets to form a decent entrance to a house. Sometimes a more permanent 'calcetum' was employed (p. 47). When Bishop Swinfield went to London a 'pavimentum' was set 'contra domos domini' (*Household Roll*, Camden Soc. p. 129). The 'stapelli' would be stakes set up to protect the entrance.

Truncus fullonis. Fuller's block. See Introduction, Note G. p. xciv.

Vetitum namium. Vé de naam. Wrongful detention of distress; refusal to release goods taken in distraint when due security was offered (Bracton, 155 b). In these Rolls the expression when extended is written 'vetitum namium,' not 'namii.'

INDEX OF MATTERS.

Affeerers, 34, 50
Agreement not to make suit, 7
Alderman of a Gild, 13
Alewives, offences of, fully described, 51
Amercements affeered by Justices of the Peace, 93
Amercements excused at request of friends, 20, 24, 26, 27, 51
Anchoress of Newbrigge, 60
Anchorite of All Saints, 6
Apples, 70
Apprentices, 55, 63, 64, 74
Archdeacon of Norfolk, 21
'Armiger,' 57
Ash, tanning with bark of, 28, 39
Assault: more fully described in fourteenth century, 66, 69
Assize, amercement for not being in, 15, 19
Avowing the goods of strangers, 15, 51, 60, 62

Bakehouse, 6, 7
Bakers, offences of, 50
'Ballivi Domini Regis,' 56, 59, 60
Barbers as medicinal bleeders, 70
Barley, 4, 40, 62, 63
Bars, 28; set up, 12, 44; withdrawn, 21
'Bayte,' 73
'Beer,' 73, 74
Beer, selling with two measures, 47
Bishop, indictment before the, 34
Bitmay, 55, 65

Blood-drawing dealt with by arrest, 57
'Bordall howse,' 87
Bounds withdrawn, 22, 23, 51
Bounds withdrawn without assent of neighbours, 71
Brawling, 87
Bread, assize of, 12, 16, 70, 72, 89
Brewers, offences of, 50, 51, 61
Butchers, offences of, 60, 80

Calcetum, 36, 47
Candlestick, drawing blood with, 23
Capital Pledges amerced. *See* Jurors
Capital Pledges amerced for flight of an outlaw, 75
Capital Pledges amerced for non-attendance, 14, 17
Capital Pledges substituted for absent ones, 17
Castle, New Fee of the, 68, 76
Castle, Steward of the, 11
Cellarer of Norwich, 3
Chamberlain of the City amerced, 88, 89, 98, 99
Chandlers, fraudulent agreement amongst, 52
Chandlers, offences of, 60
Church, amercement for not attending, 101
'Ciphe,' or cup, 42, 61, 64, 70
Cistercian Abbeys and wool, 21 *n*
'Clericus parochialis,' 70
Clerk of a church amerced for not being in tithing, 41
Climbing walls, 6

INDEX OF MATTERS.

Clothes, fraudulent working of old, 5, 55, 60, 64, 65
Cobblers, gild of, 43
'Cockey,' 6, 15, 42, 71, 92
Collectors, account rendered by, 27, 38, 43, 46, 51
Common land of Norwich, 75, 92
Composition for 'all offences,' 45
Concealing a dagger found in the highway, 67
Conspiracy, 64, 66, 68, 74
Constable of a Leet, 1
Contempt, 7, 18, 28, 36, 59, 67
Contempt of court by departing without licence, 95
Cooks, offences of, 13, 16, 32, 71
Corn, extensive forestalment of, 62, 63, 64, 65
Corn, fraudulent dealings with, 12, 13, 19, 35, 57, 58
Corrector, official, 71, 74
Corrupt meat to be burned, 80
'Cortepi,' 78
Court Christian, 3, 17, 30, 37, 45, 51, 53, 58
Crockards, 51, 53
'Cronys,' 8
Cross, meaning of mark of a, 77
Curlevasche, curlevage, curlevacher, 13, 51, 58
'Custumarii,' meaning of, 75

Day named for a person to become a citizen, 45, 89
Dead, selling meat of a cow found, 10, 47
Dean of the City of Norwich, 2, 15, 44, 58, 70, 71, 74
Debtor, release of without licence, 72
'Decenna Domini Regis,' 65
Decennaries, 44, 94 n
Default, Capital Pledge making, 3, 17, 33, 52
Default, tithingman making, 19
Defaulters ordered to be produced, 34
Deforcing the common people from mowing grass, 45
Dice-players, 66
'Discs' or dishes, 64, 70
Discharge of a Capital Pledge, 4

Distraint, domestic articles taken for, 67, 77, 88
Distraint, making, on the king's highway, 72
Distraint, making, without licence, 64, 66
Ditches, feeding animals in the City, 5
Ditches, the City, undermining, 11
Dog, killing a, in the owner's house, 48
Drain, blocking running water with a, 9
Dubbing clothes, 12, 13, 38, 55
Dutchmen, 64, 72
Dyeing, fraudulent, 47

Eaves, listening under, 70
Eels, 70
Eggs, extensive forestalment of, 63
Employer defrauding workpeople by a false weight, 91
Estrays, 2, 58, 67
Executor, assault on an, in the dead man's chamber, 59
Expenditure without income, a cause of suspicion, 16
Exporting corn, eggs etc., 63, 64, 65
Extortion and conspiracy, 64, 66, 68

Fair at the Gate of the Cathedral, 17
False presentment by three Capital Pledges, 44
Farmers of the City Gates, 75
Feathers, selling stolen, 16
Fee, wrongful avowry of, to escape toll, 24
Fine, making, for all offences, 45
Fishmongers, offences of, 14, 31, 80
Flanders beer, 21
Fleeces of sheep, stealing, 5
Forbarring, meaning of, 30
Forbarring the market, 5, 28, 31, 32, 48
Forbarring the river, 44
Foreigners, permitting, to trade in a citizen's shed, 38
Forestalment, extensive, of butter, corn, eggs etc., 62, 63, 64, 65, 71
Forestalment on the bailiffs and their serjeants, 3, 15, 19, 42, 45

Forestalment, on the sub-bailiffs, 58
Freemen, 88, 91
Footpath, wrongful, 40
Friars: of St. Augustine, 36, 42—
 Carmelites, 19—Minors, 20, 36
 —Preachers, 59
Fripperers, 55, 60, 64, 65
'Fry' or 'yongfry,' 42, 73
Fugitive, harbouring son when a, 40
Fullers' blocks, 5, 12, 38, 46
Fullers, gild of, 43
Fulling, fraudulent, 47, 53

Gaol, casting a man into the dungeon of, 11
Garendon Abbey, 21
Gates of the City farmed, 75
Gild of cobblers, 42
Gild of fullers, 43
Gild of saddlers, 43
Gild of tanners, 13, 39
'Gogge,' a calf, 6, 28, 52
Going outside the city to buy fish, 14, 47
Gold pennies, 19
Gutter, climbing a, to steal lead, 18

Half bushels, corn divided into, to avoid toll, 57
Hamsoken, 18, 40, 48, 50, 56, 57, 58, 59, 62, 64, 67, 69, 70, 74
Harbouring thieves, 5, 15
Harlots led out of the City, 59
'Haukynnes,' fish called, 70
Hides, selling ill-tanned, 9, 10
Hides, whitening, outside the City, 21, 39, 55
Horses: blocking them from the river, 44
Horses: leaving one dead in the highway, 75
Horses, stealing, 73
Household, an extensive, 38
Hue, not pursuing the, 7, 11, 15, 16, 17

Imprisoning a man in a house, 71
Indenture or roll indented, 77, 78, 79

Intervening to obtain remission of amercements, 20, 26, 27, 28, 29, 43
Irish yarn, 75
Island, a common, 37, 45

Jewish meat called 'trefa,' 28
Jewry, pawning stolen goods in the, 10
Jurors, amercement of, 2, 11, 12, 14, 15, 17, 22, 25, 31, 37, 57
Jurors compelled to make a presentment, 12
Justices of the Peace, 93, 98

King's beam, not using, 52, 60
'Knyghts of y² turne,' 92

'Lagena,' a vessel or flagon, 52
Landgable, 21 n, 31, 36, 44, 48 (?), 55
Larceny, indictment for, 4
Larceny, redemption of, 39
Leet, non-attendance at the, 63, 65, 70, 94, 95, 97, 98, 100
Leet, 'residue of y²,' 88
Leet, withdrawing to escape the, 52, 58
'Leges' or 'lege people,' 86, 87
'Lekman,' meaning of, 44, 71
Leper, 57, 59, 68, 71, 72
Leper ordered to leave the City, 68
Leper, trading with a, not forbidden, 59
'Leta Domini Regis,' 85
Linen thread wrongfully put into cloths, 30
Lot and scot, 48

Malt, women making, 19, 49, 55
Mainpast, 40, 57, 60, 66
Mainpast amerced for not being in tithing, 52
Mass of the Blessed Virgin, the hour for commencing market, 31, 80, 81
Measure, buying by greater and selling by less, 13, 30, 72
Measure, refusing bare, 12, 45
Measures, unsealed, 64, 72, 93
Meeting laden vessels on the river, 14

'Milites Turni,' 92
Mill, buying corn at a, to avoid toll, 13, 28, 40
Miller stealing flour, 65
Miller stealing wheat, 74
Mixing good and bad whelks, 10
Mixing herring, oysters and other goods, 48
Money kept back for want of heaped-up measure, 11, 12
Murder, presentment of, 35, 44

Nets contrary to the assize, 2, 34, 42
New, or Castle, Fee, 68, 76, 79, 96
Night-rovers, 5, 10, 64, 68, 70
Non-attendance, 46, 47, 48
Non-delivery of planks cast up by the river, 4
Non-delivery of treasure trove, 52
Nuisance, neighbours pray the removal of a, 66
Nuisance to a single neighbour, 8, 28, 43, 45, 51, 56

Oath, declining to take the, when elected sub-constable, 18
Oath, refusal to take the, as juror, 4, 7, 11, 36
Offences of bakers, 50; brewers, 50, 51, 61; butchers, 60
Offences of chandlers, 52, 60; cooks, 32, 40, 60
Offences of fishmongers, 32, 80, 81
Offences of fripperers, 60
Offences of poulterers, 32, 60
Offences of tanners, 50, 60
Oil, fraudulent sale of, 47
Oil, mixing two kinds of, 92
'Olla,' size of the measure, 33
Outlaw, 75
Oysters, price of, 63, 65

Panel of Capital Pledges (?), 50
Partnership with a servant out of tithing, 44
'Paste,' 75
Pawning stolen goods, 10
Pears, 70
Peas, white, 63
'Peddys,' 73

'Pekkes,' 60
Pennies, finding two gold, 19
'Perches' (perch), 70
Philip and Mary, their official titles, 90
Pig, selling meat of a mad, 57
'Pikerelles' (pike), 70
Pillory, butcher adjudged to the, 80
Pleas, Roll of, 9
Ploughing up the highway, 8
Pollards, 50, 51, 58
Pork, measly, 10, 24
Poulterers, offences of, 32, 60
Presentment by a single Capital Pledge, 2
Presentment, false, of murder, 44
Presentment traversed as incorrect, 18, 26, 27, 28, 29, 30, 31, 45
Prime, hour to begin purchases in market, 31, 56, 60, 80
Prior: his Sunday market, 17, 72
Prior, fishermen of, 42
Private nuisance, 8, 28, 43, 45, 51, 56
Procuring customers for the farmers of the City Gates, 75
Procuring pleas for the Court Christian, 45, 51, 71
Profits, sharing with another trader, 16, 48
Puddings and sausages, unwholesome, 8

Quest of Wards, 101

Rape, 6
Rape (violent seizure), 52
Receiving back stolen goods, 45, 65
Receiving stolen goods punished by amercement, 40, 64, 66
Redemption of larceny, 39
Reeds and tiles, 73
Refusal of Capital Pledge to take the oath, 4, 7, 11, 36
Refusal to make presentment, 2
Regraters of cheese, 60
Regraters of oats, 60
Release of distraint without licence, 64
Remission of amercements by request, 20, 24, 26, 27, 28, 29, 43

INDEX OF MATTERS. 109

Rent, a tenement so-called, 2, 15, 25, 30
Rescue, 57, 58, 59, 67
'Residue of y° Lete;' 88
'Respectuatis,' meaning of, 77, 78, 79
Reward taken for a stolen ox-hide, 45
River blocked by sinking a boat, 67
Robbery of the Dean's chest, 2
'Roches' (roach), 70
Roll of pleas, 9
Rye, 4, 62

Saddlers, gild of, 43
Sausages and puddings, unwholesome, 8
'Sawyngpit' set in the highway, 76
Scavenger of the City amerced, 99
Scoutheres or leather-dressers, 12, 21
Seal: setting none on beer, 28
Seal, a private, 56
Seal of taxers, 67
Secreting corn to avoid toll, 12, 35, 53
Sharing the profits of another's goods, 16, 48
Sheaves of wheat, stealing, 75
Sheep, pulling the fleeces of, 4
Sheep, selling drowned, 16
Signs, leading merchants to a house by, 48
Silk, 56, 66
Smelts, 55
Sons: father harbouring them out of tithing, 19, 34, 39
'Stalsite lether,' 39
'Statutum de falsa moneta,' 50
'Stokks and blokks,' 92
Strangers, avowing the goods of, 15
Strangers, letting a stall to, 9
Strangers, meaning of, 1
Strangers, selling corn to, 29
Straw, bushels made of, 40, 41
Streets, not paving or cleaning, 93, 98
Sub-bailiffs, 57, 58
Sub-constable elected by the jurors, 18
Suit, agreement not to make, 7
Suit by the constable of a Leet, 1

Surety, mutual, entered into by fraudulent fishmongers, 81
Suspicion, reasons for, 5, 10, 13, 15, 16

Taking back stolen goods without a licence, 65
Tallage, 58
Tallow, 30, 52, 53, 60
Tallow, fraudulent making of, 75
Tally, buying and selling by, 8, 19, 28, 45, 55, 57
Tanners, gild of, 13, 39
Tanning, fraudulent, 50, 61
Taverner suffering servants to loiter in his house, 91
Taxers: breaking their seal set on goods, 67.
Taxers of the common tax, 67
Tenting-frames, 38, 47
'Thefbote,' 63, 66
Theft, making fine with a servant accused of, 52
Thieves, receiving gifts from, 19
Tiles and reeds, 73
Tipplers, 73, 74, 86
Tithings, amercement of, 47, 48
Tithings, obligation to be in, after a year and a day, 20, 50
Tolhouse, hue pursued to the, 5
Toll, amercement for voluntary payment of, at fairs, 29
'Trebuchettum' (tumbrell), 53
Traverse of presentment as not true, 26, 27, 28, 29, 30, 31
Treasure trove, 2, 19, 39, 52
'Trefa' (Jewish meat), 6, 28
Trespass, making, on a serjeant, 39, 40
'Trona Domini Regis,' 52, 60

Use (opus), 51
Usury, 35, 38

Vetitum namium, Vé de naam, 41, 42, 45
Victualler denying ale without just cause, 91
'Villani de Conesford,' 34
'Visus ffranciplegii Domini Regis,' 93

Waifs cast up by the river, 4
Wall, feeding pigs on the king's, 37
Wands of the serjeants, 45
Warrant of a purchase, refusal to vouch the, 44
Watercourse diverted, 24, 39
Watercourse, making new, 8, 9
Weights, false and unjust, 30, 71, 72, 91
Wheat: getting it ground to avoid toll, 57
Wheat, price of, 64, 74
Wheat, selling, in a house, 12
Whelks, 9, 10
Whitening hides outside the City, 21 n, 39, 55
Wife carried off with her husband's goods, 52, 67
Wine, 72
Women admitted to the freedom of the City, 40, 55
'Woof and warp,' 63
Woollen yarn, forestalling, 49
'Worstede yarn,' 92

'Yardswann' (yard measure), short, 98
'Yongfry,' 73

INDEX OF PERSONS.

Abbot, Rogerus, 18, 31
Acre, Bartholomeus de, 22, 34
    Walterus de, 7
Acrys (Acres), Henricus, 74
gullier (Nedler), Thomas le, 8
Agulyer, Clement le, 40
    Edmund le, 30
    Semanus le, 36
Alberd, Egidius, 76
    Johannes, 74
Aldeby, Adam de, 27
    Robertus de, 33
Alderford, Humfridus de, 6, 7
Alderman, Thomas, 76
Alexander, John, 98
All Saints, anchorite of, 6
Alunday, Richerus, 30
    Alicia, 38
Alverthate, Galfridus de, 14
Alysham (Aylsham), Ricardus de, 6, 7
    Rogerus filius Ricardi de, 6
    vid. Aylesham
Andes, Johannes, 65
    uxor Johannis, 65
Antingham, Richerus de, 10
Antyngham, Ricardus de, 9
Appyngg, Johannes de, 56
Armourer, Ricardus, 64
Aschele (Ashill), Johannes de, 4, 25
Aschewell (Ashwell), Emma de, 11, 12
    Johannes de, 8, 9
    Joh. de, jun., 9
Aslakton, Radulphus de, 4
Asshfeld (Ashfield), Simon, 70, 74

Aswardeby, Walterus de, 13, 53
Attebothe, Nicholaus, 14
Attegatehend, Johannes de, 28
Attegates, Milicentia, 12
Attegore, Petrus, 19
Attegrene, Asselina, 69
    Claricia, 40
Atteker, Johannes, 70
Attemeer, Willelmus, 70
Atterowe, Henricus, 1, 22, 33, 34
Attewater, Willelmus, 74
Atteyates, Claricia, 59
    Robertus, 4
Attleburth (Attleburgh), Ricardus de, 80
    Willelmus de, 7, 17, 48
Aula, Laurentius de, 27
Avenant, Christiana, 56
Aylesham, Thomas de, 47
    vid. Alysham
Aylemerton, Nicholaus de, 19

Bacur, Galfridus le, 25
    Robertus le, 25
Bad, Adam, 78
Baddyng, Walterus, sen., 4
Bagwell, Galfridus, 67
Baker, Isabella, 54
    Richardus, 95
Bakestere, Rogerus le, 40
Baketon, Alanus de, 4, 22, 33
Bald, Rogerus le, 37
Baldewyne (Baldwin) Galfridus, 4, 25
    Ricardus, 60
    Walterus, 67
Balle, Hausya, 6

VOL. V.   O

INDEX OF PERSONS.

Balle, Ranulphus, 28
   Willelmus, 28
Ballif, Johannes le, 43
Ballye, Johannes le, 26
Banham, Johannes de, 67
   Nicholaus de, 52
Barber, Walt. fil. Walt. le, 3
Barbur, Henricus le, 10
   Reginaldus le, 13
   Robertus le, 52
Barburg, Johannes le, de Castelhacr', 57
Barlesel, Alanus, 7
Barsham, Adam de, 5, 23
Bateman, Alanus, 16
   Hugo, 12
   William, 59 n
Batesford, Rogerus de, 50
Bawburgh, Simon, 70
   Thomas de, 9
Baxster, Hugo, 70
   Robertus, 72
Bayfield, Simon de, 72
Becclys, Johannes de, 66
Bedford, Johannes de, 3
Bedingham, Willelmus de, 14
Bedyngham, Robertus, 69
Bekles, Henricus de, 6
Belache (Belaugh), Simon de, 9
Bele, Alicia, 17
   Ida, 45
   Rogerus, 28, 29
   Willelmus, 8
   uxor Willelmi, 61
Belle Ranulphus, 32, 43
Belleyetere, Martin le, 42
Bely, Walterus, 6
Bendish, Robert, 94
Bene, Hugo, 12
Benedicite, Adam, 46
   Paulus, 7, 52
Beniamin, Rogerus, 9, 23, 24
Berd, Adam, 17
   Benedictus, 17, 48
   Thomas, 66
Berere, Agatha uxor Johannis le, 23
Bergh, Johannes de, 26
   Robertus de, 40
Bergham, Rogerus de, 62, 64
Bernham, Johannes de, 59

Berningham, Walterus de, 47
Berstrete, Johannes de, 40
Berth, Thomas de, 12, 13
Berton, Ricardus de, 52
Berwick, Johannes de, 22
Berwyk, Johannes de, 2, 3
Betts, John, 89
Beumund, Beatrice, 5
   Johannes, 9, 11
   Ricardus, 17
   Robertus, 5
   Rogerus, 6
Bietlee (Bectley), Nich. de, 63
Bilneye, Cristiana de, 23
Biltham, Andreas de, 8
   Rogerus de, 8
Bintre, Galfridus de, 40
Bird (vid. Brid)
Birkelee, Johannes de, 57
Birks, Johannes, 57
Birston, Radulphus de, 53
Bischop, Johannes, 45
   Willelmus, 45
Bissop, Willelmus, 37
Bixton, Galfridus de, 62
Blackberd, Rogerus, 18
Blacomoor, Willelmus le, 62
Blafeld, Galfridus de, 52
Blakberd, Nicholas, 44
Blake, Henricus, 64
Blakene, Johannes de, 4
Blekestere (Bleacher), Johannes le, 14, 51
   Ranulphus le, 12
Bliclingg, Willelmus de, 53
Blithburth   ⎧ Johannes fil. Seman
Blitheburgh   ⎩ de, 34
   Seman de, 14, 34
Blo, Matilda, 38
Blofield, Galfridus de, 16
Bloker, Thomas, 74
Blower, Walterus, 75
   Willelmus le, 9
Blynde, Bartholomeus le, 9
Bogris, Johannes, 13
Bokenham, Hugh, 94
Bond, Walterus, 68
Bone, Milicentia, 78
Bonewell, Robertus de, 77
Bookbynder, Agnes, 66

INDEX OF PERSONS. 113

Boteler, Robertus, 64
Bothe, Odo de la, 15
Botiler, Galfridus, 80
Botman, Alexander, 1
  Ricardus, 1, 22, 33, 34
Bradfield, Hugo de, 17
  Johannes de, 24
Brakendenne, Alexander. de, 4
Brakne (Bracon), Benedict. de, 15
  Stephanus de, 11
Brandon, Johannes de, 18
Breton, Johannes, 72
Brid (Bird), Johannes, 10, 44
  Radulphus, 28, 29
Brok, Thomas de, 58
  Willelmus de, 11
  Willelmus, 80
Bromholm, Hugo de, 1
Brooke, Johannes de, 24
Brown, Hewe, 87
Brundale, Margareta de, 46, 58
Brunne (Brune), Lucas de, 10
  Matheus, 28, 29
Buk, Henricus, 16
Bukenham, Johannes de, 17
  Prior of, 11
  Willelmus de, 12
Bullok (Bullock), Constancia, 67
  Johannes, 16
  Radulphus, 10
Bungay, Galfridus de, 10
Bunthequel, Johannes, 52
Bures, Johannes de, 21
Burgate, Johannes, 74
Burgh, Johannes de, 10
  Thomas de, 12, 13
Burgeys, Rogerus, 6
Burghwode, Johannes de, 63
Burlingham, Laurentius de, 36
Burtoft, Walterus de, 40
  Willelmus de, 6, 25
But, Henricus, 31
  William, 59 *n*

Cabel, Adam, 9, 10, 17
  vid. Kabel
Calf, Johannes, 54
  Rogerus, 63, 65
  Willelmus, 4
Caly, Rogerus le, 17

Cann, Robertus, 4
Canon, Alicia, 56
Cantebrigge, Henricus de, 19
Canum, Johannes, 40, 51
Canun, Johannes, 26
Capellanus, Robertus, 19, 40
Capellani, Henricus fil., 31
  Johannes fil., 44
Carectere, Eudo le, 26
  Hugo le, 43
  Johannes le, 29
  Rogerus le, 21
  Stephanus le, 6, 28
  Willelmus le, 25
Carl, Thomas, 7
Carleton, Henricus de, 78
  Willelmus de, 23
Carpentarius, Simon, 20
Carrow, Prioress of, 5, 8, 40, 54 *n.*, 55
Carter, Galfridus, 74
Cartere, Johannes le, 48
Castleacre, Johannes de, 57
Castre (Caister), Hugo de, 10
  Johannes de, 58
  Radulphus de, 28
  Willelmus de, 56
Castro, Ernald de, 1
Catbye, John, 92
Catton, Alanus de, 2, 16
  Reginaldus de, 18, 31
  Ricardus de, 59
Caumbys (Campesse), Henricus de, 5
Causton, Alicia de, 48
  Johannes de, 38
  Rogerus de, 6
Chaluner, Johannes le, 40
Chapeller, Nicholaus le, 28
  Sarra le, 9
Chapman, John, 98, 99
Chaumpanye, Rogerus, 47
Chilman, Johannes, 16
Chyrry, Johannes, 19
Cknapeton, Henricus de, 9
Clakeston, Rogerus de, 5
Claxton, Rogerus de, 24
Clericus   ⎱ Alanus, 19
  (Clerk)   ⎰ Galfridus, 43 *n.*
  (le Clerk) ⎱ Henricus, 5, 43
  Johannes, 13, 50, 51

o 2

INDEX OF PERSONS.

Clericus (Clerk, le Clerk), Johannes de Rugham, 57
Laurentius, 26
Margaret, 50
Ricardus, 51, 66
Robertus, 87
Thomas, 82
Cluhoth, Ricardus, 45
Cobb, Reginaldus, 73
Cobelere, Emma le, 24
Rogerus le, 60
Cocke, Johannes, 100
Cokard, Ricardus, 5
Cokyschanke, Laurentius, 14
Colde, Johannes, 64
Cole, Henricus, 71
Coleman, Ricardus, 12
Collys, Stephanus, 69
Colneye, Amicia de, 19
Andreas de, 50
Rolandus de, 8
Willelmus de, 12
Coltishall, Johannes de, 14
Colton, Radulphus de, 10
Walterus de, 26
Willelmus de, 8
Colvyston, Robertus de, 58
Colyn, Willelmus, 2, 3
Combere, Ricardus le, 51
Combistere, Johannes le, 9
Conye, Mestres, 91
Coo, Johannes, 64
Cook, Robertus, 71
Coreston, Rogerus de, 43
Coslanye, Ricardus de, 18
Costeseye, Alanus de, 15
Galfridus de, 47
Robertus de, 67
Costinoble, Galfridus, 15
Henricus de, 9, 12, 39, 39 n., 42 n.
Olyva, 12, 42, 42 n.
Cote, Robertus, 19
Coteler, Henricus, 66
Coutesale (Coltishall), Johannes de, 14
Coventry, Nicholaus de, 3
Cowell, John, 90
Cowhell, Thomas, 98
Coyt, Willelmus, 62
Crabbe, Symond, 92
Craddok, Galfridus, 3

Crakeford, Willelmus de, 69
Cringelthorp, Beatrice de, 58
Crisp, Willelmus, 12
Crispelok, 30
Croke, Johannes, 6
Crostweyt, Johannes de, 25
Croyde, Gregorius, 35
Crysp, Willelmus, 38
Cubyt, Henricus, 16
Culley Alexander, 6
Cuppere, Vincentius le, 24
Currycour, Henricus, 63
Curthose, Johannes, 7
Cuttyng, Thomas de, 56

Daleby, Robertus de, 2, 50
Dalby, Robertus de, 26
Daubere, Henricus le, 13
Robertus le, 7
Rogerus le, 56
Walterus le, 7
Daumesson, Ricardus, 60
Davy, Robert, 95, 96, 100
Debenham, Johannes, 74
Dencok, Thomas, 66
Denham, Willelmus de, 48
Denne, Willelmus de, 4
Denton, Thomas de, 57
Depham, Thomas de, 31, 48
Dereday, Johannes, 59
Derham, Galfridus de, 11
Deuelcreys, Isak fil., 9
Dey, Johannes, 74
Diggard, Margaret, 66
Disce, Johannes de, 11, 29
Disse, Johannes, 64
Donnewyco, Robertus de, 18, 19, 31
Donston, Adam de, 9
Dormur, Ricardus le, 12
Downing, Edmundus, 89
Draheswerd, Petrus, 8
Drawer, Willelmus, 75
Dukke, Margaret, 60
Dun, John, 78
Dunham, Thomas de, 88

Eccles, Persona de, 48
Edythorp, Walterus de, 8, 9
Eggemere, Herveus de, 64, 66
Eldrytche, Johannes, 85

INDEX OF PERSONS.

Ellingham, Gilbertus de, 8
Ellis, Thomas, 99
Elmham, Estrilda de, 60
    Thomas de, 7
Ely, Johannes de, 5, 26
Erlham, Johannes de, 12, 74
    Stephanus de, 28
Ern, Martin, 55
Erych, Ricardus, 1, 2
    Richer, 34
Especer, Gerard le, 17
Espensor du Chastele, Willelmus le, 11
Eston, Margarota de, 49
    Willelmus de, 11
Ethil, Rogerus de, 9
Eton, Willelmus de, 65
Everard, Willelmus, 69
Everich, Ricardus, 22, 33
    Thomas, 34
Eye, Walterus, 24

Faber, Hamo, 6
    Johannes, 17
    Robertus, 27
    Rogerus, 8
Faderman, Galfridus, 14
Farrier (*vid.* Marechal)
Fastolf, Nicholaus, 70
Fegge, Adam, 18, 31
Felipps, Margareta, 17
Foltewelle, Thomas de, 14
Fenning, Johannes, 40
Fesant, Willelmus, 65
Fovere, Rogerus le, 39
Ffchis, Willelmus, 12
Ffrend, Adam, 13, 16, 47
Fhis, Ricardus, 58
Fish, Ricardus, 78
Fishmonger, David, 80
    vid. Pessoner
Flaxman, Thomas, 11
Flegghe, Willelmus, 58
Flesshewer, Robertus, 66
Flordon, Gocelin de, 13
Foly, John, 72
Forestre, Galfridus le, 15
Fornessete, Alicia uxor Ricardi de, 57
    Ricardus de, 57
    Willelmus, 58

Fourloves, Henricus, 16
Framingham, Ricardus de, 63
    Rogerus de, 14
    Willelmus, 72
Franke, Johannes, 27, 71
Fransham, Johannes de, 21, 22, 23, 34, 35, 42
Fraunceys, Johannes, 73, 74
    Philippus, 17
Freton, Alanus de, 3
Friston, Alanus de, 21
Fuler, Robertus le, 16, 19
Fultled, Thomas, 16
Fullere, Nicholaus, 64
Fuystor, Thomas, 71, 72
Fychs, Rogerus, 34
Fyppes, Nicholaus, 64

Gadthorp, Willelmus, 77
Galfridus, filius Baldewini, 4
Galiz, Willelmus, 16
Gamago, Johannes, 9
Gamen, Johannes, 19
Gaywode, Johannes de, 63
Geggard, Johannes, 9, 10, 28
Gole, Katerina, 17
Gente, Rogerus, 56
Gerard, Johannes, 54
    Willelmus, 59, 62, 75
Gerbeye, Willelmus, 55
Gernedene, Fratres de, 21
Gerthmakere, Hugo le, 25
Gervasii, Robertus filius, 18, 31
Gerveys, Robertus, 2, 5, 24
    Thomas, 5
Giber, Johannes, 25
Gilur, Johannes, 9, 23
Glasen, Willelmus, 71
Glasmyth, Thomas le, 59
Glene, Thomas, 91
Godesman, Johannes, 16
    Thomas, 59
Godewyne, Nicholaus, 3
    Ranulphus, 19
Godynou } Willelmus, 4, 25
Godynow
Godyng, Johannes, 70
Goldesmith, Walterus, 72, 73
Gonthorp, Ranulphus de, 17
Gosonthegrene, Thomas, 30

116 INDEX OF PERSONS.

Gossibe, Angnes, 13
Goutorth (Gunthorp), Willelmus fil. Ricardi de, 5
Grange, Thomas, 81
Graunt, Gervase le, 28
Gocelin le, 14
Gressenhall, Claricia de, 23
Walterus, 72, 74
Grey, Reginaldus le, 14
Walterus le, 27, 57
Grund, Henricus, 37
Ricardus, 19
Grungelthorp, Ricardus de, 48
Gurnay, Andreas, 63
Gylur, Edmundus, 40
Henricus, 5, 23, 40
Johannes, 5
Gyn, Radulphus, 11, 44
Gyssyng, Johannes de, 65

Hadesco, Robertus de, 35
Hakeford, Johannes de, 35
Hall, Laurence of the, 27
Hamund, Willelmus, 55
Hant, Johannes, 64
Happesburch, Thomas de, 15
Happing, Johannes de, 56
Happisburgh, Willelmus de, 58
Harpel, Ricardus, 78
Hasard, Robertus, 17
Hattere, Sarra le, 9, 53
Hauberger, Johannes le, 10
Hauteyn, Emma, 2, 5
Haylesham, Ricardus de, 7
Hecham, Cassander de, 10
Robertus de, 9
Hedenham, Hugo, 74
Hee (Eye), Walterus, 5
Hegham, Robertus, 75
Hekyngham, Thomas de, 22
Helwys, William, 95, 96, 100
Helwyse, Margareta, 56
Hem, Johannes, 11
Hemelington, Oliva de, 44
Hemenhale, Ricardus de, 6, 25
Willelmus de, 3
Hemesby, Johannes de, 22
Hemmyng, Robert, 90
Hengham, Johannes, 71
Herlewyne, Clemens, 16

Herre, Thomas, 23
Herryson, George, 89
Hert, Johannes, 75
Johannes, sen., 6
Thomas, 69
Hervy, Willelmus, 40
Hethel, Rogerus de, 9
Hevingham, Radulphus de, 31, 37
Heye, John le, 54
Heywarde, Robertus, 87
Hibil, Walterus, 40
Hickling, Robertus de, 52
Hidirsete, Hamon de, 7
Hidys, Ricardus, 11
Hindringham, Alan de, 53
Hiningham, Thomas de, 16
Hirdler, Nicholaus le, 25
Ho, Galfridus de, 4
Ricardus de, 44
Thomas de, 24
Hodys, Matilda, 7
Holand, Hugo de, 62, 69
Holveston, Robert de, 14, 59 n.
Honeworth, Rogerus de, 31
Hoo, Richerus de, 78
Hope, Willelmus, 39
Horsford, Johannes de, 15
Horstead, Adam de, 68
Hoveton, Henricus de, 17
Howard, Johannes, 4
Howe, Galfridus de, 4
Robertus de, 4
Hoylaunde, Henricus de, 4, 26
Hoyn, Margareta, 12
Hubberd, Mr., 89
Hunewine, Hubertus, 4
Hunne, Walterus, 6
Huntingfeud, Robertus de, 28
Hunworthe, Roger de, 18, 59
Hydhef, Ricardus, 33
Hykeling, Walterus de, 23
Hyndryngham, Adam de, 68
Simon de, 17

Ides, Willelmus, 70
Iklyngham, Lucas de, 71
Isabella uxor Luce de, 71, 71 n.
Inge, Willelmus, 1, 22, 33
Ingham, Johannes de, 17
Innkeeper, John the, 10

INDEX OF PERSONS.

Intewodde, Willelmus de, 16
Irstede, Adam de, 26 n.
  Beatrice de, 26
  Willelmus de, 3, 22, 23, 35
Isak, Margareta, 14
Isoud, Willelmus, 17
Ive, Johannes, 11

Jakes, Jacobus, 65
Jakesham (Yaxham), Persona de, 16
Janne, Johannes, 9, 16, 30
Jay, Nicholas le, 1, 3
Jelverton, Galfridus de, 12
Jobbe, Ricardus, 68
Jolyf, Walterus, 8, 39
Judeus, Deuelcreys, 9
Ju, Reykynt le, 9
Jurye, Johannes de la, 7
Justice, Willelmus, 3
Jyce, Thomas, 40

Kabel, Adam, 28
Kade, Gocelina, 40
Kebbe, Thomas, 64
Kempe, Margaret, 64
Kempster, Johanna, 65
Kenningham, Nicholaus de, 11
Kep, Robertus, 57
Kesewyk, Willelmus de, 6
Keteringham, Johannes de, 7
  Willelmus de, 51
Ketyll, Andreas, 72
Keye, Johannes, 6, 57
  Stephanus, 59
Kibel, 29
King, Willelmus, 22, 33, 34
Kinggesman, Johannes, 10
Kirkby, Willelmus de, 43
Knapeton, Adam de, 9
  Henricus de, 9
  Ricardus de, 48
  Ricardus de, jnr., 10
  Robertus de, 9
Knicht, Johannes, 18, 45
Knights, Timothy, 99
Ko, Johannes, 34
Koc, Johannes, 57
Kutere, Alicia, 66
Kyng, Willelmus, 33
Kyningham, Nicholaus de, 11

Kyrkeby, Galfridus de, 8
  Ricardus de, 53

La Bothe, Odo de, 15
Lacebreydere, Willelmus le, 53
Ladde, 78, 79
Lakenham, Hugo de, 63
  Reginald de, 6, 9, 24, 25
  Rogerus de, 6, 7
  Willelmus de, 6
Lant, Henricus, 72
Lanternemaker, Andreas, 66
Lardner, Robertus, 71
Latimer, Johannes, 62
Ledbettere, Johannes le, 25
  Matilda le, 5
Le Fevere, Roger, 39
Lek, Ricardus de, 17
  Willelmus de, 35
Lekman, Hugo, 44
  Johannes, 71
Le Neve, Thomas, 4, 26
Lenn, Galfridus de, 10
  Johannes, 70
  Robertus de, 2
  Rogerus de, 38
  Walterus de, 2, 40
Letherkervere, Gregorius le, 10
Lewin, Ricardus, 28
Lewyne, Thomas, 57
Liard, Rogerus, 25
Lincoln, Adam de, 56
Lindraper, Johannes le, 3, 35
  Walterus le, 58
Ling, Ricardus de, 12
  Simon de, 16
Lingwode, Galfridus de, 3, 22, 35
Linn, Johannes de, 78
Linnite, Willelmus le, 6
Lippard, Willelmus, 1
Litecope, Robertus, 16
Litel, John, 24
Litelcope, Matilda, 19
Lodne (Loddon), Robert de, 15
Loksmith, Johannes le, 31
Lomb, Cecilia uxor Johannis, 35
London, Gilbertus de, 25
  Hugo de, 28
Longg, Johannes, 73
Longspy, Johannes, 67

INDEX OF PERSONS.

Lopham (Loppam) } Estrelda de, 10, 30
Johannes de, 15
Robertus de, 59 n.
Rogerus de, 59
Lothale, Johannes, 54
Lowe, John, 86, 95, 96
Lucas, Isabella, 72
Ludham, Willelmus de, 14
Luke, 39
Lumbard, Philippus, 70
Luminer, Johannes le, 26
  Willelmus le, 30, 37, 45
Lymmes, Johannes, 75

Machun, Alexander le, 3
Madelmarkette, Johannes de, 48
Makabe, 28, 29
Malby, Thomas, 90
Man, Johannes le, 26, 26 n., 35, 43
  Thomas le, 25
Mangrene, Radulphus de, 7
  Ranulphus de, 6
Marche, Thomas, 14
  William, 92
Marechal, Nicholaus le, 3, 35
  Rogerus le, 3, 35
Markesale, Rogerus de, 13
Marlingford, Johannes de, 78
Marsham, Johannes, 88
Massyngham, Robertus de, 66
Masjon, Johannes, 69
Matishale, Galfridus de, 50
Matteshall, Willelmus, 71
Melton, Hugo de, 17
  Milicentia de, 12
  Ricardus de, 3
  Rogerus de, 51
  Thomas de, 51
Mendham, Katerina de, 23
  Robertus de, 4
Mentel, Robertus, 58
Mercer, Galfridus le, 16
  Johannes le, 15
Merkesale, Nicholaus de, 13
Mersh, Thomas of the, 68
Merston, Adam de, 59
Merygo, Johannes, 69, 70
Metcalfe, Augustine, 100
Metton, Edmund de, 66

Metton, Rogerus, 72
Mey, Robertus le, 16
Michael, 20, 27
Middey, Edmundus, 4, 34
Milkegos, Herveus, 12
Miller, Andreas, 65
  Johannes, 74
  Rogerus le, 83
  Stephanus, 74
Mingay, John, 94
Mitenmaker, Robertus le, 18
Molendinarius, Willelmus, 51
Molle, Johannes, 5
  Thomas, 42
Monjoye, Humfridus le, 18
Monner, Nicholaus le, 16
  Walterus le, 14
Morle, Andreas de, 58
  Johannes de, 2, 26
  Johannes fil. Rogeri de, 22
  Hubertus fil. Rogeri de, 22
  Rogerus de, 2, 3, 22
Morley, Thomas, 85, 87, 88
Moreman, Ranulphus, 64, 66
Mounfort, Johannes, 81
Mouton, Thomas de, 4
Muddok, Radulphus, 7
Munne, Galfridus, 5, 23
  Matilda, 23
Mustarder, Petrus le, 8
Mychell, Jaffrey, 89
Myngey, Willelmus, 90
Mytenmaker, Robertus le, 31

Nade, Jacobus, 11, 14
Nedham, Rogerus de, 8
Needler (vid. Agulyer)
Nel, Rogerus, 60
Nelond, Johannes de, 46
Neloth, Johannes, 66
Nethyrde, Petrus, 63, 77
Neve, Thomas le, 4, 26
Newebrid, Johannes le, 26, 51
Newbrigge, Annacoria de, 60
Nicolls, Thomas, 86
Norice, Alicia le, 23
  Thomas le, 55
Northik, Johannes de, 68
Northiks, Johannes de, 64
Northne, William le, 58

INDEX OF PERSONS.

Norton, Godefridus de, 2, 22
   Johannes de, 64
   Willelmus de, 16
Norwich, John, late Dean of, 2
   John le Mercer, Dean of, 15
   Thomas, Dean of, 44
   Prior of, 87
Norwye, Johannes de, 30
Nusun, Willelmus, 79
Nutteth, Willelmus, 85
Nycoll, Thomas, 89

Ollebechee, Thomas, 13
Olyf, Willelmus de, 55
Orfevre, Olyva le, 42
Oxburgh, Ricardus, 76
Oxewyk, Ricardus de, 78

Pagrave, Paulus de, 34
Palefreyman, Willelmus, 45
Palgrave, Johannes de, 66
Pallyng, Johannes, 90
Palmer, Johannes lo, 52
Pangesford, Willelmus de, 44
Pantermakere, Johannes le, 52
Papungeay, Robertus, 63
Parcheminer, Robertus le, 26
Parys, Editha de, 26
   Johannes de, 7
   Matilda de, 71
Pastemakere, Johannes le, 28
Pate, Thomas, 86
Pater, Thomas le, 9
Paternoster, Johannes, 62
Pattesle, Ricardus, 75
Paumer, Simon le, 21, 22
Pawe, Willelmus, 45
Pekok, Johannes, 6
Pelse (Pese), Ernald, 2, 8, 9
Penteneye, Rogerus de, 15, 30
Percie, Thomas del, 57
Persona (le Person), Robertus, 14
Pessoner, Ranulphus le, 14, 31, 38, 49
Pette, Ricardus, 7
Petyt, Johannes, 43
Pikenham, Robertus de, 58
Pikot, Robertus, 10
Pirkyn, John, 87
Pirmund, Petrus, 16, 48, 59
   Willelmus, 16

Pleye, Walterus, 25
Plumstede, Ricardus de, 9
Pope, Henricus, 4, 25
Popy, Willelmus, 13, 30
Poringlond ⎫ Ricardus de, 56
Porringlond ⎬ Johannes de, 29
Porynglond ⎭ Robert de, 9
Postwyk ⎫ Johannes de, 30
(Poswyk) ⎭
Robertus de, 8
Pouel, Alexander, 41
Prentys, Johannes, 64, 68
Prestesson, Robertus le, 60
Prior, Ricardus, 8
Provyns, Bartholomeus, 53
Prude, Simon e, 4, 6
Pruding, Emma, 51
Puddingwyf, Gundreda le, 6
Pulham, Johannes de, 14
   Walterus de, 8
Pundreys, Willelmus le, 43
Puttok, Ricardus, 39
Pye, Adam, 98

Quell, Walterus, 67
Quernhacker, Robertus le, 56
Quinton, Wyotus, 52
Qwyt (White), Johannes, 6
Qwyte, Beatrix, 4
Qwytsidi, uxor Martini, 12

Rakheythe, Robert de, 10, 14
Ravele, Henricus de, 14
Raven, Johannes, 9
Raymond, Johannes, 72
Redde, Ricardus le, 45
Rede, Emma la, 48
   Martinus le, 6
Redenhale ⎫ Agnes de, 3, 21
(Reddenhale) ⎭
Redeprest, Johannes le, 35
Redham, Bartholomeus de, 50
Reykynt le Ju, 9
Reymerston, Nicholaus de, 5
Ringerose, Johannes, 17
Ringgelonde, Alanus de, 12
Ringolf, Galfridus, 5
Risinge, Willelmus de, 15
Rodlond, Johannes, 51
Rokelund, Galfridus de, 17

INDEX OF PERSONS.

Rokelund, Hugo de, 3, 22, 35
Rokhathe, Roger de, 9
Rolesby (Rollesby), Johannes de, 14, 64
Roper, Robert, 90
   Willelmus, 72
Roscelin, Dominus Petrus, 46
Rounkyn, Oliverus, 66
Ruchballok, Roger, 18
Rumble, John, 98
Runham, Ricardus de, 17
Rus, Johannes le, 59
   Petrus le, 41
Russell, Radulphus, 44
Rykynghale, Jordan de, 9

Saham, Adam de, 5, 9, 15
   Vincentius de, 5
St. Augustine, Brethren of, 42
St. Edmund, Galfridus de, 3
   Robertus de, 9, 27
St. Faith, Walter de, 87
St. Faith, Galfridus de, 45
St. Katherine, Peter parson of church of, 63
St. Margaret de Westwick, Simon parson of church of, 63
St. Peter de Parmentergate, Richard clerk of church of, 41
Salehar, Isabella, 24
Salter, Willelmus, 93, 94, 95, 96, 99
Saluz, Ranulphus, 17, 18, 19, 51
Samer, Johannes, 57
Sandresson, Johannes, 64
Sandryngham, Wylliam, 89
Sartrin (Sartryn, Sarteryn, Sarterin), Alexander del, 3, 15, 51
Saxlingham, Thomas de, 14
Schelfanger, Caterina de, 58
Schepeshe, Ricardus, 2
Schepesheghee, Ricardus, 34
Schesemongere, Willelmus le, 13
Schipedham, Ricardus de, 60
Schod, Rogerus, 8
Schotesham, Johannes de, 44, 58
Schotisham, Ricardus de, 24
Schowthere, Thomas le, 5
Schuldham, Reynerus de, 18, 31
Scolthorpe, Johannes de, 10
Scot, Robertus, 2, 5, 6

Scotesham, Johannes de, 14
Scothowe, Petrus de, 65
Scotia, Johannes de, 47
Scoudere, Radulphus le, 21
   Thomas le, 21
Scriven, Henricus le, 18
Sechgeford, Gilbertus de, 66
Senges (Soething), Henricus de, 9
Ri ardus de, 45
Rogerus de, 20
Seasons, Willelmus de, 3, 21
Sewale, Galfridus, 44
Shedere, Alicia filia Roberti, 66
Shimpling, 77
Shuldham, Johannes de, 73
Sibeton, Johannes de, 26
Siger, Silvester, 1, 22, 33, 34
Silkman, Johannes, 66
Skeppere, Andreas, 6
   Galfridus le, 17
   Rogerus le, 45
Skeynkill, Willelmus, 68
Skie, Henricus, 62
Skinnere (Skynnere), Johannes le, 31
   Katerina, 63
   Ricardus le, 11
   Warinus le, 18
   Willelmus le, 29
Skip, Thomas, 78, 81
Skott, Herveus, 70
Skrike, Johannes, 24
Skriveyn, Simo, 54
Slabbard, Johannes, 1, 33
Slopere, Ricardus le, 48
Smaleberthe (Smalberth) Beatricia de, 53
   Galfridus de, 12
Smyth, Henricus, 74
   Johannes, 66
   Ricardus, 66
   Rogerus, 70
Snago, Petrus, 30
Snoringg, Ricardus de, 52
Solby, Johannes, 78
Somer, Ricardus, 21
Souter, Johannes, 70
Sparham, Alexander de, 14
   Simon de, 10
Sparwe (Sparrow), Galfridus, 20
   Thomas, 7

Sparwe, Willelmus, 15
Sperlyngg, Rogerus, 69
Spike, Johannes, 2, 9
   Thomas, 9, 10, 31, 45
Spitellond, Magister del, 37
Sprouston, Radulphus de, 53
Spycer, Clemens, 66
Stabler, Johannes, 30
Stafforth (Stafford), Edmundus de, 4
   Radulphus de, 25
Stalham, Ricardus de, 18, 19, 28, 31, 39
Stalun, Adam, 55
Stanhard (Stannard), Johannes, 23
   Paulinus, 50
   Thomas, 9, 81
   Willelmus, 40
Stannowe, Rogerus, 86
Staunford, Avicia de, 43
   Robertus de, 67
Stedefast, Willelmus, 46, 52
Sterr, Johannes, 78
Stewyns, Wylliam, 88
Stiberd, Radulphus de, 16
Stirston, Adam de, 22, 30, 53
   Willelmus de, 4
Stodeye, Petrus de, 65
Stoke, Johannes de, 4, 10
   Willelmus, 72
Ston, Adam, 44
   Johannes, 29
Stonhus, Johannes del, 29, 59
Storell, Johannes, 73
Storm, Willelmus, 8
Stotere (Stotrere), Henricus le, 18, 31
   Hugo le, 59
   Nicholaus, 81
Stowe, Robertus de, 53
Stratton, Rogerus de, 37
Strike, Johannes, 6
Stugs, Willelmus, 66
Sturgen, John, 91
Sucling, Henricus, 12
Suffield, Robertus, 47
Sugden, Gamaliel, 97
Sumer, Ricardus, 34
Sumeres, Margareta, 4
Surlingham, Johannes de, 3, 22
   Johannes filius Matildis de, 35
   Thomas de, 1, 76
Surmylk, Radulphus, 34

Sussam, Radulphus, 9
Suthfeld, Rogerus de, 52
Suthgate, Radulphus de, 1, 22, 34
   Radulphus filius Henrici de, 33
Sutor, Galfridus, 51
Swafham, Johannes de, 20
   Robertus de, 20
Swan, Adam, 75
Swanton, Persona de, 48
Swathefeld, Robertus de, 8
Swathynge, Walterus de, 9
Swerdeston, Johannes de, 31, 39, 40
Sweynsthorpe, Johannes de, 54
   Ricardus de, 19
Swyneshevnd, Johannes, 12
Sylet, Thomas, 71

Tacolston (Takelston), Johannes de 52
   Laurentius de, 7
Taillour (Taliur, Talyor, Taylur),
   Floritius, 73
   Henricus, 67
   Johannes, 52
   Ricardus le, 14, 15
   Rogerus, 55
Tanur (Tannur), Walterus le, 3, 22
   Willelmus filius Walt. le, 3, 35
Tasburg (Tassburth), Bartholomeus de, 17
   Walterus de, 11
Taverham, Cecilia de, 62
Taverner, Galfridus le, 52
   Johannes, 78
Tepede, Nicholaus, 36
Thacker, Petrus, 97
Thurbern, Thomas, jnr., 17
Thusceyns, Matheus, 50
Tiffanye, Adam, 16, 32
Tixtor, Radulphus, 30
Toftes, Clara de, 51
   Thomas, 66
Tolle, Johannes, 57
   Willelmus, 52
Totham, Willelmus de, 43
Totyngton, Ricardus de, 60
Towyt, Johannes, 8
Trewlove, Johannes, 73
Tripet, Robertus, 15
Trox (Trowse), Hamo de, 6

INDEX OF PERSONS.

Trukke, Johannes, 47
Trumpyngton, 66
Tudenham, Isabella de, 29
   Martinus de, 12, 44
   Warinus de, 57
Turner (Turnor), Johannes, 74
   Stephanus le, 7, 25
Turry, Johannes, 69
Tuschenys, Matheus, 9
Tusceynz, Matheus, 28
Tutte, Godefridus, 48
   Johannes, 45
Tweyt, Robertus de, 11
Tybenham, Eudo de, 4
Tytell (Tytel), Robertus, 75
   Thomas, 68
Tyvillie, Hugo, 57

Undermel, Ricardus, 1, 22, 33

Valeyns, Willelmus de, 56
Vanlere, Johannes, 74
Vincent, Thomas, 24
Virly, Andreas de, 50

Wake, Johannes, 70
Waleys, Thomas le, 24
Walpole, Ricardus, 74
Walres, Johannes, 17
   Thomas, 17
Walsham, Johannes, 74
   Thomas, 71
Walsingham, Johannes de, 65
Walswymman, Isabella, 67
Walters, Johannes, 85, 87, 88
Warde, Robertus, 4
Ware, Herveus de, 19
Warinhale, Ricardus, 7
Warkhouse, Samuel, 100
Warner, Johanna, 67
Warwyk, Johanna, 62

Wayte, Willelmus le, 58
Wearing, John, 98
Webster, Johannes, 86
Well, Johannes de, 74
Wenge, Robertus, 10
Westhorpe, John, 93, 94, 95, 96
Weston, Godefridus de, 16
   Jacobus de, 9, 11
   Johannes de, 24, 47, 51
Whylwryght, William, 89
Wichard, Hugo, 32
Wigemaker, Alicia, 66
Wilby, Ricardus, 71
Witton, Johannes de, 1, 3
Wolterton, Ricardus de, 37
Wonder, Margeria, 71
Worstede, Alicia de, 18
Wortes, Rogerus, 35
Worthsted, Johannes, 75
Wratham, Adam de, 30
Wreningham, Renerus de, 11
Wro, Henricus de le, 33
   Henricus del, 84
Wrong, Rogerus, 19
Wroxham, Willelmus de, 19, 31
Wylde, Henricus, 74
Wyleby, Galfridus de, 18
   Petrus de, 29
Wymer, Johannes, 74
Wymundham (Wymondham), Hugo
   de, 7
   Robertus de, 45, 52
   Rogerus de, 8
   Willelmus de, 17
Wyndel, Alexander, 17
Wytton, Johannes de, 20
   Ricardus de, 16
   Rogerus de, 10

Yntte, Willelmus, 28
York, Nicholaus de, 29
Yve, Johannes, 29, 78

INDEX OF PLACES.

Brakendele, 2, 5, 21, 24
Brundall, 14

Carrow, 47
Claxton, 38, 40
Cromer, 73

Dunston, 43

Earlham, 3, 10
Eccles, 48

Forncett, 72

Hartford Mill, 13, 28
Hellesdon, 75

Horning, 73

Irstead, 3

Keswick Hall, 73
Kirkby, 23

Lakenham, 13

Marsham, 57
Morley, 43

Oulton, 34

Pakefield, 65
Pulham, 11

Rougham, 57

Scottow, 57
Shipden, 73 n.
Sprowston, 8
Surlingham, 4, 42
Swanton, 48

Thorpe, 65
Trowse, 5, 6, 21, 24, 25, 51, 55, 74, 88, 90, 93, 96, 99

Whitlingham, 70

Yarmouth, 3, 16, 44, 65
Yaxham, 16

NORWICH.

Berstrete, 4, 8, 26, 46, 54, 56, 70, 77, 87, 88, 90, 93, 95, 96, 97, 99, 100
Bishop's Bridge, 67

Calkmills, 37, 74
Castle Bridge, 96
Castle Fee, 15, 68, 76, 79, 100
Chapel Field, 38 n.
Cockey, 6, 15, 42, 47, 71, 86, 99
Common [Town Close], 75, 92
Conesford, 1, 7, 20, 26, 33, 42, 46, 50, 54, 55, 66, 69, 77, 88, 90, 93, 94, 96, 99, 100, 101

Cookrowe, 17
Coslany, 15, 95, 98, 100

Dallingfleet, 46

Fibrigge, 47, 59, 95, 98, 100
Fibriggate, 12, 18, 71
Friars Carmelites, 19
Friars Minors, 20
Friars Preachers, 59

Guildhall, 85, 87, 88, 90, 93, 94, 97

Heigham Gate, 99
Holdthor, 58
Holy Trinity [Cathedral], 17, 72, 80
Hosyergate, 42 n.

Jewry, 7, 10

Lothmere, 29

Mancroft, 7, 28, 39, 43, 46, 52, 56, 61, 91, 95, 99, 101
Muspol, 59

Nedham, 28, 43, 46, 52, 56, 61, 79
Nedham Gates, 64
Nedler-row, 8
Nether Conesford, 42, 56 n.
Newbrigge, 60
Newgate, Great, 79
Newgate, Little, 54
Newgatesend, 71
Normanspitel, 37, 45, 68

INDEX OF PLACES.

Oldeswinemarket, 5
Pottergate, 13
Raton-rowe, 8
Risgate, 8
St. Augustine's Gates, 59, 60, 99
St. Bartylmew's Lane, 88
St. Bennett's Gates, 99
St. Giles' Gates, 8, 99
St. Giles, Hospital of, 48, 53
St. Martin's Gates, 99
St. Myhell's Lane, 88
Swynemarket Gate, 8

Teppeystathe, 36
Tolhouse, 5
Tombland, 17 n.

'Ultra Aquam,' 31, 37, 45, 48, 53, 59, 79, 91, 92, 96, 99

Wastlegate, 71
Westwyk, 29, 38, 44, 47, 53, 58
Wheatmarket, 14
Wymer, 29, 38, 44, 47, 53, 58, 85, 88, 96, 99, 101

Churches and Parishes.

All Saints, 6, 54
All Saints (Fibriggate), 18
St. Andrew, 14, 74, 78, 95, 98, 100
St. Augustine, 18
St. Bartholomew, 54
St. Benedict, 11, 95, 97, 100
St. Botulph, 18, 76
St. Clement, 18, 75, 79
St. Clement in Conesford, 33
St. Cross, 14, 86
St. Cuthbert, 35
St. Edmund, 18
St. Edward, 33
St. Etheldreda, 33
St. George (Colegate), 17, 98
St. George (Tombland), 16, 75, 78, 95, 98, 100
St. Giles, 11, 73, 79, 101
St. Gregory, 12, 73, 78, 85, 86, 89, 95, 97, 100
St. James, 18
St. John (Maddermarket), 14
St. John (Timberhill), 54
St. Julian, 33
St. Katherine, 63
St. Lawrence, 12, 86
St. Margaret (Westwick), 11, 63
St. Margaret (Fibriggate), 18

St. Martin (in the Baily), 6, 54, 87
St. Martin (Coslany), 17, 98
St. Martin (at Palace), 16, 75
St. Mary (Combust), 18
St. Mary (Coslany), 17
St. Mary (the Less), 35
St. Michael (Berstrete), 54
St. Michael (Conesford), 33, 35
St. Michael (Coslany), 17, 75, 79, 98
St. Michael de Motstowe (at Plea), 14
St. Olave, 18, 19
St. Peter (Hungate), 14
St. Peter (Mancroft), 8, 78, 95, 97, 100, 101
St. Peter (Conesford, or de Parmentergate), 35, 41
St. Peter (Southgate), 4, 33
St. Saviour, 18
St. Sepulchre, 54
St. Simon and St. Jude, 16
St. Stephen, 7, 58, 70, 72, 78, 95, 97, 100, 101
St. Swithun, 11, 99
St. Vedast, 35
St. Wynwaloy, 54

PUBLICATIONS.

OBJECTS AND WORK OF THE SELDEN SOCIETY. With an Account of the Principal Classes of Manuscripts with which the Society proposes to deal. 4to. 28 pp. Price to non-members, One Shilling.

I. (FOR 1887).
SELECT PLEAS OF THE CROWN. Vol. I., A.D. 1200–1225, from the Rolls preserved in H.M. Public Record Office. Edited, with a Translation and complete Indexes of Subjects and of the Names of Persons and Places, by F. W. MAITLAND, Downing Professor of the Laws of England, Cambridge. Crown 4to. Price to non-members, 28s.

II. (FOR 1888).
SELECT PLEAS IN MANORIAL AND OTHER SEIGNORIAL COURTS. Vol. I., Hen. III. and Edw. I., from the earliest Rolls extant. Edited, with a Translation and complete Indexes of Subjects and of the Names of Persons and Places, by Professor F. W. MAITLAND. Crown 4to. Price to non-members, 28s.

III. (FOR 1889).
SELECT CIVIL PLEAS. Vol. I. A.D. 1200–1203, from the Plea Rolls preserved in H.M. Public Record Office. Edited, with a Translation and complete Indexes of Subjects and of the Names of Persons and Places, by W. PALEY BAILDON, of Lincoln's Inn, Barrister-at-law. Crown 4to. Price to non-members, 28s.

IV. (FOR 1890).
PRECEDENTS OF PLEADING IN MANORIAL AND OTHER LOCAL COURTS. Edited from MSS. of the XIV. and XV. Centuries, by Professor F. W. MAITLAND and W. PALEY BAILDON. Crown 4to. Price to non-members, 28s.

V. (FOR 1891).
THE LEET JURISDICTION IN THE CITY OF NORWICH DURING THE THIRTEENTH AND FOURTEENTH CENTURIES. Edited from the Leet Rolls in the possession of the Corporation, by the Rev. W. H. HUDSON, M.A. Crown 4to. Price to non-members, 28s.

VI. (in preparation). (FOR 1892).
THE MIRROR OF JUSTICES. Edited from the MS. at Corpus Christi College, Cambridge, by J. W. WHITAKER, M.A., Trinity College, Cambridge. Crown 4to. Price to non-members, 28s.

Non-members can obtain the Publications of the Society from Mr. BERNARD QUARITCH, 15 Piccadilly, London, W., who has been appointed Agent for the Sale of the Society's Publications.

ACCOUNTS OF THE SELDEN SOCIETY FROM NOVEMBER 1, 1889, TO OCTOBER 31, 1891.

RECEIPTS.

	£	s.	d.
Balance brought forward ...	392	17	9
Subscriptions	438	18	0
Interest on Investments ...	12	0	0
	£843	**15**	**9**

PAYMENTS.

	£	s.	d.
Spottiswoode & Co. ...	303	14	3
F. W. Maitland ...	78	15	0
W. P. Baildon	34	2	6
Balance ...	427	4	0
	£843	**15**	**9**

Examined and found correct,

(Signed) R. CAMPBELL, *Auditor.*

CAPITAL ACCOUNT.

		£	s.	d.			£	s.	d.
Invested	... ...	195	0	0	Balance...	... ...	273	0	0
Uninvested	...	78	0	0					
	£273	0	0			£273	0	0	

Examined and found correct,

(Signed)   R. CAMPBELL, *Auditor.*

October 1892.

I have audited these accounts alone, Mr. H. Hall being unable through illness to join in the audit. I have compared the entries in Treasurer's books with the vouchers from November 1, 1889, to October 31, 1891, and find them correct, showing the receipts (inclusive of £392. 17s. 9d. brought forward from the last account) to have been £843. 15s. 9d., and the payments to have been £416. 11s. 9d., leaving a balance in favour of the Society of £427. 4s. 0d.

(Signed)   R. CAMPBELL, *Auditor.*

October 1892.

Selden Society.

OFFICERS AND COUNCIL.

Patron:
HER MAJESTY THE QUEEN.

President:
†THE LORD CHIEF JUSTICE OF ENGLAND.

Vice-President:
†THE RT. HON. SIR EDWARD FRY.

Council:
H.R.H. THE PRINCE OF WALES.
H.R.H. THE DUKE OF CONNAUGHT.
*THE LORD CHANCELLOR.
THE LORD CHIEF JUSTICE OF ENGLAND.
*THE MASTER OF THE ROLLS.
*THE PRESIDENT OF THE PROBATE DIVORCE AND ADMIRALTY DIVISION.
THE CHIEF JUSTICE OF THE UNITED STATES.
*THE ATTORNEY-GENERAL.
*THE SOLICITOR-GENERAL.
*THE TREASURER OF THE MIDDLE TEMPLE.
*THE TREASURER OF THE INNER TEMPLE.
*THE TREASURER OF LINCOLN'S INN.
*THE TREASURER OF GRAY'S INN.
*THE PRESIDENT OF THE INCORPORATED LAW SOCIETY, U.K.
        * *Ex officio*, when willing.
THE MARQUIS OF SALISBURY, K.G.
THE EARL OF DERBY, K.G.
THE LORD BISHOP OF OXFORD.
THE LORD ABERDARE, G.C.B.
THE LORD HANNEN.
THE LORD HERSCHELL.
THE LORD PENZANCE, Dean of Arches.
†THE LORD JUSTICE LINDLEY.
†THE LORD JUSTICE BOWEN.
THE LORD JUSTICE KAY.
MR. JUSTICE CAVE.
MR. JUSTICE CHARLES.
MR. JUSTICE CHITTY.
MR. JUSTICE DAY.
MR. JUSTICE GRANTHAM.
MR. JUSTICE JEUNE.
MR. JUSTICE KEKEWICH.
MR. JUSTICE NORTH.
MR. BARON POLLOCK.
MR. JUSTICE ROMER.
†MR. JUSTICE STIRLING.
†MR. JUSTICE WILLS.
THE HON. SIR THOMAS GALT, Chief Justice, Ontario.
THE HON. HORACE GRAY, Justice of the United States Supreme Court.
THE HON. SIR S. W. GRIFFITH, Q.C., K.C.M.G., Premier of Queensland.
THE HON. SIR CHARLES LILLEY, Chief Justice of Queensland.
THE HON. O. W. HOLMES, Jun., Justice of the Supreme Court, Massachusetts
THE HON. RUSSELL S. TAFT, Supreme Court, Vermont.
THE HON. S. J. WAY, Chief Justice of South Australia.
THE HON. J. S. WILLIAMS, Judge of the Supreme Court, Dunedin, New Zealand.
      † Executive Committee.

[Continued on next page.

OFFICERS AND COUNCIL—continued.

JAMES W. ALSOP, Solicitor, Liverpool.
Professor JAMES BARR AMES, Harvard.
Sir W. R. ANSON, Warden of All Souls College, Oxford.
J. ANSTIE, Q.C.
MELVILLE M. BIGELOW, Boston, Mass.
†S. R. SCARGILL BIRD, F.S.A., Public Record Office.
GEORGE TUCKER BISPHAM, Dean of Law School, University of Pennsylvania.
The Hon. S. H. BLAKE, Q.C., Toronto.
G. H. BLAKESLEY, Lincoln's Inn.
J. B. BRAITHWAITE, Lincoln's Inn.
SEWARD BRICE, Q.C.
E. W. BYRNE, Q.C., M.P.
†R. CAMPBELL, Lincoln's Inn.
S. J. CHADWICK, F.S.A., Solicitor.
†HYDE CLARKE, V.P.R.Hist.S.
ALFRED COCK, Q.C.
ARTHUR COHEN, Q.C.
†MONTAGUE CRACKANTHORPE, Q.C.
The Right Hon. Sir R. COUCH.
BRINTON COXE, Philadelphia.
†R. CUNLIFFE, Solicitor.
Rev. W. CUNNINGHAM, D.D., F.R.Hist.S., University Lecturer on History, Cambridge.
JOHN CUTLER, Professor of Law, King's College, London.
Sir HORACE DAVEY, Q.C.
Professor A. V. DICEY, Oxford.
His Honour Judge KENELM E. DIGBY.
†P. EDWARD DOVE, Lincoln's Inn.
Professor T. W. DWIGHT, Dean of the Law School, Columbia College, New York.
His Honour Judge EDDIS, Q.C.
†H. W. ELPHINSTONE, Lincoln's Inn.
CHARLES ELTON, Q.C., M.P.
Sir JOHN EVANS, T.R.S.
R. I. FINNEMORE, J.P., F.R.Hist.S., Natal.
Professor JOHN CHIPMAN GRAY, Harvard.
HUBERT HALL, F.R.Hist.S., Public Record Office.
W. J. HARDY, F.S.A.
Professor J. I. CLARKE HARE, Philadelphia.
T. HODGKIN, D.C.L.
Professor T. E. HOLLAND, Oxford.
Professor NOBUSHIGE HOZUMI, Tokyo.
J. INSKIP, Solicitor, Bristol.

A. R. JELF, Q.C.
E. K. KARSLAKE, Q.C.
†GRINHAM KEEN, Solicitor.
Professor W. A. KEENER, Harvard.
COURTNEY S. KENNY, Downing College, Cambridge.
†B. G. LAKE, Solicitor.
Professor C. C. LANGDELL, Harvard.
HENRY C. LEA, Philadelphia.
W. A. LINDSAY, Middle Temple, Portcullis Pursuivant of Arms.
His Honour Judge VERNON LUSHINGTON, Q.C.
†H. C. MAXWELL LYTE, F.S.A., Deputy Keeper of the Public Records.
†JOHN MACDONELL, Master of the Supreme Court.
†Professor F. W. MAITLAND, F.R.Hist.S., Cambridge.
†C. TRICE MARTIN, F.S.A., Public Record Office.
ROKUICHIRO MASUJIMA, Tokyo.
H. S. MILMAN, F.S.A., Director of the Society of Antiquaries.
†STUART MOORE, F.S.A., Inner Temple.
The Rt. Hon. Sir G. OSBORNE MORGAN, Bart., Q.C., M.P.
J. FLETCHER MOULTON, Q.C.
†FRANCIS K. MUNTON, Solicitor.
†Professor Sir FREDERICK POLLOCK, Bart.
G. W. PROTHERO, King's College, Cambridge.
WILLIAM HENRY RAWLE, Philadelphia.
The Hon. HENRY REED, Philadelphia.
JOHN RIGBY, Q.C., M.P., Solicitor-General.
Professor ROGERS, Michigan.
F. E. SAWYER, F.S.A., Solicitor, Brighton.
WM. A. SHORTT, New York.
Professor W. W. SKEAT, Cambridge.
Professor GOLDWIN SMITH, Toronto.
†HUGH STIRLING, Solicitor.
Sir WHITLEY STOKES, K.C.S.I., Inner Temple.
Sir ROBERT STOUT, K.C.M.G., Dunedin.
Professor J. B. THAYER, Harvard.
Professor TIEDEMANN, Missouri.
†W. M. WALTERS, Solicitor.
Professor JOHN WESTLAKE, Q.C.
†F. MEADOWS WHITE, Q.C.
J. C. WILSON, Exeter College, Oxford.
The Hon. GEO. B. YOUNG, Minnesota.

Honorary Secretary for America :

EZRA R. THAYER, Cambridge, Mass.

Honorary Secretary and Treasurer :

† P. EDWARD DOVE, 23 Old Buildings, Lincoln's Inn, London, W.C.

† Executive Committee.

www.ingramcontent.com/pod-product-compliance
Lightning Source LLC
Chambersburg PA
CBHW022053230426
43672CB00008B/1154